The Lords' Jews:

Magnate-Jewish Relations
in the Polish-Lithuanian Commonwealth
during the Eighteenth Century

Center for Jewish Studies, Harvard Judaic Texts and Studies, VII
Harvard Ukrainian Research Institute, Monograph Series

Cambridge, Massachusetts

M. J. Rosman

The Lords' Jews

178

Magnate-Jewish Relations in the

Polish-Lithuanian Commonwealth

during the Eighteenth Century

Distributed by the Harvard Ukrainian Research Institute
and the Center for Jewish Studies, Harvard University

ISBN: 1364226

Publication of this volume was made possible by the Yanoff-Taylor Lecture and Publication Fund and a generous donation from the late Wasyl Melnyk.

ISBN 0-916458-18-0
ISBN 0-916458-47-4 (pbk.)
Library of Congress Catalog Number 89-84704
Printed in the United States of America

For my Parents-in Law
Emil Ratz Reed
and
Eda Silberman Reed

Contents

Preface

Historians have frequently emphasized the development of close ties between the Polish nobility and the Polish Jews during the sixteenth, seventeenth, and eighteenth centuries. Jews lived and worked in nobility-owned towns, leased nobility-controlled rights, and served in noblemen's administrations. They also gained a reputation as specialists in supplying income and services to noblemen. The consequences of these ties have received different emphases, usually depending on the ethnic background of the writer.

Polish historians have tended to stress the way in which the use of Jewish commercial services freed the nobility from the need to patronize the royal towns and their merchants. This contributed to the ability of the agriculturally oriented nobility to determine the direction of economic development in Poland, resulting in the stifling of commercial and industrial progress. It also significantly hampered the development of the large royal towns, thereby weakening the nobility's rivals for political power—the townsmen and the king. Employment of the Jews as administrators or lessees inhibited the cultivation of a professional Polish managerial class and resulted in gross inefficiency. Moreover, the Jews, dependent upon the nobility's good graces, proved to be a dependable ally of the latter in their struggle to maintain control over the peasantry.[1]

[1] This is espoused in many works. A few examples are: J. Bergerówna, *Księżna pani na Kocku i Siemiatyczach* (Lviv, 1936), pp. 8–9, 26, 307–308; J. A. Gierowski, ed., *Rzeczpospolita w dobie upadku 1700–1740* (Wrocław, 1955), pp. xvi–xviii; J. Rutkowski, *Historia gospodarcza Polski* (Warsaw, 1953), pp. 176–86; R. Rybarski, *Skarb i pieniądz za Jana Kazimierza, Michała Korybuta i Jana III*, pt. 2 (Warsaw, 1939). English readers can find a modified version of the traditional Polish view in N. Davies, *God's Playground: A History of Poland*, vol. 1 (New York, 1982), pp. 213, 290, 306, 319, 350, 444. For the opinion of Jewish historians on these aspects of nobility-Jewish relations see: B. Z. Dinur, *Bemifne Hadorot* (Jerusalem, 1955),

This emphasis on the Jews as the tool of the nobility in their political and economic battles with the other segments of Polish society relegates the Jews to a secondary (and unsavory) role. As a catalyst, not a protagonist, their existence was incidental to the central processes of Polish history, and the historian need scarcely take notice of them. In monographs and articles about the Polish economy or the nobility-owned latifundia, the Jewish role is usually mentioned, if at all, in general terms. In contrast, the main focus of these studies, the relationship between the nobility and the serfs, is explicated in great and often quantified detail.[2] The subject of the Jews is dispensed with by comments like: "Town merchants, mainly Jews, vegetated on the margin of the latifundium economy";[3] or "The Jews had to carry on a struggle with the town population occupied in commerce. From this they emerged successful, completely dominating trade and industry."[4]

Such pronouncements yield an impression of the Jewish role and its significance, but they do not reveal the basis of such an impression. The problem deserves more serious treatment.

If Polish historians have buried the subject of nobility-Jewish relations in the context of what they consider to be the larger issues of Polish history, for Jewish historians the important aspect of the nobility-Jewish link was its effect upon Jewish life in Poland. They have established that during the sixteenth through eighteenth centuries the foundation of Jewish existence in Poland increasingly consisted of the settlement and economic opportunities offered by the nobility in their private towns. If it had been limited to the royal towns, domi-

---

p. 104; M. Kremer, "Leheker Hamelakha Vehevrot Baalei Hamelakha Etzel Yehudei Polin," *Zion* 2 (1937), pp. 269 (n. 8), 299–301.

[2] Among the works fitting this description are: A. I. Baranovich, *Magnatskoe khoziaistvo na iuge Volyni v XVIII v.* (Moscow, 1955); Z. Guldon, *Związki handlowe dóbr magnackich na prawobrzeżnej Ukrainie z Gdańskiem w XVII w.* (Toruń, 1966); W. A. Markina, *Magnatskoe pomeste pravoberezhnoi Ukrainy vtoroi poloviny XVIII veka* (Kiev, 1961); W. A. Serczyk, *Gospodarstwo magnackie w województwie podolskim w drugiej połowie XVIII wieku* (Wrocław, 1965).

[3] J. Burszta, "Handel magnacki i kupiecki między Sieniawą nad Sanem a Gdańskiem od końca XVII do połowy XVIII wieku," *RDSG* 16 (1954), p. 218.

[4] Bergerówna, p. 307. Even a book devoted to urban life, M. Bogucka and H. Samsonowicz, *Dzieje miast i mieszczaństwa w Polsce przedrozbiorowej* (Wrocław, 1986), does not go much beyond a characterization of Jewish demographic development.

nated by the non-Jewish townsmen, the Jews' field of operation would have been greatly restricted. Moreover, politically, the Jews' best, if inconsistent, allies against anti-Jewish measures continually proposed in the *Sejm* (Diet) were noblemen who benefited from Jewish economic activity.

These historians also accentuate the fact that Jewish dependence on noblemen for political support and residential and economic opportunities entailed some undesirable side effects. It made Jews subject to the capriciousness and arbitrariness of their noble lords and resulted in terrible suffering for individual Jews.[5]

The sources behind these assertions are Jewish communal record books, rabbinic works, Polish legal sources, famous proverbs and anecdotes, traveler's reports, memoirs, and anti-Jewish tracts. As valuable as these sources are, they tend to present either generalities or a very small number of fortuitous examples, which the historian must accept as typical. Most of them, by their very nature, are likely to be tendentious. These types of sources must be supplemented by other materials. Since the usual sources are often unrelated in time or space, it would be useful to employ sources that are connected to each other geographically and chronologically. New sources presenting a large quantity of concrete cases would enable generalizations to be based on detailed, quantifiable data. Perhaps most important, it is desirable to obtain more sources that are "neutral" in character, not written to address the question of Jewish-nobility relations per se, but bearing on those relations nonetheless.

When combined with the published sources, material of this nature can shed new light on several issues. Which commercial positions did

[5] M. Bałaban, *Beit Yisrael Bepolin*, vol. 1, I. Halpern, ed. (Jerusalem, 1948), pp. 95–98; S. W. Baron, *A Social and Religious History of the Jews*, vol. 16 (New York, 1976), pp. 28, 122–25, 162, 214, 375 (n. 50); S. M. Dubnov, *Toldot Hahasidut* (Tel Aviv, 1931 [1975]), pp. 9–12; idem, *History of the Jews in Russia and Poland*, vol. 1 (Philadelphia, 1916), pp. 69, 77, 93, 170; J. Goldberg, "Bein Hofesh Lenetinut—Sugei Hatlut Hafeiudalit shel Hayehudim Bepolin," *Proceedings of the 5th World Congress of Jewish Studies*, vol. 2 (Jerusalem, 1972), pp. 107–108; R. Mahler, *Toldot Hayehudim Bepolin* (Merhavia, 1946), pp. 224, 246, 252–53; B. D. Weinryb, *The Jews of Poland* (Philadelphia, 1973), pp. 10–11, 112, 117–18, 120; S. Ettinger, "Maamadam Hamishpati Vehahevrati Shel Yehudei Ukraina Bameiot Ha-15-17," *Zion* 20 (1955), pp. 145–47; idem, "Helkam Shel Hayehudim Bekolonizatzia Shel Ukraina," *Zion* 21 (1956), pp. 139–40.

Jews occupy? How did Jewish commerce fit into the overall economy
of the nobility and of Poland? Why did Jews dominate the field of
leasing? How did the leasing process work? Which administrative
posts did Jews occupy? What were their qualifications and responsibilities? How did noblemen treat individual Jews? How did they
relate to the Jewish community? What was life like for Jews in
private towns? Due to either lack of interest or lack of sources, these
issues have not been examined systematically and the resulting
lacunae formed the genesis of this study.

In writing this book I posed two questions: What were the principal spheres of interaction between the Jews and the nobility? What
was the significance of this interaction for each party? Dealing with
these questions, I have treated each of the issues raised in the preceding paragraph—where possible from a quantitative perspective.

The Polish nobility was not a monolith and, concomitantly, relations with Jews varied among the different groupings. Hence, in order
to ensure focus, I have limited the scope of this study to representatives of the nobility group that was politically and economically most
important, that is most commonly the subject of nobility studies in the
literature, and that left the best documentation—the aristocratic magnates.

My approach to the subject is that of a case study. I chose the
example of the Sieniawski-Czartoryski family and its holdings
because this family exemplifies the aristocratic magnate group by generally accepted standards of measurement: kinship, wealth, heritage,
office-holding, prestige, life-style, and attitudes. The administrative
structure and social organization of their huge latifundium were typical, and their holdings included all of the elements represented on the
Polish feudal complexes. The Sieniawskis and Czartoryskis were
faced with the full array of challenges, problems, and rewards that
confronted all magnates. Moreover, their latifundium's large Jewish
population (approximately thirty thousand)[6] makes the Sieniawski-
Czartoryski case a particularly apt one for the exploration of
magnate-Jewish relations. I have tried to present a detailed study of
the situation of the Jews in this representative latifundium over a
period of almost fifty years, at a time when Jews were gravitating

---

[6] See Appendix 1.

increasingly to magnate latifundia. My intention has been to lay the foundations for a more precise perception of the nobility-Jewish relationship.

My experience with the Sieniawski-Czartoryski archive began in 1977 in Jerusalem. A few of the files are on microfilm there, and by studying them I was able to familiarize myself with the nature of the material and the methodological difficulties. Thus primed, I spent about half of the academic year 1978–79 collecting material in archives in Cracow and Warsaw. The Sieniawski-Czartoryski documents include inventories, financial statements, freight records, contracts, court protocols, correspondence, petitions to the latifundium owners, decrees, and orders to administrators.

While I have drawn some conclusions about the attitudes of the magnates toward the Jews, the sources, with the exception of certain choice remarks, generally were not intended to express opinions, but rather to serve as instruments in conducting business. Therefore I have concentrated on the question of relationships as expressed through actions and not through attitudes.

My findings document what has heretofore been asserted only on an impressionistic basis: that the Jews interacted with the magnates through their commercial, leasing, and administrative activities, and magnates wielded great influence over the Jewish community. Furthermore, the source materials I utilized allowed for an exposition of the nature of these activities and influence and for an appreciation of their place within the latifundium context.

What emerges is that the Jews were one of several identifiable socio-economic groups that played central roles in the Polish-Lithuanian Commonwealth. Like the nobility, peasants, townsmen, and clergy, the Jews had interests to defend and allied themselves with the forces that could help them achieve their objectives. This book is an attempt to analyze the Jews' relationship with at least one of those groups as well as the significance of their activity. I hope that it will contribute to a broader understanding of both Jewish history and the history of Poland.

In the course of researching and writing this study many individuals and institutions shared their resources with me. I take this opportunity to express my thanks.

The institutions that saw fit to lend financial support to my research were The Charles Revson Foundation through the Revson Fellowship

Program at the Jewish Theological Seminary of America; The
Fulbright-Hays Fellowship program administered by the United States
Department of Health, Education and Welfare; The International
Research and Exchanges Board (IREX); The Memorial Foundation
for Jewish Culture; The National Foundation for Jewish Culture; and
The Abraham and Edita Spiegel Foundation through the Spiegel Prize
of Tel Aviv University.

During the process of converting my doctoral dissertation into this
book I was fortunate to receive a second Spiegel Fellowship as well as
the Allon Prize of the Israel Council for Higher Education, the Jefroy-
kin Prize of the Jewish National Fund and the Hebrew University, and
a grant from Bar Ilan University where I teach.

My interest in the academic study of Jewish civilization was kindled by my teachers at the Jewish Theological Seminary of America.
Their combination of passionate commitment with dispassionate
scholarship makes this institution a unique one, and has served me as
an ideal. My appreciation of Poland and her culture was cultivated in
the classrooms and libraries of Columbia University. I hope my
interpretations of Polish history ring true to what I learned there.

For their expert guidance I am indebted to Professors Józef Andrzej
Gierowski, Jacob Goldberg, Andrzej Kamiński, and Ismar Schorsch.
Each man enriched my knowledge, refined my thinking, and honed
my skills in his own inimitable fashion.

Yaacov Hisdai graciously shared his index of eighteenth-century
rabbinic literature. Richard Cohen favored me with a valuable cri-
tique of an early draft of the manuscript. Zvi Volk and Rochelle
Furstenberg made stylistic suggestions, and Władysław Bartoszewski
and David Moss helped with the finishing touches. Danuta Talanda
and Jennie Bush drew the maps. Judy Goldberg typed the final
manuscript with patience and diligence. Michael Loo compiled the
index.

The archives where I conducted my research were Archiwum
Główne Akt Dawnych in Warsaw; Biblioteka Czartoryskich and the
Wojewódzkie Archiwum Państwowe, both in Cracow; and the Central
Archive for the History of the Jewish People in Jerusalem. The per-
sonal interest taken by the archivists, especially Dr. Adam Homecki,
Dr. Teresa Zielinska, and Mgr. Anna Palarczykowa, in my project
made my task much easier and more enjoyable than it might otherwise
have been.

I would also like to thank the staffs of the libraries where I carried out most of my secondary research: Biblioteka Jagiellońska in Cracow, Biblioteka Narodowa in Warsaw, The Jewish National and University Library in Jerusalem, and the libraries of the Jagiellonian and Warsaw Universities and of the Jewish Theological Seminary of America. During part of the period I spent writing this book I benefited from the hospitality and facilities of the Diaspora Research Institute of Tel Aviv University.

I am also grateful to the Polish Ministry of Science, Higher Education, and Technology for granting me the necessary credentials for and ensuring the success of my research trip to Poland, as well as to the diplomatic staff of the United States Consulate in Cracow for all of their help.

I am particularly beholden to Professors Jacob Katz, Omeljan Pritsak, and Isadore Twersky for their interest in my work and their efforts to see that it be published. George Mihaychuk and Kathryn Taylor of the Harvard Ukrainian Research Institute have faithfully shepherded the book to press.

Some of the material in Chapters 4 and 6 has been incorporated, in different form, in articles that have appeared in: *Danzig: Between East and West*, I. Twersky, ed., Cambridge, 1985, *Gal-Ed* 7–8, *Nation and History*, vol. 2, S. Ettinger, ed., Jerusalem, 1984, and *Sobótka* 22. The manuscript was prepared for publication in 1984. Despite the intervening delay, technical considerations have permitted only a partial update of the footnotes and bibliography.

My parents, Norman and Elayne Rosman, who afforded me the experiences and education that made an academic career in Polish-Jewish studies a live possibility were silent partners in my research and writing. I have dedicated the book to my parents-in-law, who have given me boundless encouragement and who survived the final, tragic chapter in the story of Polish Jewry. They remain a living link to the people and society described here.

Finally, my most humble and heartfelt thanks I offer to my wife, Lynne, who chose to view this project and all of the hardships it placed upon her as but one more joint endeavor of our marriage.

M. J. Rosman
Jerusalem
September, 1987
Elul, 5747

List of Maps, Tables, and Figures

Maps

Tables

Figures

Geographic Names

Placenames are transliterated according to the country in which they are presently located, except when standard English forms exist, such as Warsaw, Cracow, Lviv, Kiev, Vilnius, and Dnieper. Thus, Ukrainian placenames are used for all geographical references in the Ukraine and Belorussian for all references in Belorussia. In footnotes, when a placename is part of a reference to source material in Polish archives, the placename is given in Polish, regardless of the present location. A partial list of placenames in present-day Ukraine and Belorussia and their Polish equivalents is provided below.

I. The Ukrainian Soviet Socialist Republic

Ukrainian	Polish
Antonivka	Antonów
Berezhany	Brzeżany
Bratslav	Bracław
Buchach	Buczacz
Burshtyn	Bursztyn
Chyhyryn	Czechryn
Halych	Halicz
Ivankiv	Iwanków
Kalush	Kałusz
Kam''ianets'-Podil's'kyi	Kamieniec Podolski
Khodoriv	Chodorów
Klevan'	Klewań
Liatychiv	Latyczów
Medzhybizh	Międzybóż
Mikolaiv	Mikołajów
Nemyriv	Niemirów
Nesterov (Zhovkva)	Żółkiew
Nova Syniava	Nowa Sieniawa
Ovruch	Owrucz

Peremyshliany	Przemyślany
Sataniv	Satanów
Stanyslaviv	Stanisławów
(now Ivano-Frankivs'ke)	
Stara Syniava	Stara Sieniawa
Stavnytsia	Stawnica
Stryi	Stryj
Ternopil'	Tarnopol
Ternoruda	Tarnoruda
Trebukhivtsi	Trybuchowce
Zin'kiv	Zinków
Zvenyhorod	Dźwinogród

II. Belorussian Soviet Socialist Republic

Belorussian	*Polish*
Aleksandryia	Aleksandria
Mahilioŭ	Mohilew
Panevežis	Poniewież
Shkłoŭ	Szkłów
Slutsk	Słuck
Slabodka	Słobódka
Zubrevichy	Zubrewicze

CHAPTER ONE

Poland and the Magnates

To anyone whose consciousness of Poland has been formed in the post-World War II era, the configuration of the Polish-Lithuanian Commonwealth in the mid-seventeenth century comes as a surprise. The Poland of modern times is usually perceived as a medium-sized country, politically subjugated, militarily inconsequential, economically weak, and religiously and ethnically homogeneous. In 1634, however, Poland was the largest country in Europe, stretching from the Brandenburg and Silesian borders to a line some one hundred miles east of the Dnieper and from the Baltic to within one hundred miles of the Black Sea. Sixty percent of its population of ten million was not ethnically Polish. It included such diverse groups as Germans, Ruthenians or Ukrainians, Lithuanians, Belorussians, Armenians, Turks, Italians, Scots, and the largest concentration of Jews in the world at that time.

In this "State Without Stakes"[1] Protestant, Catholic, Orthodox, Armenian, Muslim, and Jew managed to practice their respective religions in close proximity without being drawn into holy warfare. This was a remarkable record of ethnic pluralism and religious toleration, considering the seething religious strife in Western Europe and the religious exclusivity and xenophobia of Poland's Russian neighbor.

Economically, Poland's rich farmlands and forests had given her a lucrative role as the main supplier of food and natural products to Western Europe. Her upper classes, at least, were able to enjoy a standard of living as opulent as any in Europe.

On the field of battle, over the previous two hundred years Poland's armies had tested their mettle against Germans, Muscovites, Swedes, Tartars, and Turks, maintaining and even expanding the borders of

---

[1] This is the title of a book by J. Tazbir (New York–Warsaw, 1973) describing Polish religious toleration in the sixteenth and seventeenth centuries.

their country. In its political structure the Commonwealth might be termed an incipient democracy where the elected king's power was tempered by a representative two-house body. This Diet or *Sejm* had to approve any constitutional changes, vote on budgetary and taxation matters, and agree to army mobilization.

I call Polish democracy "incipient" because the electoral franchise was held by just 10 percent of the population. This was the same 10 percent that held most of society's privileges in Poland: the nobility. The nobility controlled the political power, commanded the economic resources, and possessed the symbols of social status. While noblemen could be rich or poor—and some were very poor—the road to wealth, power, and prestige passed through nobility status. A poor nobleman had at least the potential for attaining high status,[2] while a rich nonnoble aimed for nobilitation.

Together with the crown and the church the nobility owned all of the land, and hence the wealth, of what was an agrarian country. The grain and other natural products exported to the West were largely nobility-owned, and noblemen were the primary users of the imported goods. This being the case, a merchant's suppliers and customers were mainly noblemen. He had little choice but to buy from them and sell to them. If a merchant needed to borrow capital, he could turn only to the monasteries or the nobility. In order to market his goods he had to pay tolls, customs duties, and market taxes—often to a nobleman. By contrast, noblemen transporting their own products, or goods intended for their own use, were exempt from all taxes, duties, and tolls. Under such conditions noblemen who marketed their products or purchased goods by themselves or through their representatives effectively undermined the development of the merchants in independent royally chartered towns.

On the other hand, the private towns, owned by noblemen, flourished under their owners' guiding hands. The lords invested in their towns' commercial life and often delegated to their resident merchants the nobility trade privileges to which they themselves were entitled. Hence, even though Polish noblemen generally shunned direct involvement in commerce as a distasteful, unnoble pursuit, the nobility actually determined the contours of Polish commercial life.

---

[2] For example, King Stanisław August Poniatowski's grandfather was a minor nobleman who owned only one village.

The nobility-owned estates that produced most of Poland's agriculturally based wealth were inhabited and cultivated by peasants who, after serfdom's demise in the West, continued in ever more burdensome feudal villeinage to their nobility masters.[3] These peasants paid feudal dues in labor, kind, and money. They also were bound to respect the nobleman's hereditary monopoly rights—to buy his liquor only, to patronize his mills exclusively, to keep out of his forests and meadows, and to submit to his judiciary.

Neither the peasants nor the merchants held any perquisites of power. Delegates to the *Sejm* and holders of state office were either noblemen or high clergy (who usually came from nobility families). Even the king was limited by his obligations to consult with and obtain the consent of the *Sejm*. In sum, Poland by the mid-seventeenth century was indeed a "Commonwealth of the Nobility."

By the eighteenth century the persistent nobility domination of feudal agrarian Poland, in a world where absolutism and mercantilism were in the ascendant, became a point of pride. An ideology, called Sarmatism, previously developed to justify expansion and war, was employed to rationalize and reinforce the status quo. Sarmatism posited that Poland was sui generis. As descendants of the original ancient population of Sarmatia—i.e., Poland—the Polish nobility was a chosen people. Their liberties, privileges, religion, economic and political structure, and culture, different from West European models, bore an aura of holiness. Foreign influences were by definition pernicious. The suggestion that Poland should transform its feudal agrarian economy, which assured the continued domination of the high nobility, was greeted as heresy. To claims that Poland should learn from its powerful neighbors, centralize power in the hands of the king, and end the incessant power plays by the various magnate coteries, came the famous reply: *Polska nierządem stoi*: Poland exists *by virtue* of its chaotic political structure. Otherwise, it would not be Poland, but some degenerate absolutist state.[4]

---

[3] See: A. Kamiński, "Neo-Serfdom in Poland-Lithuania," *Slavic Review* 34 (1975), pp. 253 – 68; L. Makkai, "Neo-Serfdom: Its Origin and Nature in East Central Europe," *Slavic Review* 34 (1975), pp. 225 – 38.

[4] On Sarmatism, see: S. Cynarski, "The Shape of Sarmatian Ideology in Poland," *APH* 19 (1968), pp. 5 – 17.

Sarmatism reached its ultimate articulation in the Saxon period (1697–1763), precisely when the deteriorating state of the country necessitated an ideological prop for the traditional Polish structures. At a time when the polity and economy seemed to be breaking down, Sarmatism provided a means of viewing internal developments in the best possible light, while blaming problems solely on Poland's meddlesome neighbors.

If proponents of Sarmatism tended to explain away Poland's difficulties, historians are unanimous in characterizing Poland between the mid-seventeenth and mid-eighteenth centuries as a country mired in crisis. Words like "eclipse," "decay," and "decline" are usually chosen to describe the pitiable state of the Polish-Lithuanian Commonwealth, particularly from 1700 on.[5]

This crisis was played out in a string of natural and man-made disasters. Beginning with the partially successful Cossack revolt and Ruthenian peasant uprising in 1648 and continuing with a series of invasions, wars, peasant rebellions, and nobility confederations,[6] the period between 1648 and 1763 was a time of turmoil, violence, and danger.

The strength of the country was also sapped by political dislocations such as the first use of the *liberum veto* (1652),[7] the Lubomirski

---

[5] For documents and discussion on the eighteenth-century crisis in Poland, see: J. A. Gierowski, ed. *Rzeczpospolita w dobie upadku 1700–1740* (Wrocław, 1955); idem, *Między saskim absolutyzmem a złotą wolnością* (Wrocław, 1953); J. Gierowski and A. Kamiński, "The Eclipse of Poland," *The New Cambridge Modern History*, J. S. Bromley, ed., vol. 6, (Cambridge, 1970), pp. 681–715.

[6] A confederation was a temporary military union of a large group devoted to redressing or preventing what they viewed as an injustice. Usually this meant forcing the government to adopt a certain policy. Strictly speaking, confederations were not revolutionary in that they were an accepted form of political expression and did not aim to overthrow the government, only to pressure it. For example, the Confederation of Tarnogród (1715–17) was formed to prevent the king from adopting absolutist powers and to force him to keep his Saxon troops out of Poland. See: G. Grodecki, "Konfederacje w Polsce xv w.," *Sprawozdania PAN* 52 (1951).

[7] Liberum Veto was the right of any single member of the *Sejm* to veto legislation and dissolve the house. Once employed, in 1652, the Liberum Veto hung as an often activated Damocles' Sword over every session of the *Sejm*. See: W. Konopczyński, *Liberum Veto: Studyum porównawczo-historyczne* (Cracow, 1918); W. Czapliński, *Dwa Sejmy w roku 1652: Studium z dziejów rozkładu Rzeczypospolitej Szlacheckiej* (Wrocław, 1955), pp. 115–30.

Rebellion (1665–66), the abdication of King Jan Kazimierz (1667), the double election of Augustus II and Prince Conti (1697), and the royal claims of Stanisław Leszczyński for most of the first four decades of the eighteenth century. A *Sejm* that could scarcely reach a decision and a king who had to spend much of his time defending his right to the throne could not provide forceful leadership. On top of all of these problems, in the early eighteenth century there was a concatenation of plagues, fires, and floods that wreaked havoc with fields, homes, and human lives.[8]

All of the fighting and political maneuvering required money, which, as always, was obtained by more efficient—and usually high-handed—exploitation of both the rural and urban components of the feudal estates. Even existing feudal dues, however, could not be borne by peasants and townsmen whose properties and crops were decimated by war, fire, or flood; whose food and money were confiscated by passing armies; and whose persons were threatened by the constant conditions of violence and disease. The combination of events in the field and increased demands by the owners served to pauperize many a town and village.[9]

In general the feudal-style, agrarian-based economy was failing. Royal towns, always forced to compete with the closed market system dominated by the nobility, were confronted with additional burdens under new adverse conditions. As a result the towns were losing population and lacked the skilled labor, financial resources, and political power needed to develop industry and commerce on a level comparable to that emerging in Western Europe. The Polish royal towns languished and their inhabitants sank into poverty. Peasants, far from

---

[8] A. Homecki, *Produkcja i handel zbożowy w latyfundium Lubomirskich w drugiej połowie XVII i pierwszej XVIII wieku* (Wrocław, 1970), pp. 16–18 and list of natural disasters on p. 118; S. Namaczyńska, *Kronika klęsk elementarnych w Polsce i w krajach sąsiednich w latach 1648–1696* (Lviv, 1937).

[9] *Historia Polski,* T. Manteuffel, ed., vol. 1, pt. 2, H. Łowmiański, ed. (Warsaw, 1957), pp. 616–24; Gierowski, *Między,* pp. 9–24; idem, *Rzeczpospolita,* pp. x–xii, xvi–xviii; L. Wiatrowski, "Z dziejów latyfundium klasztoru Klarysek z Starego Sącza," *Zeszyty Naukowe Uniwersytetu Wrocławskiego,* Ser. A, no. 13 (1959), pp. 133–35. The vicissitudes referred to by Meir b. Eliakim Getz in the Introduction to *Even Hashoham Umeirat Einaim,* (Dyhernfürth, 1733) and by Yaacov Yoshua Falk, *Penai Yehoshua,* (Amsterdam, 1730), in his Introduction are Jewish testaments to the turmoil of the times.

well-off in good times, were squeezed harder as the inhospitable conditions developed. Rising feudal dues and falling crop yields forced
many peasants to abandon their plots and wander through the countryside. Even many petty and middle noblemen found that they could no
longer afford to keep up their manors and turned to working as
managers for their richer brethren who could do so.

Currency was in short supply and was continually being debased in
order to stretch it further. The most popular investments were relatively safe enterprises like moneylending, revenue farming, and lease-
holding, rather than long-term, high-risk industrial and commercial
ventures. Consequently, Poland continued to import most of its
manufactured goods while, to pay the bills, it depended upon unstable
markets for its shrinking supplies of raw materials.

By the mid-eighteenth century, such features as the undiversified
agrarian economy, the dearth of skilled labor, the weak central
government, and the lack of a large, standing, professional army rendered Poland impotent in the environment of absolutist, mercantilist
Europe. Yet, fundamental transformations that might have recast the
economic and political structure were prevented by a sharp conflict of
interest in Polish society.

To the people who lived through it, this conflict was perceived as
the opposition of "Majesty and Liberty." That is, the claims of the
king and the central government to sufficient power to rule decisively
and effectively were pitted against the demands of the nobility, as
elaborated by Sarmatist ideology, that their traditional freedoms and
prerogatives be preserved. Any moves to increase the king's authority, such as the institution of hereditary succession or the strengthening of the standing army, or any attempt to limit nobility "liberties,"
for example the abolition of the *liberum veto,* were met with fierce and
successful opposition on the part of the nobility.[10]

There was also an economic facet to this conflict. The primary
beneficiaries of the feudal system in Poland were the aristocratic
noblemen. When their system was strained by the adverse conditions
in the mid-seventeenth to mid-eighteenth centuries, the nobles did not

---

[10] Gierowski and Kamiński, "Eclipse," pp. 704, 709–15; Gierowski, *Rzeczpospolita,* pp. xxv–xxxiv, 151–54; S. Grodziski, "Les devoirs et les droits politiques de la
noblesse Polonaise," *APH* 36 (1977), pp. 163–76; H. Olszewski, *Doktryny prawno-
ustrojowe czasów saskich* (Warsaw, 1961), pp. 34–67.

conclude that the system needed reform, which might have imperiled their own economic position. Instead, they worked the system harder, concentrating more land in their own hands, exporting more raw materials, pressing the peasants further, and developing their own marketing capabilities more intensively at the expense of the towns.[11]

The Magnates

The elite of the nobility who took the lead in furthering its political and economic interests consisted of the most powerful and wealthy noblemen, designated by most twentieth-century historians as "magnates," but probably more precisely termed "aristocratic magnates." This group consisted of ten to twenty families in each generation who were distinguished by ongoing high economic standing, several generations of service in the Polish Senate, marriage connections with other aristocratic families, a high level of education, and recognition accorded by contemporaries.[12] Although they represented only a small

[11] *Historia Polski,* vol. 1, pt. 2, pp. 624–51, 659–61; J. Topolski, "La regression économique en Pologne du XVI au XVII siècle," *APH* 7 (1962), pp. 45–49; L. Żytkowicz, "Okres gospodarki folwarczno-pańszczyźnianej XVI–XVIII w.," *Historia chłopów polskich,* S. Inglot, ed. (Częstochowa, 1970), p. 251; S. Śreniowski, "Oznaki regresu ekonomicznego w ustroju folwarczno-pańszczyźnianym w Polsce od schyłku XVI wieku," *KH* 61 (1954), pp. 165–96. For a somewhat different interpretation of this period of Polish history, see Kamiński, "Neo-serfdom."

[12] The principle of equality of all noblemen prevented sixteenth–eighteenth century noblemen from labeling the elite among them. There is no doubt, however, that noblemen who owned scores of villages and sat in the Senate were on a completely different plane from landless or one or two-village owning noblemen. The problem, however, is in precisely defining a group that was not rigorously defined by its contemporaries. The description offered here is based upon the work of W. Dworzaczek, *Genealogia* (Warsaw, 1958), pp. 4–7, 11–12, and charts, pp. 93–193; idem "La mobilité sociale de la noblesse Polonaise aux XVI et XVII siècles," *APH* 36 (1977), pp. 147–61; A. Kersten, "Les magnats—élite de la société nobiliaire," *APH* 36 (1977), pp. 119–33; T. Zielińska, *Magnateria polska epoki saskiej* (Wrocław, 1977), pp. 5–6, 195–97. Polish historians have not been rigorous in their use of the term "magnates." They apply it to the small elite group of which families like the Sieniawskis and Czartoryskis were a part as well as to a larger group of wealthy but much less established and politically powerful noble families. See, for example, W. Czapliński and J. Długosz, *Życie codzienne magnaterii polskiej w XVII wieku* (Warsaw, 1976), pp. 7–11. A. Kamiński, "The *Szlachta* of the Polish-Lithuanian Com-

percentage of the total nobility,[13] their significance for the nobility
and for Poland as a whole can hardly be exaggerated. To their noble
brethren these aristocrats were models, opinion-makers, and standard-
setters. Beyond this they were patrons who provided economic opportunities in the form of property leases, administrative jobs, and court
sinecures. The dependency relationship thus created gave each aristocratic magnate control of blocs of loyal noblemen who were willing to
fight for their patron's interests in the *sejmiki* (dietines) and the *Sejm*.
Individual magnates became the heads of the interest groups or parties
that vied with each other in the *Sejm* and the royal court for influence
and power. In order to rule, the king was forced to come to terms with
these political rivals. So powerful were the magnates that some Polish
historians have dubbed the Polish state of this period the Magnate Oligarchy. Whether such a formal designation is warranted or not, it is
beyond dispute that 1648–1763 was the heyday of magnate power in
Poland.[14]

As influential as he may have been at the royal court, the magnate
was still only one of many contenders for power there. Within his
own latifundium, however, a magnate had absolute authority far
exceeding that of the Polish kings over Poland as a whole. As a common proverb put it, "God rules in Heaven but *Pan* X rules in
_____.'' Particularly in the eastern two-thirds of the country,

---

monwealth and their Government,'' *The Nobility in Russia and Eastern Europe*, I.
Banac and P. Bushkovitz, eds. (New Haven, 1983) has pointed out this imprecision.
In the present work, the term ''magnate'' refers to the small group of aristocrats.

[13] Dworzaczek cited a total of seventy-nine families between the fifteenth and
nineteenth centuries that could be considered to be among the elite.

[14] Czapliński and Długosz, pp. 178–86; Gierowski and Kamiński, ''Eclipse,'' pp.
705–706; W. A. Serczyk, *Gospodarstwo magnackie we województwie podolskim w
drugiej połowie XVIII wieku* (Wrocław, 1965), pp. 19–20; Żytkowicz, ''Okres gospodarki,'' pp. 253–56. On the concept of Poland as a magnate oligarchy see: W.
Czapliński, ''Rządy oligarchii w Polsce nowożytnej,'' *PH* 52 (1961), pp. 445–65; Z.
Kaczmarczyk, ''Oligarchia magnacka w Polsce jako forma państwa,'' *Pamiętnik VIII
powszechnego zjazdu historyków polskich w Krakowie* (Warsaw, 1958), pt. 1; H.
Olszewski, *Sejm Rzeczpospolitej epoki oligarchii* (Poznań, 1966), pp. 9–21. For a
dissenting view, see: A. Kersten, ''Problem władzy w Rzeczypospolitej czasu
Wazów,'' *O naprawę Rzeczypospolitej*, J. A. Gierowski, ed. (Warsaw, 1965), pp.
23–26; and Kamiński, ''Szlachta.'' Historians who use the designation ''magnate
oligarchy'' usually choose to apply the term ''magnate'' to a very large group of
noblemen (see note 12).

magnates ruled as potentates over feudal estates that were in effect principalities consisting of hundreds of villages and towns, containing tens of thousands of inhabitants, and representing hundreds of thousands of *złoty* in annual income and expenditures.

On his domain a magnate was sole legislator, chief executive, commander in chief of his private army, supreme judge, and the source of all authority and benefice. His main interest was the economic well-being and profitability of the lands he owned, but he also had to be concerned with social, religious, judicial, military, and even foreign policy questions.[15]

Aspiring to princely power was only half the story. Tradition dictated that magnates should live like princes as well. Conspicuous consumption was a highly developed art among them. Each magnate possessed several palatial residences, usually designed by Italian architects and built and furnished at fantastic expense. Once built, each residence had to be maintained and supplied with a full complement of butlers, maids, cooks, grooms, soldiers, and so forth, totaling as many as several hundred people.[16]

Of course, once the residences were built and staffed they had to be enjoyed. Magnates regularly hosted balls and prodigious feasts that afforded the opportunity for showing off expensive imported clothing, gourmet delicacies, silver and crystal tableware, and private orchestras and entertainers.[17]

In order to maximize the good times, magnates were constantly on the road, traveling among their own residences and those of their friends. Elżbieta Sieniawska changed residences at least twenty times between January 1, 1719, and January 3, 1720. Such trips were not made unaccompanied. A magnate's entourage could be very large: in exceptional cases, it included as many as sixty to seventy wagons and one thousand people, all of whom had to be fed, housed, and clothed.[18] Moreover, magnates did not just spend money on them-

---

[15] S. W. Baron, *A Social and Religious History of the Jews,* vol. 16 (New York-Philadelphia, 1976), p. 165; Czapliński and Długosz, pp. 83–87.

[16] P. Bohdziewicz, ed., *Korespondencja artystyczna Elżbiety Sieniawskiej z lat 1700–1729* (Lublin, 1964); Czapliński and Długosz, pp. 12–18.

[17] Czapliński and Długosz, pp. 105–107.

[18] BC 2677, BC 5945; J. Burszta, *Wieś i karczma* (Warsaw, 1950), pp. 125–30; Czapliński and Długosz, pp. 99–104.

selves and their entourages. They prided themselves on their patronage of the arts, literature, architecture, theater, and music as well as their contributions to religious institutions and to charities.[19]

But the buildings, staff, trips, banquets, and patronage did not exhaust the magnates' expenses. There were also legal expenses from the many disputes that arose with other magnates, money required to purchase new lands in order to expand the latifundium, and the operating budget of the productive side of the latifundium—the manors. All of these expenses created an insatiable need for cash. If a magnate could not spend, he could not maintain his standard of living nor his standing with his fellow magnates. To be secure he needed a constant, dependable supply of cash. The source of this supply was his latifundium.[20]

The Latifundium

A magnate derived virtually all of his wealth from his latifundium, which was organized into complexes called *klucze*. Each complex might contain two to ten manors (*folwarki*), a town or two, as many as twenty or more villages, and a residence (*dwór*), utilized by the owner or by his general manager. Several such contiguous complexes or an extremely large one were usually called a territory (*dobra, włość*), barony (*hrabstwo*), or, after the mid-eighteenth century, a district (*komisariat*). Often, however, these complexes were not contiguous, and very wealthy magnates like the Sieniawskis and Czartoryskis possessed complexes in many regions of Poland. Map 1.1 shows the boundaries of Poland and the location of the Sieniawski-Czartoryski holdings within it in 1731. This was of course subject to change as properties were purchased, sold, inherited, or given away, or as royal leases were acquired or lost. Maps 1.2 – 1.5 illustrate what each point on Map 1.1 represents—namely, a complex with its town, villages, and manors.

The central component of the latifundium from the subjective

---

[19] Czapliński and Długosz, pp. 39 – 41, 141 – 75.

[20] Czapliński and Długosz, pp. 71, 75 – 82; W. Brablec, "Elżbieta z Lubomirskich Sieniawska," doctoral dissertation, Jagiellonian University (Cracow, 1949), p. 139; W. Kula, *An Economic Theory of the Feudal System*, L. Garner, trans. (Bristol, England, 1976), p. 37.

perspective of its owner and inhabitants, as well as from the objective fact of the amount of time and labor invested, was the manors, which were centers of many types of labor-intensive agriculture and industry. The important activities were apiculture, cattle, poultry and fish, field crops, forest industries, liquor production and sale, mills, and mines. The key to their successful operation was the feudal labor system, which guaranteed the owner a reliable, cheap supply of peasant *courvée*.[21]

The second component of the feudal complex was the village. For the owner, this was both the labor pool for the manors and a good source of income paid either in money rent or in kind. Each peasant household was obliged to provide some combination of labor, money rent, and payments in cloth, poultry, wax, and so on, in varying proportions depending on the region, local tradition, and the owner's needs. While the villagers, as serfs, were subject to the rule of the lord and his representatives, they did have a modest measure of control over village matters through their traditional village council (*gromada*). The council controlled the use of village forest and meadow lands and had a treasury at its disposal to cover public expenditures or aid to individuals. Its executive arm collected taxes, served some judiciary functions, divided the *courvée* burden fairly among the villagers, and kept peace and order. In theory, the council served as liaison between the villagers and the owner. In reality, this usually meant enforcing the owner's edicts in the village.[22]

---

[21] A. Baranovich, *Magnatskoe khoziaistvo na iuge Volyni v XVIII v.* (Moscow, 1955), pp. 36–67; J. Bergerówna, *Księżna pani na Kocku i Siemiatyczach* (Lviv, 1936), pp. 131–41; W. Kula, "L'histoire économique de la Pologne du XVIII siècle," *APH* 4 (1961), pp. 133–36, 141–45; J. Majewski, *Gospodarstwo folwarczne we wsiach miasta Poznania w latach 1582–1644* (Poznań, 1957), pp. 51–69; J. Rutkowski, *Badania nad podziałem dochodów w Polsce w czasach nowożytnych,* pt. 1 (Warsaw, 1938), pp. 41–46, 92–219; Serczyk, pp. 49, 80, 120–25; M. B. Topolska, *Dobra szkłowskie na Białorusi wschodniej w XVII i XVIII wieku* (Warsaw, 1969), pp. 84–87; Żytkowicz, "Okres gospodarki," pp. 249–50, 303.

[22] C. Bobińska, ed., *Studia z dziejów wsi małopolskiej w drugiej połowie XVIII w.* (Warsaw, 1957); J. Rafacz, *Ustrój wsi samorządnej małopolskiej w XVIII wieku* (Lublin, 1922); W. Rusiński, *Uwagi o rozwarstwieniu wsi w Polsce XVIII wieku* (Poznań, 1953); Rutkowski, *Badania,* pp. 30–41, 246–55; idem, *Przebudowa wsi w Polsce po wojnach z połowy XVII wieku* (Cracow, 1916); idem, "Studya nad położeniem włościan w Polsce w XVIII wieku," *Ekonomista* 14 (1914); E. Trzyna, *Położenie ludności wiejskiej w królewszczyznach województwa krakowskiego w XVII wieku* (Wrocław, 1963).

Map 1.1: The Properties of Maria Zofia
Sieniawski and August Alexander
Czartoryski at the Time of their Marriage
(1731)

scale (approximate) 1:3 622 000

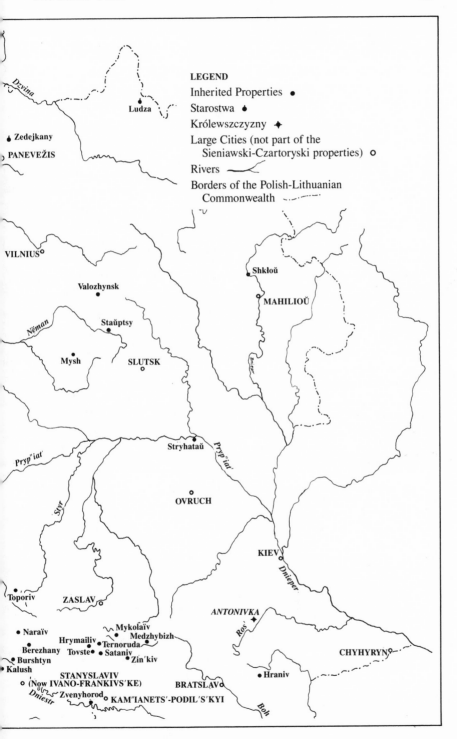

LEGEND

Inherited Properties •

Starostwa ⧫

Królewszczyzny ✦

Large Cities (not part of the
   Sieniawski-Czartoryski properties) ○

Rivers

Borders of the Polish-Lithuanian
   Commonwealth

Map 1.2: The Medzhybizh Klucz (1730–1736)

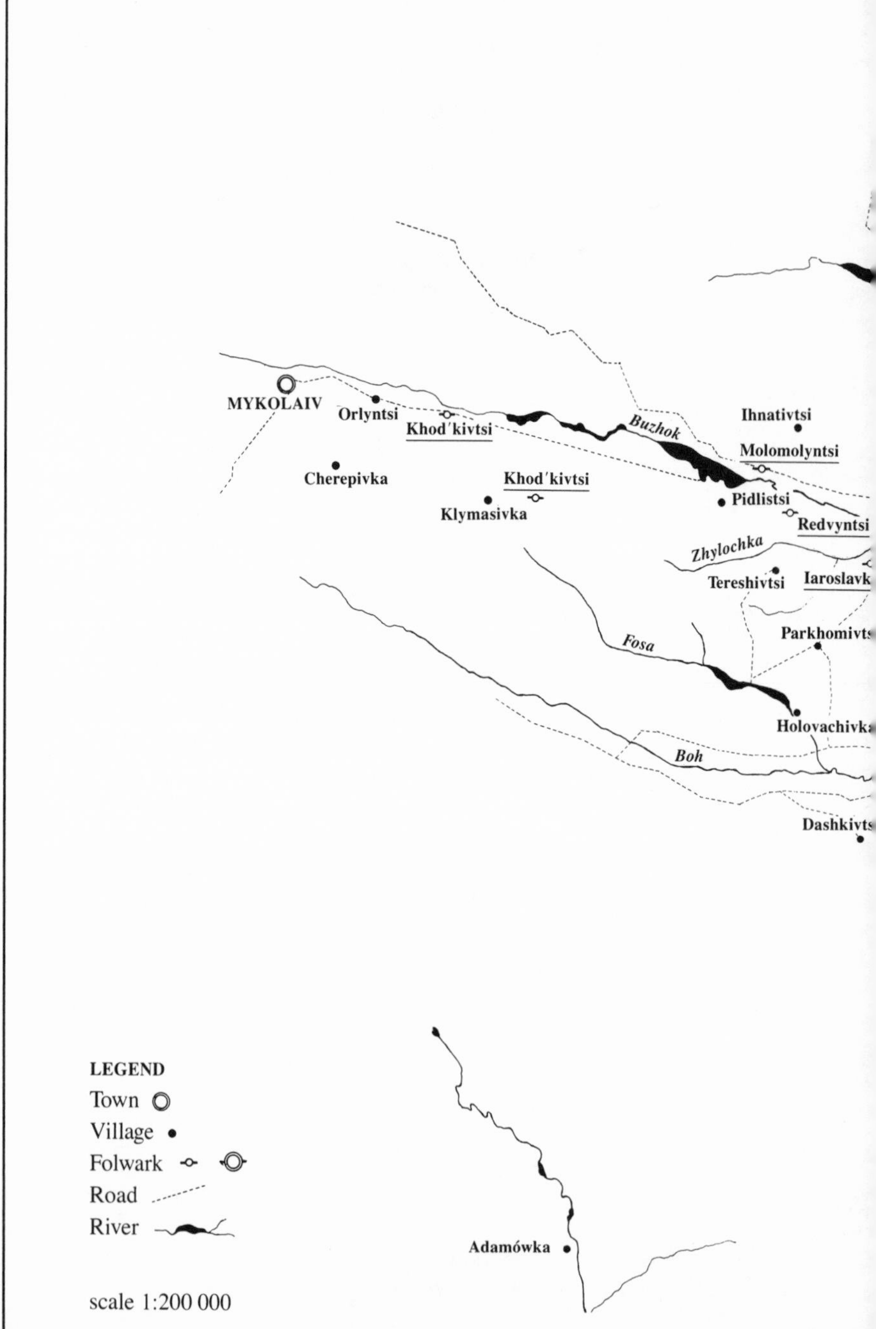

MYKOLAIV   Orlyntsi
                    Khod´kivtsi   *Buzhok*   Ihnativtsi
                                                                Molomolyntsi
        Cherepivka   Khod´kivtsi
                        Klymasivka   • Pidlistsi
                                                                  Redvyntsi
                                                    Zhylochka
                                                    Tereshivtsi   Iaroslavk

                                        Fosa   Parkhomivts

                                                                Holovachivka
                                        Boh

                                                                  Dashkivts

LEGEND
Town   ○
Village   •
Folwark   -○-   ◎
Road   ------
River

scale 1:200 000

Adamówka •

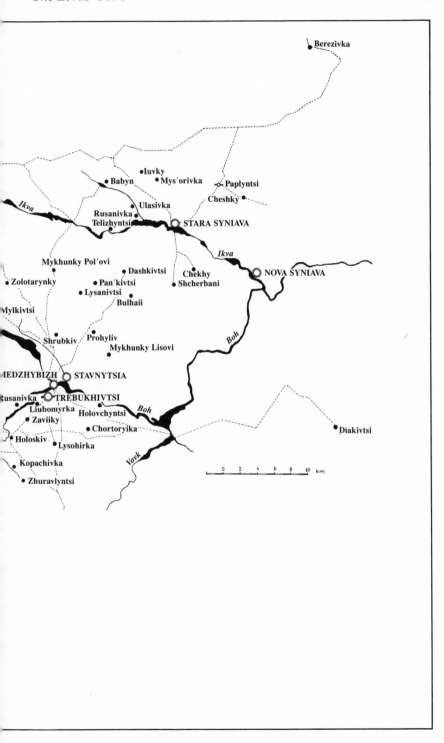

Berezivka

Iuvky
Babyn • Mys'orivka • Paplyntsi
Cheshky •
Ulasivka
Rusanivka
Telizhyntsi
STARA SYNIAVA

Ikva

Ikva

Mykhunky Pol'ovi
Zolotarynky • Dashkivtsi
Pan'kivtsi Chekhy
Shcherbani
Lysanivtsi
Mylkivtsi
Bulhaii

NOVA SYNIAVA

Boh

Shrubkiv Prohyliv
Mykhunky Lisovi

MEDZHYBIZH STAVNYTSIA

Rusanivka TREBUKHIVTSI
Liubomyrka Holovchyntsi *Boh*
Zaviiky
Chortoryika
Holoskiv Lysohirka
Kopachivka
Zhuravlyntsi

Diakivtsi

Vovk

0 2 4 6 8 10 km

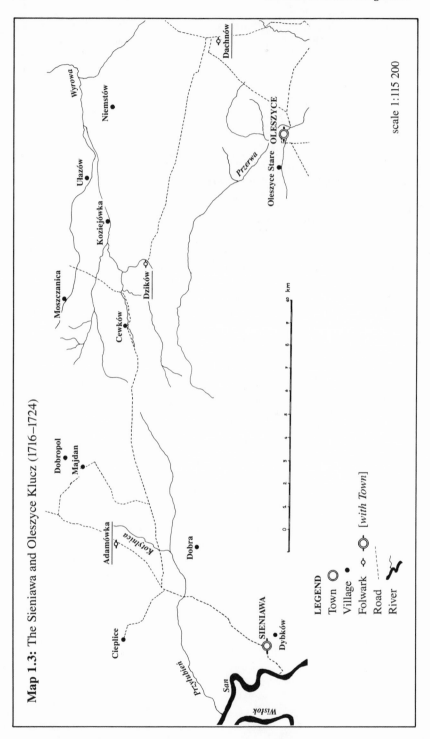

Map 1.3: The Sieniawa and Oleszyce Klucz (1716–1724)

scale 1:115 200

LEGEND
Town ◎
Village ●
Folwark ◇
Road ---
River

◇ Ⓞ [with Town]

40 km

Dachnów
Niemstów
Wyrowa
Ulazów
Koziejówka
Moszczanica
Cewków
Dzików
Oleszyce Stare
OLESZYCE
Przerwa
Dobropol
Majdan
Adamówka
Korybnica
Dobra
Cieplice
SIENIAWA
Dybków
Przyłubień
San
Wisłok

The third unit in the feudal complex was the town. It served as the commercial and administrative center for the surrounding manors and villages. Towns were usually granted privileges based on the so-called "German Law." These privileges allowed for a large measure of autonomy in judicial and administrative matters. As in the village, however, the town council was ultimately subservient to the owner and his representatives. Town residents contributed tax money to the owner's coffers and were obliged to perform specific services such as guard duty, hauling products by wagon, and shoveling snow. Besides new taxes and obligations, residents of villages and towns provided revenue by patronizing liquor and mill monopolies controlled by the owner, by buying latifundium products (voluntarily or by coercion), and by giving traditional "gifts" to the magnate.[23]

The residence or court was more or less developed, depending on whether the owner and his entourage utilized it frequently. There were many facets to running a proper residence, and, as already noted, the staff could number in the hundreds.[24]

The latifundium was administered through an elaborate structure. Each branch of activity on the manor was directed by an employee or lessee: stackyard supervisor, *gospodyni* in charge of dairy and poultry production, *leśnik* in charge of the forest, shepherd, lessee of the mill and/or liquor monopoly, foreman of field workers, and so forth. Each of these reported either to the officials in charge of the manor, the *podstarosta* and his assistant, the *dwornik,* or directly to the two officials in charge of the entire complex, the general manager and comptroller.[25]

[23] T. Opas, "Miasta prywatne a Rzeczpospolita," *KH* 78 (1971), pp. 28–48; idem, "Powinności na rzecz dziedziców w miastach szlacheckich województwa lubelskiego w drugiej połowie XVII i w XVIII wieku," *Rocznik Lubelski* 14 (1971), pp. 121–44; A. Prochaska, *Historja miasta Stryja* (Lviv, 1926), pp. 36–39; Serczyk, p. 49; A. Wyrobisz, "Rola miast prywatnych w Polsce w XVI i XVII wieku," *PH* 65 (1974), pp. 19–46; Żytkowicz, "Okres gospodarki," p. 253.

[24] BC 2626 1703, pp. 11–15, 1706, pp. 37, 42–44, BC 4044, 1725 p. 16 (payrolls); BC 2904 no. 51 (uniform orders); cf. I. Rychlikowa, *Szkice o gospodarce panów na Łańcucie* (Łańcut, 1971), pp. 121–22.

[25] A. Pośpiech and W. Tygielski, "Społeczna rola dworu magnackiego XVII–XVIII wieku," *PH* 69 (1978), pp. 215–16; Rutkowski, *Badania,* pp. 67–76, 308–12; Serczyk, pp. 31–35; Z. Szkurłatowski, "Organizacja, administracja i praca w dobrach wielkiej własności feudalnej w Polsce w XVII i XVIII wieku w świetle instruktarzy ekonomicznych," *Zeszyty Naukowe Uniwersytetu Wrocławskiego,* Ser. A, no. 7 (1957), pp. 150ff.

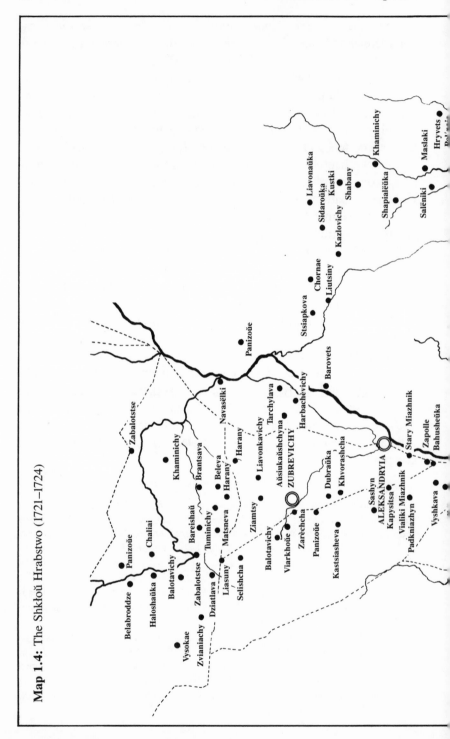

Map 1.4: The Shkłoŭ Hrabstwo (1721–1724)

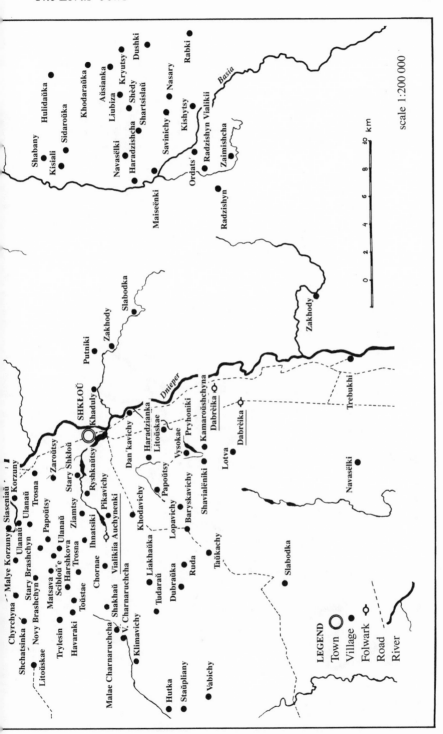

scale 1:200 000

Basia

40 km

Dnieper

Basia

Rabki
Dushki
Kryutsy
Aŭsianka
Khodaraŭka
Šhèdy
Nasary
Liubiza
Shartsislaŭ
Kishytsy
Radzishyn Vialikii
Savinichy
Zaimishcha
Hulidaŭka
Sidaroŭka
Shabany
Navasëlki
Ordats'
Kisiali
Haradzishcha
Radzishyn
Maiseënki

Slabodka
Zakhody
Zakhody
Putniki
Trebukhi
SHKŁOŬ
Khaduly
Kamaroŭshchyna
Dabrèika
Dabrèika
Haradzianka
Pryhoniki
Dan'kavichy
Litoŭskae
Navasëlki
Zaroŭtsy
Ryshkaŭtsy
Vysokae
Chyrchyna
Malye Korzuny
Siaseniaŭ
Korzuny
Pikavichy
Papoŭtsy
Lotva
Stary Shkłoŭ
Ulanaŭ
Ulanaŭ
Trosna
Khodavichy
Shaviaëŭniki
Stary Brashchyn
Papoŭtsy
Ziamtsy
Ihnatsiki
Vialikiia Auchynenki
Lopavichy
Baryskavichy
Shchatsinka
Matsava
Ulanaŭ
Harshkova
Chornae
Slabodka
Novy Brashchyn
Sciblou''e
Trosna
Taŭkachy
Litoŭskae
Trylesin
Toŭstae
Shakhaŭ
Liakhaŭka
Ruda
Havaraki
Malae Charnaruchcha
Tudaraŭ
Dubraŭka
V. Charnaruchcha
Klimavichy
Hutka
Vabichy
Staŭpliany

LEGEND
Town
Village
Folwark
Road
River

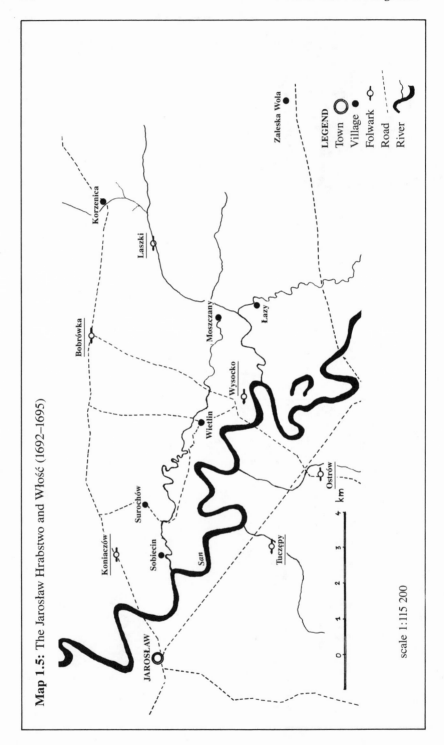

Map 1.5: The Jarosław Hrabstwo and Włość (1692–1695)

scale 1:115 200

Every feudal complex or group of complexes had a general manager, usually called a *komisarz, ekonom,* or *gubernator,* who had overall responsibility for every facet of the section of the latifundium under his control. He supervised all personnel, oversaw each branch of latifundium activity and marketing, and was the owner's representative in every sense. In the owner's absence—that is, most of the time—he was the highest authority for village and town inhabitants, issuing edicts and rendering justice.[26]

The general manager was assisted by the general comptroller (*pisarz prowentowy*), who was in charge of accounting for all income and expenses in cash, labor, and kind. Although he worked closely with the general manager, he was not quite subordinate to the latter, for he periodically reported directly to the owner. This semi-independence was intended to mitigate collusion between the executive and accounting officials.[27]

The residence, although dependent on the rest of the complex for supplies and labor, was administered separately. Its staff was headed by the *marszałek*.[28]

Keeping in mind that every magnate owned more than one complex, frequently far apart geographically, it is apparent that keeping such an extensive administration efficient and honest was a formidable task. Historians have not given the Polish magnates much credit for succeeding at it. Typically, they are portrayed as egotistical, dissolute louts who were concerned only with the cash they could wring out of their holdings, hardly aware of the necessity for investment, supervision, economy, or maintenance if their property were to remain profitable.[29]

It is hard to understand how such behavior could sustain the luxurious magnate life-style described above for even one generation. In cases where fortunes continued to prosper, it makes sense to expect that this would be the result, at least in part, of good management by

---

[26] See Chapter 6.

[27] Serczyk, p. 31.

[28] Pośpiech and Tygielski, pp. 215–17, 223, 224.

[29] Burszta, *Wieś,* pp. 45–53, 198–202, 204–205; Czapliński and Długosz, pp. 80–82; Z. Kuchowicz, "Społeczne konsekwencje postępującej degeneracji możnowładztwa polskiego w XVII i XVIII w.," *KH* 76 (1969), pp. 21–43, especially pp. 22–29.

the owner. As we shall see, this certainly was true with regard to the Sieniawski-Czartoryski latifundium.[30]

The Sieniawski-Czartoryski family and latifundium illustrate everything said here about the magnates and their holdings. Their genealogy, wealth, power, and behavior patterns made them aristocratic magnates par excellence. Since the story of the Jews in their territories serves as the focus of this study, it is important to become acquainted with them and their latifundium.

---

[30] There were several sixteenth-eighteenth century agricultural texts that advocated rational economic behavior and were read by the magnates; see: A. Gostomski, *Gospodarstwo*, S. Inglot, ed. (Wrocław, 1951); K. Kluk, *O rolnictwie, zbożach, łąkach, chmielnikach, winnicach, i roślinach gospodarskich*, S. Inglot, ed. (Wrocław, 1954); A. Podraza, *Jakub Kazimierz Haur, pisarz rolniczy XVII wieku* (Wrocław, 1961).

CHAPTER TWO

The Sieniawskis and Czartoryskis and Their Latifundium

When August Aleksander Czartoryski married Maria Zofia Sieniawska Denhoffowa in 1731, she owned more land than any other person in Poland.[1] Her fortune began accumulating centuries earlier through land purchases, grants, opportune marriages, and royal privileges like the early sixteenth-century decree granting Mikołaj Sieniawski permission to make the village of Berezhany into a town.[2] By the time her grandfather, Mikołaj Hieronim Sieniawski, married Cecylia Radziwiłł in 1622, he possessed more land and serfs than most German princes.[3] This already huge fortune was increased by the union, in 1686, of Adam Mikołaj Sieniawski, Maria Zofia's father, with her mother, Elżbieta Lubomirska, heiress of one of the richest and most powerful families in Poland. As part of her dowry, she brought into the marriage the complexes of Puławy and Końskowola. In 1704, Elżbieta Sieniawska inherited four complexes in the Cracow and Sandomierz regions worth more than three million *złoty* from her uncle, Stanisław Opaliński. In the same year, she purchased the Starosielski and Skolski complexes. She added half of the city of Jarosław and environs in 1706. By 1720, when she purchased Wilanów, the magnificent residence of the Sobieski family near Warsaw, whole

[1] A. Gieysztor et al., *A History of Poland* (Warsaw, 1979), p. 250; K. Buczek, "Z dziejów polskiej archiwistyki prywatnej,' *Studia historyczne ku czci Stanisława Kutrzeby*, vol. 2 (Cracow, 1938), p. 50, n. 4 contains a list of Maria Zofia's holdings in 1731. Map 1.1 is based on this enumeration.

[2] B. Puczyński, "Ludność Brzeżan i okolicy w XVII i XVIII w.," *Przeszłość Demograficzna Polski* 4–5 (1971–72), p. 179 gives the date as 1507; cf. M. Maciszewski, *Brzeżany* (Brody, 1910), pp. 13–14, who gives the date as 1530.

[3] Maciszewski, p. 69; M. B. Topolska, *Dobra szkłowskie na Białorusi wschodniej w XVII i XVIII wieku* (Warsaw, 1969), pp. 14–16.

regions of Poland were divided between the Sieniawskis and their relatives, the Lubomirskis.[4]

In addition to all of these hereditary territories, the Sieniawskis also possessed many royal land leases and nonhereditary grants (*królewszczyzny* and *starostwa*). Moreover, when Maria Zofia was widowed in 1728, after four years of marriage to the heirless Stanisław Denhoff, she received further hereditary and other territories, particularly in the Northwest. By the time of her second marriage, to Czartoryski, she owned more than twenty complexes, including some thirty towns and seven hundred villages, in addition to leases and grants. As Map 1.1 indicates, her possessions were spread throughout the Commonwealth, although the largest concentrations were in Royal Prussia, Mazowia, Little Poland, Red Ruthenia, and Podillia. Included in the latifundium were vast tracts of fertile farmland, large forests, and salt, calamine, and iron mines. In addition, places like Sieniawa, Berezhany, Jarosław, and Shkłoŭ were situated on main roads or near rivers, placing them in advantageous positions economically, militarily, and politically.[5] There were also several palatial residences in addition to Wilanów, which was, in the words of Sieniawska, merely a place "where I will be able to stable my horses while the *Sejm* is in session."[6] The other palaces regularly used by the owners during this period were in Sieniawa, Oleszyce, Medzhybizh, Puławy, and Lviv. Others, such as those in Berezhany and Rytwiany, were rarely if ever visited.[7]

The Owners

The four people who ruled the latifundium during the period covered by this study were Adam Mikołaj Sieniawski, Elżbieta Sieniawska, Maria Zofia Czartoryska, and August Aleksander

[4] Brablec, pp. 57–58, 125–26; Z. Guldon, *Związki handlowe dóbr magnackich na prawobrzeżnej Ukrainie z Gdańskiem w XVIII w.* (Torun, 1966), p. 1; L. Powidaj, *Rytwiany i ich dziedzice* (Cracow, 1880), pp. 47–49.

[5] Brablec, p. 125; Buczek, p. 50, n. 4; *Historia Polski*, vol. 1, pt. 2, p. 648; Puczyński, p. 170; Topolska, pp. 16–17.

[6] Brablec, p. 126.

[7] Brablec, pp. 40–41.

Czartoryski. Adam Mikołaj Sieniawski's vast economic wealth was matched by his political and military power. Born in 1666 into a family with a tradition of serving as hetman (grand marshal)[8] of Poland's army, he was educated in Poland and France. In 1702 he was elevated to the position of hetman of Crown Poland. In 1710 he was nominated to be *kasztelan* (palatine) of Cracow, the most prestigious secular seat in the Polish Senate. At the time he became hetman, this institution had reached the apex of its power. Since, on the one hand, the large *hibernia* tax intended to finance provisioning the army was at his disposal, and, on the other, the monarchy was being contested by Augustus II and Stanisław Leszczyński, Sieniawski was not answerable to anyone for the military and budgetary decisions he made. He had free reign in running the army and even determined his own policy with regard to Russia and other countries. Possessing so much power, it is no wonder that he was considered a candidate for king.[9]

Sieniawski's power as hetman kept growing, especially after the organization of the Sandomierz Confederation, which he headed, and Augustus II's abdication in 1706. Yet, except to enrich himself, he did not utilize the power at his disposal, allowing it to dissipate until it was finally taken from him by acts of the Russian-controlled "Silent *Sejm*," in 1717.[10] He was one of the least efficient hetmans in Polish history. Having reached his position through family connections and ambition, he lacked the requisite talent to make the most of it when he arrived. His efforts at improving the army met with no more than modest success.[11] At crucial moments during the Sandomierz

[8] There were four such hetmans at any given time: a grand marshal and field marshal each for both Crown Poland and Lithuania.

[9] *AGZ* vol. 22, nos. 94.8, 95.3, 97.2, 180; vol. 25, nos. 37, 49, 53, 55 all reflect Adam Mikołaj Sieniawski's great power and high standing with other noblemen; cf. Brablec, pp. 43–44, 86, 88–89, 101; A. Bruckner, *Dzieje kultury polskiej*, vol. 3 (Warsaw, 1958), p. 16; J. A. Gierowski, *W cieniu Ligi Północnej* (Wrocław, 1971), p. 29; A. Kamiński, *Konfederacja Sandomierska wobec Rosji w okresie poałtranstadzkim, 1706–1709* (Wrocław, 1969), pp. 21 (n. 21), 77, 95, 99, 111; Maciszewski, pp. 70–74, 170; J. Wimmer, *Wojsko Rzeczpospolitej w dobie Wojny Północnej* (Warsaw, 1956), pp. 345–46.

[10] Gierowski and Kamiński, "Eclipse," pp. 93 (n. 3), 95; Maciszewski, pp. 70–74.

[11] A. Kamiński, "Piotr I a wojsko koronne w przededniu szwedzkiego uderzenia na Rosję w. 1707," *Studia i materiały do historii wojskowości* (Warsaw, 1969), pp. 43–46, 55.

Confederation he vacillated, failing to rally his men for decisive battles.[12] A moody person, Sieniawski was prone to depression and pro-
crastination and was easily swayed by assertive people like his wife
and Peter the Great.[13]

Elżbieta Sieniawska possessed the strengths that her husband
lacked. She was bright, decisive, efficient, and alternately charming
and ruthless as required. Whether representing the interests of the
king of France or tsar of Russia, the Hungarian nobleman Rakoczy, or
would-be-kings Stanisław Leszczyński and Stanisław Poniatowski,
she was respected as a deft politician.[14] Sieniawska was an acquaintance of King Jan Sobieski, confidante to Queen Marysieńka, and
lover of Prince Aleksander. Such proximity to the center of power,
combined with her family background as daughter of Stanisław
Herakliusz Lubomirski, Grand Marshal of Poland, and her status as
wife of the hetman and *kasztelan* of Cracow, conferred power on
Sieniawska and made her unafraid to enter into the politics and
conflicts of the time. She so thoroughly pervaded the social, court,
and political life of the period that her biographer did not exaggerate
in calling her "a queen without a crown."[15] Her activity elicited
strong feelings. King Charles XII of Sweden referred to her as "that
most accursed woman,"[16] while others would have concurred in the
opinion of the eighteenth-century chronicler, Otwinowski, that she
was "a great, insightful, clever genius of a woman."[17]

Unlike her husband, who was burdened by official duties, Elżbieta
Sieniawska's main concern was the latifundium, as she was the titular

---

[12] Brablec, pp. 43–44, 73, 85, 89; Gierowski and Kamiński, "Eclipse," pp.
701–704, 711; Gierowski, *W cieniu*, pp. 60–64; idem, *Między*, pp. 106–107; A. F.
Grabski et al., *Zarys wojskowości polskiej do roku 1864* (Warsaw, 1966), p. 170;
Maciszewski, pp. 70–74; L. Powidaj, *Rytwiany i ich dziedzice* (Cracow, 1880), pp.
50–51.

[13] Brablec, pp. 9–11, 141–42; Gierowski and Kamiński, "Eclipse," p. 708;
Gierowski, *W cieniu*, pp. 29, 50, 53; Kamiński, *Konfederacja*, p. 21.

[14] Brablec, Introduction, pp. 9–11, 26, 62–128, 137; Gierowski, *W cieniu*, pp. 32,
47, 54–55, 67; idem, "Wrocławskie interesy hetmanowej Elżbiety Sieniawskiej,"
Studia z dziejów kultury i ideologii (Wrocław, 1968), pp. 222–23.

[15] Brablec, Introduction, pp. 29–30.

[16] Brablec, pp. 76–78.

[17] E. Otwinowski, *Dzieje Polski pod panowaniem Augusta II* (Cracow, 1849), as
quoted by Maciszewski, p. 82.

owner of a large part of it. Turning her considerable talents to managing this enterprise, she enjoyed nurturing the family lands and fortune. Her efforts were assiduous and the results successful.[18]

In addition to working hard as estate manager, Sieniawska loved to enjoy the good life of a Polish magnate. She regularly hosted and attended balls, spent huge amounts of money renovating buildings and staffing palaces, and was known as a generous maecenas who sponsored many artists and musicians.[19]

When Elżbieta Sieniawska died on March 24, 1729 (some three years after her husband), her widowed thirty-year-old daughter, Maria Zofia, became the sole owner and ruler of the tremendous latifundium. In his memoirs, her grandson Adam Jerzy Czartoryski described her as "a lady of rare intelligence and extreme wealth."[20] She apparently was endowed with her mother's brilliance and single-mindedness and her father's moodiness. As the richest heiress in Poland and an attractive woman in her own right, she was inundated with proposals. Her first marriage, in 1724, was to Stanisław Denhoff, who was more than twice her age. This was a political match arranged by her father. It brought her more property as well as status as both daughter and wife of hetmans.[21] Once her husband, father, and mother died, Maria Zofia was left alone to manage the latifundium. She evidently tried to make the transition as smooth as possible by retaining old personnel and following her mother's policies.[22] Being relatively young, and now the possessor of an immense fortune, she was once again the object of much ardent courting. Everyone realized that the prize at stake went beyond her hand and even her wealth to considerable political power.

Maria Zofia's choice of a second husband was somewhat surprising. August Aleksander Czartoryski came from one of the oldest and

[18] Brablec, pp. 43–44, 76, 127–34, 138, 142–45.

[19] Bohdziewicz, *Korespondencja artystyczna Elżbiety Sieniawskiej*; Brablec, pp. 133, 130–45; Gierowski, "Wrocławskie interesy," pp. 222–23; J. Gajewski, "Elżbieta Sieniawska i jej artyści. Z zagadnień organizacji pracy artystycznej i odbioru w XVIII w. w Polsce," *Mecenas, Kolecjoner, Odbiorca* (Warsaw, 1984), pp. 281–302.

[20] A. J. Czartoryski, *Memoirs,* A. Gielgud, ed. and trans., 2 vols. (London, 1888), vol. 1, p. 2.

[21] Brablec, pp. 146–53; *PSB* 4, pp. 248–49.

[22] See the correspondence with the administrators, e.g., BC 5767, 5806, 5881–83, 5897, 5934–35, 5943–46.

most distinguished, but also one of the poorest, Polish magnate families.[23] Czartoryski himself, born in 1697, had pursued a military career as a Maltese Knight and as an officer in the Austrian army. He possessed neither office nor fortune in Poland, and his ancestral holdings did not go beyond his share in the family estate at Klevan'.[24] Nevertheless, Maria Zofia preferred him to scions of much richer houses. Her choice was vindicated, for Czartoryski proved to be a superior manager of the latifundium, and the marriage was apparently a happy one.[25] The subsequent prominence of the Czartoryskis at the center of Polish politics over the next century or so was in large part a result of this marriage. The stature of "The Family" of later eighteenth- and nineteenth-century Polish history was immeasurably enhanced by the opportunities resulting from the acquisition of the Sieniawski fortune.[26]

The Owner's Task

Historians describing Polish land-owning noblemen have usually emphasized their involvement in politics, their temper and fighting spirit, their philanthropic activity, and their love of high living and drink. Polish magnates have not typically been depicted as efficient managers. The extant sources from the Sieniawski-Czartoryski latifundium, however, show that Elżbieta Sieniawska, Maria Zofia Czartoryska, August Aleksander Czartoryski, and even Adam Mikołaj Sieniawski were practical, conscientious, and appreciative of the relationship between income and all the elements that went into generating it. They knew that current investment in buildings enhanced profits in future years, and so they insisted on repairing damaged buildings quickly. They approved loans to individuals who had to rebuild homes or businesses as a result of fire or some other calam-

---

[23] Dębicki, *Puławy*, vol. 1 (Lviv, 1887), pp. 3–23; M. Dernalewicz, *Portret familii* (Warsaw, 1974), pp. 7, 22–26.

[24] Dernalewicz, pp. 22–26; *PSB* 4, pp. 272–75.

[25] Czartoryski, p. 2; Dernalewicz, pp. 26–29.

[26] Gieysztor et al., p. 250; Topolska, pp. 15–16.

ity.[27] Since discontented peasants were unproductive, the Sieniawskis and Czartoryskis accepted petitions from their serfs and took them seriously.[28] They even realized that at times it was desirable to forego short-term income in order to assure the productive capacity of their property.[29] It is also apparent that economic decisions were usually made on the basis of economic factors.[30] These magnates were particularly careful about preserving law and order in their territories so as to guarantee the orderly conduct of business and agriculture.[31]

The basic problem for the owners—especially these owners—in administering the latifundium did not lie in formulating judicious policies or in setting the proper priorities. For them the difficulty was to ensure the execution of these policies and the observance of the priorities. Since the size of the latifundium prohibited the owners' personal presence, their primary managerial task was to supervise those entrusted with on-site management.

The first step in supervision was having a clear idea of what was required and communicating it to the administrators. For example, Elżbieta Sieniawska knew how much income she expected each territory to produce annually and demanded detailed answers if her expectations were disappointed.[32]

Second, the Sieniawskis and Czartoryskis tried to avoid surprises in the financial reports submitted to them periodically by closely monitoring the situation in each complex. They required accurate financial statements, sent auditing teams to visit the complexes, culled information bearing on management from petitions submitted by residents,

[27] EW 189 *Supliki:* Hercyk Dawidowicz, Maier Jakubowicz, Jakob Moszkowicz, Jakob Krakowski et al.; Brablec, pp. 134, 137, 142–45; Maciszewski, p. 17.

[28] BC 5881 Łukszyński to ES 1.23456 undated. Brablec, pp. 136–37, maintained that harsh treatment of serfs contravened the policy of the owner. According to her, when it occurred it was due to the malice of administrators.

[29] EW 525 Szkłów *Informacje* 1725, BC 5881 Łukszyński to ES 1.23458 undated.

[30] BC 5943 ES to Marysieńka 1.37135 8/7/1703, for example, demonstrates that ES would rather give a lease to a Jew, despite the fact that a nobleman wanted it, because in her estimation the Jew would more surely generate profit.

[31] BC 5945 ES to Morzycki 1.37720 2/5/1721; see also the *Supliki* and the correspondence between ES and Chaim Tywlowicz, BC 5972; cf. R. Haim Rapoport, *Responsa* (Lviv, 1861), Even Haezer no. 27.

[32] BC 5945 ES to Morzycki 1.37624 4/12/1719, 1.37629 5/22/1719.

made occasional visits themselves, and, most of all, carried on a lively and frequent correspondence with subordinates.[33]

In the case of the Sieniawskis and Czartoryskis, these letters demonstrate the owners' memory of orders given, mastery of detail, and careful scrutiny of reports and other sources of information. Administrators were kept on the spot with streams of questions concerning the performance of orders, the progress of projects, and the propriety of certain expenses.[34] Excuses for failure to perform were not met kindly. In one instance, a plea of powerlessness to gain an increase in income from a lease renewal was answered with a threat of irons.[35] In another, an alibi of misunderstanding with regard to improper refining of calamine was rebuffed with the sarcastic response, "Either you are stupid or you suppose that I am."[36] Administrators who were incompetent or found guilty of malfeasance were dismissed or punished. Conversely, loyal, efficient, honest administrators were rewarded with material benefits and the owner's attention and confidence—valuable commodities in dealing with other people.[37]

In addition to supervision, there were certain tasks that the owner performed personally. Decisions regarding investment, marketing, and allocation of resources had to be approved by the owner.[38]

[33] BC 5934 R to ES 1.34737 7/10/1722; BC 5946 ES to Morzycki 1.37899 10/27/1723; ES to Zabagłowicz 1.37965 7/16/1725, 1.37968 8/5/1725; EW 189, 525 various *supliki* complaining about administrators where the responses are signed personally by AMS; EW 525 Szkłów *Informacje* 1716; Brablec, pp. 30–32, 134–38; Maciszewski, p. 124; Serczyk, p. 31.

[34] BC 5934 R to ES 1.34571 3/5/1705; BC 5943 ES to R 1.37211 6/1/1708; BC 5945 ES to Morzycki 1.37639 9/3/1719, 1.37755 9/15/1721, 1.37759 9/29/1721, 1.37769 11/5/1721; BC 5946 ES to Morzycki 1.37908 12/1/1723.

[35] BC 5946 ES to Morzycki 1.37899 10/27/1723.

[36] BC 5945 ES to Morzycki 1.37781 1/14/1722; cf. BC 5945 ES to Morzycki 1.37777 12/16/1721.

[37] The administrators Lublicki and Trojanowski were both dismissed; see: Brablec, pp. 30–32, 135; Gierowski, "Wrocławskie interesy," p. 224. On rewards for loyal service, see: BC 5945 R to ES 1.34767, 2/21/1723; Czapliński and Długosz, pp. 66–69; Gierowski, "Wrocławskie interesy," p. 235; Pośpiech and Tygielski, pp. 224–31.

[38] BC 5945 ES to Morzycki 1.37759 9/29/1721, 1.37762 10/12/1721, 1.37777 12/16/1721, 1.37781 1/14/1722, 1.37786 2/3/1722; BC 5946 ES to Zabagłowicz 1.37965 7/16/1725.

Elżbieta Sieniawska was particularly strict about this. Once, when Morzycki, the administrator of Tenczyn, received an order to give grain to the arrendator of Tenczyn, who had suffered a calamity, he did not dare to decide the amount on his own but requested a second order from Sieniawska specifying the quantity.[39]

Another area in which the owner participated directly was leasing. Since the specter of collusion between agent and lessee was ever-present, the Sieniawskis and Czartoryskis tried to negotiate personally as many leases as possible and oversaw the rest through correspondence. Sieniawska once complained to her husband that she had been prevented from traveling as planned, because "until now I could not settle with these arrendators."[40]

Latifundium Income

The latifundium was the source of a magnate's wealth, and measuring the revenue generated by latifundia would shed much light on magnate behavior and on Polish economic history. Unfortunately, producing a reliable balance sheet akin to a modern corporate report for any latifundium, including the Sieniawskis' and Czartoryskis', is virtually impossible. This is so because neither the tools nor the concepts underlying such a modern capitalistic device existed in Poland during the sixteenth, seventeenth, and eighteenth centuries.[41]

---

[39] BC 5897 Morzycki to ES 1.26544 9/16/1719 BC 5945 ES to Morzycki 1.37645 9/24/1719.

[40] BC 2514 ES to AMS 6/10/1702. For other examples of owner involvement in *arenda* negotiations see Chapter 6; cf. Brablec, pp. 41, 135–36; A. Leszczyński, *Żydzi ziemi bielskiej od połowy XVII wieku do 1795 r.* (Wrocław, 1980), pp. 206–208.

[41] The methodological problems connected with surviving latifundium financial records are numerous. They include: omission and distortion of data, lack of detail, inconsistent use of terminology, general currency confusion in Poland (see Appendix II), and the impossibility of reducing labor and kind dues to monetary terms. For examples of these problems see EW 133–34; cf. A. Burzyński, "Struktura dochodów wielkiej własności ziemskiej XVI–XVIII w.," *RDSG* 34 (1973), pp. 44–45; J. Leskiewiczowa, *Próba analizy gospodarki dóbr magnackich w Polsce* (Warsaw, 1964), pp. 15–24, 49; R. Łukasik, *Rachunkowość rolna w dawnej Polsce* (Warsaw, 1963), pp. 42, 45–47; Rutkowski, *Badania,* pp. 67–78, 234–38; 246–51, 263–66;

Even where relatively full documentation is extant, it does not address the concerns of modern accountants. Magnate financial records may have been complex in detail but not sophisticated in concept. A Polish magnate measured the profitability of his property by a simple equation: Income = Receipts - Expenses.[42] His attention was focused almost exclusively on cash transactions. The value of items such as the cost of credit and inventory, liabilities, accounts receivable, interdepartmental transactions, fixed asset value, and depreciation was not accounted for unless cash expenditures were entailed. The records were designed to show receipts and disbursements, not to give an accurate description of the financial health of the property in modern terms.

Even in the area of receipts, however, the records are uneven. In most cases there is a clear distinction made between payments in cash and receipts in kind, with the latter usually not being reduced to monetary terms. This is so because, in spite of the obvious fact that receipts and expenditures of labor, animals, and products were no less real than money, the owner's primary interest was in cash. The uses of kind were limited. The lists of disbursements indicate that agricultural products not sold for cash were used primarily to pay salaries and for services; to provide for the food needs of the staff, guests, or passing army units; to supply seed for peasants; or to give raw material to lessees. Occasionally, they were used to pay debts, but they were almost never bartered for goods. Yet, being a magnate necessitated consuming conspicuously and having all the things money (that is, cash) could buy. This need, coupled with the serious lack of circulating currency in this period, put a premium on cash.[43]

Another reason that the owner preferred cash is the matter of direct benefit. The amount of products sent from outlying complexes to the

---

I. Rychlikowa, *Produkcja zbożowa wielkiej własności w Małopolsce w latach 1764–1805* (Warsaw, 1967), pp. 118–26; Topolska, pp. 134–41.

[42] Burzyński, p. 31 n. 2; Kula, *Economic Theory*, pp. 28–36; Rutkowski, *Badania*, p. 66; I. Rychlikowa, *Klucz wielkoporębski Wodzickich w drugiej połowie XVIII wieku* (Wrocław, 1960), pp. 170–76.

[43] This is evident from the lists of expenditures of products, e.g., BC 4046, BC 4075, GOSP 340, 478, 853, 1014, 1015, Krzesz. 137, 141. See also BC 3502, Skole July 26, 1706, the shopping lists that ES gave to her skippers to fill for her in Gdańsk, and BC 4814–19. Similarly, see: Gierowski, *Między*, pp. 76–77; Kula, *Economic Theory*, pp. 30–31 (n. 3), 40, 122, 141–42, but cf. p. 51.

main residence for the consumption of the owner was very small or nonexistent. The owner knew about his noncash wealth, but he did not normally enjoy it personally. Cash profit, however, was sent to the main treasury to be spent as the owner saw fit, or was kept in reserve at the complex so that the owner could write vouchers against it.

Thus, the foremost question in the mind of a lord reading financial reports was, "How much cash is there at my disposal?"[44] Given this bias, it is impossible to determine accurately the "true"—in the modern accounting sense—financial state of the latifundium. It is possible, however, to obtain a reasonably correct picture of the cash flow. This is important because the owner was, in large measure, guided by this picture. The owner was neither aware of nor interested in the "true" state of affairs,[45] but he did want to maximize cash income. Hence, the records of the cash flow can aid in understanding how the owner decided economic policy.

Such records are available for six of the Sieniawski-Czartoryski complexes for periods ranging from six to twelve years between 1700 and 1739. The average annual revenues from each of these six complexes ranged between 30,000 and 85,000 zł. and came from three main sources: leases, fixed payments (taxes, rents, fees), and sale of products (grain, wax, cloth, hides, potash, and so forth).[46]

The proportion of the total revenue represented by each of these elements varied. As postwar monographic work has shown, the amount of latifundium produce·available for marketing was heavily dependent on factors of geography, soil, climate, and access to markets. In the majority of complexes far away from large population and export centers, most production was diverted to internal use or given over to lessees who sold it locally. In areas where soil or climate were

---

[44] BC 5945 ES to Morzycki 1.37624 4/12/1719; 1.37629 5/22/1719; BC 5934 R to ES 1.34579–80 4/10–13/1710; BC 5943 ES to Leymin 1.37126 4/26/1700; cf. Kula, *Economic Theory,* p. 32; Rychlikowa, *Szkice,* p. 91.

[45] Kula, *Economic Theory,* pp. 33–35; Leskiewiczowa, *Próba analizy gospodarki,* pp. 25–29.

[46] The complexes are: Jarosław, Medzhybizh, Rytwiany-Lubnice, Sieniawa-Oleszyce, Shkłoŭ, and Tenczyn. The information is derived from Krzesz. 141, BC 4041, BC 4048, AKP D.S. 84, EW 133, 135, GOSP 59, Topolska, Table 40.

inhospitable to agriculture, production was decreased and taxes increased as a means of collecting revenues.[47]

This pattern is at least partially borne out by the Sieniawski-Czartoryski latifundium. In Tenczyn, for example, which was very close to Cracow, income from product sales was approximately 45 percent of the total. In cold, distant Shkłoŭ, it was apparently never more than 25 percent, with taxes composing 45–60 percent. Medzhybizh, far from market, but with ample grain to be sold as liquor, was distinguished by the high percentage (more than 60 percent) of revenue produced by leases. For reasons that need to be clarified, leases were also the leading component in Rytwiany-Lubnice (58 percent), Jarosław (48 percent), and Sieniawa-Oleszyce (61 percent).

It would be difficult to rank the sources of revenue according to their value to the owner; each had advantages. The significant point is that every magnate had diverse sources of cash revenue and could shift emphasis as conditions changed. Such a shift meant, among other things, shifting the burden of revenue production from one group of latifundium inhabitants to another. For example, the groups primarily responsible for product sales were the serfs and their administrative supervisors who produced the goods, with a secondary role played by other administrators who handled the marketing. On the other hand, leases were mainly within the purview of the Jewish lessees with secondary participation—in the form of supervision—by the administrators. Taxes were paid by serfs, Jews, and townsmen, and were collected by administrators or lessees. Thus a shift from sales to leases involved placing more pressure on the Jews, while a shift from taxes to sales would mean that the peasants and administrators would have to work harder.

Of course, making demands on any group created a reciprocal claim on the owner to help eliminate obstacles and to provide the means by which the group in question could fulfill the demands. With each group striving to meet the rigorous requirements placed upon it,

[47] Baranovich, pp. 3–6, 61; Z. Guldon, *Związki handlowe dóbr magnackich na prawobrzeżnej Ukrainie z Gdańskiem w XVII w.* (Toruń, 1966), pp. 27, 30–31, 71–72; Homecki, pp. 33–34, 54–57; S. Hoszowski, "Handel Gdańska w okresie XV–XVIII wieku," *Prace z Zakresu Historii Gospodarczej* 11 (1960), p. 10; Leskiewiczowa, *Próba analizy gospodarki*, p. 50; Rychlikowa, *Szkice*, p. 94; Topolska, pp. 40–59, 77–79.

these claims could—and did—come into conflict. One of the central problems with which the owner had to deal was balancing these legitimate, conflicting claims.

The owner was constantly faced with choosing between the leaseholder who claimed that peasants violated his monopoly and the peasants who said that the lease-holder overcharged; or between the administrator who tried to maximize tax collection and the Jews who claimed that they needed to husband their resources in order to invest in commerce. In such disputes, each side was, in addition to serving its own interests, attempting to fulfill its obligations to the owner. The owner was forced to choose between two elements, both of which interlocked with the latifundium profit machine. Such choices were difficult to make because the owner's interests lay with both parties and he risked a loss regardless of whom he favored.

Dilemmas of this nature point up the fact that a large latifundium like that of the Sieniawskis and Czartoryskis was complex not only from the perspective of the range of activities it housed, but also because of the complicated relationships that developed among the constituent groups residing there. Successful management of such a latifundium required skillful integration and balancing of these groups.

One of the groups essential to the life of the latifundium was the Jews. As residents, leaseholders, merchants, and administrators, Jews provided many of the services and much of the income that made the latifundium profitable for the owner. We turn now to a characterization of their role on the latifundium and their relationship with the magnates.

CHAPTER THREE

The Jews as Latifundium Residents

Background: Jews in Poland

The roots of the Jewish community in seventeenth- and eighteenth-century Poland go back to the twelfth century, when the first signs of organized, albeit small and not very financially secure, communities appear. The indications are that the nuclei for the Jewish settlements were wealthy Jews from Ashkenaz who worked for the Polish kings as minters, bankers, or commercial agents. Such rich individuals probably attracted a complement of petty servants, tradesmen, merchants, and religious functionaries who formed the early communities. Poland's atmosphere of religious toleration made it an attractive land of settlement for Jews aiming to avoid religiously inspired persecution in Western Europe.[1]

These Jews typified a general trend in Poland during the twelfth, thirteenth, and fourteenth centuries—the so-called foreign colonization. Advances in agricultural technology and the integration of peasant lands into the nobility estates brought more land under cultivation, increased the number of villages, and produced more wealth. Increasing political stability under a crystallizing monarchy provided a climate conducive to maximum exploitation of this wealth through trade. As a result many people from Germany, Bohemia, and Moravia—including a large number of Jews—were attracted to the growing towns and cities of Poland and filled the commercial –

---

[1] While there may have been some pre-Ashkenazic Jewish settlement on Polish territory, the community that succeeded in perpetuating itself demographically and culturally was that begun by the Ashkenazic immigrants from the West. See: Baron, *History*, vol. 3, pp. 217–20; vol. 10, pp. 31–49; B. D. Weinryb, *The Jews of Poland* (Philadelphia, 1973), pp. 18–29; P. Wexler, "The Reconstruction of Pre-Ashkenazic Jewish Settlements in the Slavic Lands in the Light of Linguistic Sources," *POLIN* 1 (1986), pp. 3–18.

urban – entrepreneurial niche in this country of nobility and serfs.[2]

Historians estimate that by 1500 the Jewish community numbered between ten thousand and thirty thousand, a respectable size by European standards. Compared to Western Europe, the Jews in Poland enjoyed an agreeable legal and economic status. Notwithstanding certain minor feudal obligations in privately owned towns (obligations that were shared by other townspeople) the Jews were free men entitled to travel, change residence, swear and sue in court, bear arms, and own homes and businesses. In principle, they were allowed to deal in any commodity and could sell retail as well as wholesale. Jewish religious practice was completely licit and church-inspired restrictions on Jewish dress or behavior were rarely taken seriously.[3]

Local Jewish communal autonomy was a fact of European life for centuries. In Poland, this autonomy was more ramified and more highly developed than anywhere else.[4] Each main Jewish community (*kehilla*), with its satellite communities, constituted a medieval-style corporation run by an oligarchic group of about twenty men called the *kahal*. These *kehalim* were organized into regional councils (*vaad galil*), which were in turn loosely confederated on the seminational level as the Council of Four Lands (Poland's *Vaad Arba Aratzot*) and the Council of the State of Lithuania (*Vaad Medinat Lita*).

The local *kahal* was responsible for the organization of the life of its community: administrative, judicial, legislative, and educational functions were all within its purview. The *kahal* collected taxes; determined membership, housing, and fiscal policies; and hired all communal employees. Its regulations extended to economic activities, religious practice, and the family and social life of community members.

Each regional council concerned itself chiefly with distribution of the Jewish head tax burden among the communities in its district, with

[2] Gieysztor et al., pp. 80 – 89.

[3] Baron, *History,* vol. 16, pp. 146 – 61; Weinryb, *Jews,* pp. 33 – 55, 119 – 55.

[4] On the Jewish communal organization in Poland-Lithuania see: S. W. Baron, *The Jewish Community,* vol. 2 (Philadelphia, 1942 [Westport, Conn., 1972]), pp. 267 – 73; A. I. Braudo et al., *Istoriia evreiskogo naroda,* vol. 11 (Moscow, 1914), pp. 132 – 205; J. Katz, *Tradition and Crisis* (New York, 1971), pp. 79 – 134; R. Mahler, *Toldot Hayehudim Bepolin* (Merhavia, 1946), pp. 190 – 215, 357 – 415; I. Trunk, "Der Vaad Medinas Rusya" *YB* 40 (1956), pp. 63 – 82.

intercommunal disputes—for example, about jurisdiction over satellite communities—and with matters of general concern such as communal defense, regional economic regulations, and aid in time of disaster. The national councils concentrated on relations with the government, tax collection, and adjudication or arbitration of intractable and important matters.

Of course the salutary status of the Jews in Poland outlined here reflects only the intent of royal laws and declarations. In practice, paper privileges did not always hold up. When a Jew found himself under the jurisdiction of a powerful, despotic nobleman, when a royally chartered town's patriciat convinced the king to grant their town a privilege *de non tolerandis Iudaeus,* or when a clergyman incited a blood libel, the nominal legal status of the Jews did not count for very much. Moreover, as time went on the Jews' main antagonists, the petty nobility and the royal town patriciats, were more successful in eliciting official restrictions on Jewish settlement and economic rights. The weak bureaucratic reach of the royal government, however, meant that laws beneficial and detrimental to the Jews were enforced equally haphazardly. Jews living in privately owned territories automatically circumvented royally prescribed restrictions, and could usually expect a measure of protection, not persecution, from their lord.

Even these Jews, however, had to be mindful of underlying tensions between them and their non-Jewish neighbors, tensions that could be catalyzed into active persecution when the conditions were right. Thus, notwithstanding the putative protection of the lords, the Cossack-Ruthenian Revolt of 1648, followed by the Muscovite-Swedish Invasion in 1654, both of which assumed a strongly anti-Jewish posture, were among the most tragic events in the long history of anti-Jewish persecution. Between 1648 and 1660 scores of thousands of Jews were killed or died as a result of battle conditions. Scores of thousands more were rendered homeless and impoverished, becoming refugees. Families were separated, religious and educational institutions were destroyed, and economic and social structures were ruptured.[5]

In the eighteenth century, there arose what Dubnov termed "a frenzy of blood accusations," increased anti-Jewish religious

---

[5] Weinryb, *Jews,* pp. 181–95.

propaganda and the Uman Massacres of 1768. All of this underscored the dimension of insecurity in Polish-Jewish life.[6]

Contrasting with such horrible episodes is evidence of the hospitable side of the Polish host society. In Poland the Jews achieved impressive demographic growth and forged a prodigious cultural legacy. By 1648 there were as many as 450,000 Jews and by 1765 approximately 750,000.[7] This community developed a language—Yiddish—and folklore that still echo in Jewish culture today. Its scholars contributed many classics to the library of talmudic and Jewish legal scholarship. Its social and economic institutions, such as the *kahal*, rabbinate, *hevra*, *hazaka*, and *mamram*,[8] were ingenious adaptations of talmudic and early medieval prescriptions. They bespoke a flourishing community with the desire and ability to live by its traditions, making them work in a new environment with its fresh challenges. In the eighteenth century Polish Jewry created a new spiritual movement, Hasidism, which, despite its innovations, succeeded in remaining within and even redirecting the Jewish religious mainstream.

While Polish Jews came to Poland originally in connection with their service to Polish kings, by 1765 more than half of the 750,000 Jews in the Commonwealth lived in privately owned latifundia under the direct jurisdiction of nobility—especially magnate—owners.[9] The relationship between Jew and owner was that of a subject and his lord. In 1539, the Polish king relinquished to the noblemen full jurisdiction over the Jews resident in their lands, so that for all practical purposes a Jewish resident of a privately owned town viewed his lord or lady as his king.[10] Like other subjects, the Jews possessed rights and owed

---

[6] S. M. Dubnov, *History of the Jews in Russia and Poland,* vol. 1 (Philadelphia, 1916), pp. 172–87.

[7] For summaries of the demographic picture of the Jews in Poland, see: Baron, *History,* vol. 16, pp. 192–211, 405–18; Weinryb, *Jews,* pp. 308–20.

[8] See glossary for definitions of Hebrew terms.

[9] Weinryb, *Jews,* p. 120.

[10] Baron, *History,* vol. 16, pp. 29, 124–25; J. Goldberg, "Bein Hofesh Lenetinut—Sugei Hatlut Hafeiudalit shel Hayehudim Bepolin," *Proceedings of the Fifth World Congress of Jewish Studies,* vol. 2 (Jerusalem, 1972), pp. 108–11; Z. Kaczmarczyk and B. Leśnodorski, *Historia państwa i prawa Polski,* vol. 2, J. Bardach, ed. (Warsaw, 1966), pp. 73–74; *Volumina Legum,* vol. 1 (St. Petersburg, 1859), p. 500; Weinryb, *Jews,* p. 120.

duties. The primary rights and duties were usually included in a privilege granted to the Jews at the time they first settled in the town and periodically reconfirmed or modified.

From the sixteenth century there was a marked tendency for the Jews to concentrate in magnate-owned territories. With the 1569 Union of Lublin, Poland gained vast open territories in the Ukraine.[11] These large, sparsely populated tracts, inhabited mainly by Ruthenians, were given to the magnates, who set about organizing them as Polish feudal estates. They needed people who could serve as administrators, develop commerce, and simply fill the new towns they established. Jews, increasingly subject to pressure from the nobility and townsmen to limit their settlement and economic rights in the crown territories in western Poland, were attracted eastward to the lands of the magnates. Here they were offered free—even subsidized—settlement and abundant economic opportunity. Jews were welcomed to these territories for the administrative and commercial contributions they could make. They were not viewed as interlopers.[12] The ideal Jewish settler, as implied by the Sieniawski-Czartoryski sources, was someone with a good reputation, ready cash, and commercial skills.[13]

Moreover, as magnates sought to increase their power and control of affairs, they engaged in a struggle to break potential rivals such as the city merchants and the artisan guilds. In this effort, the Jews, who were in direct competition with these groups, were a natural partner.[14] Even in royally chartered towns, when merchant or artisan guilds

---

[11] At the Union of Lublin the Palatinates of Volhynia, Bratslav, and Kiev were annexed to the Kingdom of Poland.

[12] Baron, *History,* vol. 16, p. 28; Bergerówna, p. 307; S. Ettinger, "Maamadam Hamishpati Vehahevrati shel Yehudei Ukraina Bameiot Ha-16-17," *Zion* 20 (1955), p. 145; Mahler, *Toldot,* p. 244; Prochaska, *Historja,* p. 61.

[13] BC 5897 Morzycki to ES 1.26450 11/16/1714; EW 189 *Supl.* Gotel Berko Fajbowicz of Sieniawa, undated.

[14] B. Baranowski, *Życie codzienne małego miasteczka w XVII i XVIII w.* (Warsaw, 1975), pp. 58–59; B. Z. Dinur, *Bemifne Hadorot* (Jerusalem, 1955), p. 118; M. Kremer, "Leheker Hamelakha Vehevrot Baalei Hamelakha Etzel Yehudei Polin," *Zion* 2 (1937), pp. 299–301; Prochaska, *Historja,* pp. 47, 110; J. Rutkowski, *Historia gospodarcza Polski* (Warsaw, 1953), pp. 176–82; W. Smoleński, *Stan i sprawa Żydów polskich w XVIII wieku* (Warsaw, 1876), pp. 16–17; B. D. Weinryb, *Mehkarim Betoldot Hakalkala Vehahevra shel Yehudei Polin* (Jerusalem, 1939), p. 25.

succeeded in legally limiting Jewish economic activity or Jewish settlement rights, the magnates often rendered such limitations almost meaningless by allowing Jews to live and work freely in their privately owned suburbs (*jurydyki*) adjoining the towns.[15]

The tolerance and economic opportunity offered by the magnates encouraged the majority of Jews to become inhabitants of magnate holdings, mainly as town dwellers.[16]

The Jews in the Towns

By utilizing the Sieniawski-Czartoryski material it is possible to characterize the Jewish town-dwelling population of the eastern magnate-owned latifundia. On the basis of the 1765 census and other sources, I estimate the number of Jews living in the Czartoryski territories in 1765 at approximately 30,000.[17] If the figure of 750,000 is accepted as the approximate number of the total Jewish population in the Polish-Lithuanian Commonwealth,[18] then the Czartoryski Jews represented about 4 percent of all the Jews. Like the general Jewish population, they were settled mainly in the south-central and southeastern sections of the country (roughly between Cracow and Bratslav) with one large community, Shkłoŭ, in Belorussia (see Map 1.1). There were at least twenty communities under Czartoryski ownership, and by 1765 each boasted more than 1,000 Jews. The largest community, with more than 2,000 Jews, was in the town of Medzhybizh and suburbs. By the time of the census, this town had served, ca. 1740–60, as the home of Israel Baal Shem Tov and the center of the circle of new Hasidim that gathered around him.

---

[15] Baron, *History,* vol. 16, pp. 11, 14, 20, 254; Dinur, p. 118; J. Goldberg, "De Non Tolerandis Iudaeis," *Studies in Jewish History Presented to Professor R. Mahler,* S. Yeivin, ed. (Merhavia, 1974), pp. 42–43.

[16] There is evidence that in general the Jewish village population was on the increase in the eighteenth century; see: R. Mahler, *Yidn in Amolikn Poiln in Likht fun Tsifirn,* 2 vols. (Warsaw, 1958), vol. 1, pp. 49–58, vol. 2, Table III. As J. Goldberg has pointed out, however, a large percentage of these were temporary residents who leased an *arenda* for a few years. The Sieniawski-Czartoryski sources emphasize this point by listing all arrendators as part of the town population and listing virtually no Jews as actually resident in the villages. Thus it is hard to determine the proportion of Jews who lived in Sieniawski-Czartoryski villages.

[17] See Appendix I.

[18] Mahler, *Yidn,* vol. 1, p. 195.

Inventories of property taxpayers exist for several of the Sieniawski-Czartoryski towns for various years. The tax (*czynsz*) itself could range from less than one-half to more than thirteen *złoty* per household annually depending on the town and its significance to the overall budget.[19]

According to the available inventories of taxpayers, localities did not exhibit identical patterns of population growth. In one of the five communities reflected in the data—Sieniawa (Table 3.3)—the Jewish population held more or less steady throughout the first half of the century; in the others it grew by at least 60 percent. Obviously, local factors, on which known sources are silent, were at least as important as national and regional conditions in determining growth. On the other hand, the fact that none of these five scattered communities lost population suggests that general conditions favored Jewish numerical increase.

The inventories clarify the physical and numerical relationship of the Jews in the towns to the non-Jews. While it is conventional to speak of the Jews as composing half of the urban population of eighteenth-century Poland,[20] this figure must be understood as an average. In the towns indicated in Tables 3.1–3.5, Jews ranged from 25 to 60 percent of the population. Regardless of their percentage in the population, Jews were disproportionately represented among the owners of homes and stores on the marketplace, often to the point of being in a large majority. Even a cursory study of the tax inventories reveals that Jewish settlement was concentrated on or near the marketplace and became more dispersed as one moved farther away.[21]

---

[19] Financial significance of this tax aside, however, the lists are valuable in characterizing some of the demographic features of the towns, and, particularly, in allowing for comparison of the Jewish and non-Jewish populations (see Tables 3.1–3.5).

[20] Mahler, *Toldot*, p. 245; M. Bogucka and H. Samsonowicz, *Dzieje miast i mieszczaństwa w Polsce przedrozbiorowej* (Wrocław, 1986), pp. 364–70, 469–74.

[21] Compare S. W. Baron, "The Jewish Factor in Medieval Civilization," *Proceedings of the American Academy for Jewish Research* 12 (1942), pp. 9–10; N. M. Gelber, *Brzeżany Memorial Book,* M. Katz, ed. (Haifa, 1978), p. 22; M. Nadav, *Pinsk* (Tel Aviv, 1973), pp. 138–39, 156–57. Note, however, J. Goldberg, "Poles and Jews in the Seventeenth and Eighteenth Centuries: Rejection or Acceptance," *Jahrbücher für Geschichte Osteuropas* 22 (1974), p. 271.

TABLE 3.1
MEDZHYBIZH REAL ESTATE TAXES

Year	Potential Real Estate Taxpayers		Stores		Real Estate Taxes Paid (*zł/gr*)		Type of Housing			Jews with Christian Neighbors	
	Christians	*Jews*	*Christians*	*Jews*	*Christians*	*Jews*	*Christians*		*Jews*	*One*	*Two*
1717	508	155	3	35	686/26	713					
1725	388	112	11	30	—	—					
1730	430	204	30	45	1265/3	950/24	House 24	House 110		61	14
							Shack 402	Shack 78			
							Boarder 4	Boarder 16			
1755	544	261	37	48	1203/27	863/24	All listed in shacks	All listed in houses			

Source: BC 4035, 4045, 4047, 4117

TABLE 3.2
BEREZHANY HOMES AND STORES

	1682		1695		1709		1762	
	Christians	Jews	Christians	Jews	Christians	Jews	Christians	Jews
Homes	193	55	329*	75	460*	130	[no data]	125
Stores			0	20				

* includes suburbs

Source: M. Maciszewski, *Brzeżany*, pp. 19–20

TABLE 3.3
SIENIAWA REAL ESTATE TAXES

Year	Potential Real Estate Taxpayers		Stores		Real Estate Taxes Paid (zł/gr)		Size of House Lot		Jews with Christian Neighbors	
	C	J	C	J	C	J	C	J	One	Two
1702	96	113	0	18	436/19	702/4	a) 9 b) 73 c) 8 d) — e) 6	7 35 24 — 47	19	7
1718	64 homeowners 76; 8 boarders 27		0	30	209	1404/10	a) 3 b) 51 c) 9 d) 1	8 46 22	25	5
1734	64 homeowners 85; 16 boarders 39		—	—	—	—	a) 6 b) 51 c) 6 d) 1	9 45 29 2	17	5
1760	76	123	—	—	—	—	—	—	—	—

C = Christians J = Jews
a) = less than ½ lot b) = ½–¾ lot c) = full lot d) = more than a full lot e) = unspecified, probably boarders

Source: EW 144, GOSP, 784

TABLE 3.4

STASZÓW REAL ESTATE TAXPAYERS

Year	Potential Real Estate Taxpayers			Stores on Marketplace		Jews with Christian Neighbors		
	Christians		*Jews*	*Christians*	*Jews*	*One*	*Two*
1733	154	homeowners	29	—	—	9	8
	19	boarders	20				
1760	193	homeowners	54	0	8	19	4
	16	boarders	37				

Source: AKP D.S. 2,6

TABLE 3.5
SHKŁOŬ REAL ESTATE TAXES

Year	Taxable Pieces[1] of Property		Stores		Property Taxes Paid (zł/gr)		Size of Homes		Jews with Christian Neighbors	
	C	J	C	J	C	J	C	J	One	Two
1727	245	63	37(?)	23	590	821	3.3[4]	4.0[4]	19	9
1760	232	147	55	57	1005/5[2]	1558/2[3]	shacks 134 36		53	22
							houses 33 78			
							stone houses 1 7			

C = Christians J = Jews
(1) Property includes residences, gardens, empty lots. Breweries are not included.
(2) For 47 pieces of property no tax was paid or cannot be determined.
(3) For 16 pieces of property no tax was paid or cannot be determined.
(4) Average number of *pręty* on which an individual paid real estate tax.

Source: Ossolineum 5167/II 5168/II (=HM 7926–27)

Jews bought and sold property and expanded their geographic presence in the towns. In Shkłoŭ in 1727, for example, out of twelve real estate transactions recorded involving a Christian and a Jew, the Jew was the buyer in ten of them.[22] Jewish geographic dispersal meant that there were no ghettos and that cases of Jews and Christian living alongside each other were common.[23] In the towns indicated by the tables, 25 to 55 percent of the Jews had at least one Christian neighbor.

Economic and Occupational Structure

The tax lists also provide information about the Jews' economic position in the towns. Being concentrated on the marketplace, Jews were likely to live in the large stone houses found there rather than in the small wooden shacks common in other neighborhoods.[24] In eighteenth-century Berezhany, a stone house on the market cost 600 to 1,200 zł. while a wooden house on a side street went for 50 to 80 zł.[25] In Sieniawa, where the lists describe house lots as fractions of one, most of the full lots were owned by Jews (Table 3.3). In Medzhybizh in 1730 more than 80 percent of the houses (*domy*) belonged to Jews; while Christians occupied most of the wooden shacks (*chałupy*) (Table 3.1). This pattern was so normal that in 1755 the inventory-taker did not even bother to differentiate and simply listed all Christians in shacks and all Jews in houses.[26]

On the other hand, Jews also composed the majority of people who owned no home at all. In the towns where the inventories specify boarders (*komornicy*) (Tables 3.1, 3.3, 3.4), the Jewish boarders outnumbered the Christian ones and constituted a relatively high percen-

---

[22] Ossolineum 5167/II (HM 6678) Szkłów 1727; cf. BC 5934 R to ES 1.34791 9/28/1723, M. Maciszewski, *Brzeżany* (Brody, 1910), pp. 127–28, 132–33; Trunk, "Vaad Medinas Rusya," pp. 81–84.

[23] Compare G. D. Hundert, "Jewish Urban Residence in the Polish Commonwealth in the Early Modern Period," *Jewish Journal of Sociology* 26 (1984), pp. 25–34.

[24] Baranowski, *Życie,* p. 82.

[25] Maciszewski, pp. 121–22.

[26] In Shkłoŭ, too, the Jews owned the largest homes; see EW 525 *Supl. Kahal* Szkłów ca. 1731. Likewise, a list of the damage caused by a fire in Stryi in 1742 shows that the richest residents were Jews; see Prochaska, *Historja,* p. 24.

tage (at least 25 percent) of the Jewish taxpayers.

The fact that Jews were heavily represented both among the owners of the largest homes and among the boarders[27] reflects the two basic occupational tendencies of the Jewish populations of these towns: commerce and artisanry (Table 3.6).

The owners of the larger houses and stores on the marketplace were well-established merchants and arrendators, some of whom were active in intercity or even international trade.[28] The boarders were, in addition to poor people, young tailors, furriers, butchers, and the like. The group owning middle-size houses was composed of petty merchants, established artisans, and communal functionaries.

Table 3.6 is a list of the occupations of the Jews in these towns.[29] While an individual may have been primarily occupied as a merchant or trained in a certain craft, he could deal in a sideline in addition to his main occupation, change occupations seasonally, or engage in several complementary occupations simultaneously.

For example, Lejba Anklewicz Sukiennik, one of the communal leaders of Sieniawa, was a wealthy cloth merchant and for several years held the liquor *arenda* as well as the rights to some of the tax income from Sieniawa. The two pursuits went hand in hand. By selling large quantities of cloth, acquired in Leszno,[30] to the Sieniawskis for staff uniforms, he was able to accumulate enough capital to bid successfully on the *arenda*. In turn, the money he received from this lucrative *arenda* aided him in financing his commercial ventures. In addition, the grain grown on the fields belonging to the *arenda* was another product that Lejba could market. Like other arrendators, he probably made use of the accruing payments he received under the *arenda* contract to make petty pledge loans to noblemen and others.

---

[27] Jews were also among the owners of the most poorly built homes; cf. Baranowski, *Życie*, pp. 85–90, who indicates, but exaggerates, this phenomenon.

[28] In Sieniawa, for example, Jozef Markiewicz, Hersz Abramowicz, Hersz Szlomkowicz, Abram and Moszko Krakowski, Lejba Sukiennik, Haskiel Zelmanowicz, and Moszko Dobromilski all owned homes on the marketplace and appear in other contexts as merchants and arrendators.

[29] Compare Kremer, pp. 313–18; J. Goldberg, "Społeczność żydowska w szlacheckim miasteczku," *BZIH* 59 (1966), pp. 14–15; J. Morgensztern, "O działalności gospodarczej Żydów w Zamościu w XVI i XVII w.," *BZIH* 53 (1965), pp. 3–34; 56 (1965), pp. 3–28.

[30] BC 2904, no. 51.

TABLE 3.6
JEWISH OCCUPATIONS[31]

Apothecary	Latheturner	Tailor
Arrendator	Launderer	Tar maker
Baker	Liquor producer	Teacher
Barber-surgeon	Magnate-official	Teamster
Bathhouse attendant	Moneylender	Tinker
Blacksmith	Musician	
Bookbinder	Oculist	
Butcher	Parchment maker	
Candlemaker	Potash maker	
Cantor	Preacher	
Cloth merchant	Rabbi	
Cooper	Salter	
Doctor	Second-hand merchant	
Furrier	Sexton	
Glazier	Shoemaker	
Goldsmith	Soapmaker	
Haberdasher	Soldier	
Hawker	Storekeeper	

Note: Based on last names or appelations attached to Jewish individuals in Ossolineum 2122/II, Brzeżany 1696; BC 4035, 4047, 4117, Międzybóż 1717, 1730, 1755; EW 144, GOSP 784, Sieniawa 1718, 1734, 1760, AKP DS 2, 6, Staszów 1733, 1760.

---

[31] It is not possible to give a statistical breakdown of the Jewish occupational structure for two reasons. First, there is no way of knowing whether the attachment of occupational titles to names in the tax lists was consistent or not. Was every tailor identified as such or was the occupational tag given only in lieu of a better identifier? Second, occupational specialization as practiced in twentieth-century Europe was not the general rule in eighteenth-century Poland, and particularly among Jews. Cf. G. D. Hundert, "Security and Dependence: Perspectives on Seventeenth Century Polish-Jewish Society Gained Through a Study of Jewish Merchants in Little Poland," doctoral dissertation, Columbia University (New York, 1978), pp. 13–16.

These, of course, added to the capital he had available for commerce and *arenda* bidding.[32]

The most common supplementary occupation was brewing and distilling. In Sieniawa in 1718 all thirty-two brewing kettles were owned by Jews, but it is obvious that liquor manufacture was a sideline for many if not all of these. Most of the individuals on the list of brewers appear elsewhere as storeowners, intercity merchants, petty administrators, or arrendators. A Jew who manufactured liquor or beer might serve it in his store or even in his home, or supply someone else. For the right to maintain liquor facilities, he paid a tax or commission to the town arrendator or directly to the magnate's treasury.[33]

Commerce could also be a sideline. Among the names of the freighters, people who traveled to and from Gdańsk to market country goods and buy merchandise for sale back home, were artisans, arrendators, a doctor, a moneylender, and an administrator.[34]

Multiple employment was an important aspect of Jewish economic life. For the entrepreneurial-minded, the linking of complementary occupations provided a means of expanding one's enterprises and accumulating wealth. For the less well-off, sidelines were a means of supplementing their incomes so that they could reach an acceptable standard of living. For everyone, being able to count on several sources of income was insurance against the vicissitudes of the business cycle, nature, and social conditions.

---

[32] The price of the Sieniawa *arenda* in 1718 was 14,500 *zł.*; in 1726 it was 20,500 *zł.*; see Chapter 5. On arrendators lending out accruing payments, see BC 5897 Morzycki to ES 1.26501 5/6/1719; cf. Prochaska, *Historja,* pp. 111–12. Others who exemplify the phenomenon of combining several occupations are Fortis and Rubinowicz, described in Chapter 6, and Ber of Bolechow, who set forth all of his many activities in his *Memoirs,* M. Wischnitzer, ed. and trans. (Berlin, 1922 [New York, 1973]); cf. *SB,* pp. 225–29.

[33] EW 144 Inventories Sieniawa 1718; see also BC 3499–3500 *Arenda* Contracts; cf. H. H. Ben-Sasson, "Takanot Issurei Shabbat Shel Polin Umashmautan Hahevratit Vehakalkalit," *Zion* 21 (1956), pp. 188–90, where it is assumed that such small sellers were never connected to the general arrendator.

[34] See Chapter 4.

Rights and Obligations

In the Sieniawski-Czartoryski latifundium, as elsewhere, the relationship between Jews and the magnate lord was expressed in privileges granted by the magnate to the original Jewish settlers in any given locale. From the Sieniawski-Czartoryski territories, two formal privileges granted by Elżbieta Sieniawska have survived: one to the Jews of Międzyrzec Podlaski, the other to those in Staszów.[35]

The main obligation of the Jews emphasized in these privileges is their duty to pay various taxes punctually. As to the Jews' rights, the privileges single out two:

a) The right to live as practitioners of the Jewish religion in an organized community. Permission is granted to establish communal religious institutions, rabbinical courts, and kosher slaughtering and baking facilities, and to exempt Jewish clergy from taxes. Such permission had to be made explicit because of the potential opposition to organized Jewish communal religious life on the part of Christian clergy in the area. This was particularly true in Staszów whence Jews had been expelled in 1610 as a result of a blood libel and readmitted officially—not without controversy—only in 1690. Elżbieta Sieniawska's decision to grant a formal privilege in 1718 was probably intended to settle the question of Jewish status in the town once and for all.[36]

b) The right to engage freely in commerce and crafts; this despite complaints by the local guilds of competing merchants and artisans.[37]

These two rights—to settle as a community and to engage freely in

---

[35] The Międzyrzec Privilege, AGAD Akta Komisji Rządowej Spraw Wewnętrznych Duchownych no. 185, cards 120–21 is included in J. Goldberg, *Jewish Privileges in the Polish Commonwealth* (Jerusalem, 1985), pp. 210–13; the Staszów one, Sichów Archive 1858 no. 196, was published by N. M. Gelber, "Letoldot Hayehudim Bestaszów," in *Sefer Staszów*, E. Ehrlich ed. (Tel Aviv, 1962), pp. 34–35. Both were originally granted in 1718. The Staszów Privilege is extant only in the version confirmed by AAC in 1772.

[36] Gelber, "Letoldot Hayehudim Bestaszów," pp. 27–28.

[37] Kremer, pp. 303, 307–308.

economic pursuits—were precisely what royally chartered towns often denied to the Jews.[38]

These privileges exemplify the attraction of magnate-owned towns for Jews. The Sieniawskis, in their desire to develop their towns commercially, offered the Jews the conditions essential to the establishment of a flourishing Jewish settlement. To judge by the growth of the Jewish population in Berezhany, Staszów, Medzhybizh, and Shkłoŭ, their efforts met with some success.

The privileges establish the fundamental rights and obligations of the Jews in the magnate's town. These provisions were often elaborated or modified in the lists of duties of town citizens that were published periodically as part of the regular inventories of the latifundium complexes. While the contents of these lists varied somewhat from town to town, those from Berezhany, Medzhybizh and Sieniawa are typical. It is possible to summarize the common points:

1. All property owners or renters had to pay the property tax (*czynsz*) on their homes or stores. In most places the rate was higher for Jews than for Christians. For example, in Sieniawa, a Christian boarder paid 12 *gr.*, a Jew paid 1 ½ *zł.* In Medzhybizh, a Christian paid a flat 2 ½ *zł.* for his home regardless of size; Jews, who owned the larger homes, paid, in proportion to size, 2 *zł.* to 8 *zł.* In Shkłoŭ, Christians paid 3 or 4 *tynf;* Jews paid more than 1 *cz. zł.*

2. All householders had to pay a fee for the right to fish in the magnate's pond, and those who owned livestock paid for pasture rights in the magnate's meadow.

3. All householders were required to participate personally in maintenance work on town walls, bridges, roads, and so forth.

4. All householders had to contribute some time and equipment to projects such as hay cutting and baling, grain harvesting, and transporting the magnate's fish, honey, and grain. Jews usually had the option of hiring a substitute.

5. All householders had to maintain firearms and participate in the defense of the town.

6. All householders were responsible for fire prevention.

[38] *AGZ*, vol. 23 nos. 157.34, 168.6, 174.29; Mahler, *Toldot,* p. 288; Goldberg, "De Non Tolerandis Iudaeis," pp. 44–51; Rutkowski, *Historia,* pp. 177–84.

7. Each home had to be equipped with a ladder and water buckets and the *kahal* and municipality had to share the cost of a nightly fire watch. Fire negligence was punishable by fine or imprisonment.
8. Christian householders had to pay honey tax.
9. Both the *kahal* and the municipality were accountable to the magnate for the way in which they spent their respective budgets.
10. The magnate's court was supreme over both the *kahal* and the municipal courts.
11. Frequently, millers, shoemakers, tailors, furriers, and weavers were required to provide the magnate with a specified amount of free material or labor.
12. Jews were often warned to serve good quality liquor and to pay the required liquor tax (*czopowy*).[39]

To some extent the lists of duties reflect the differences between the Jewish and Christian communities in the towns. Such provisions as higher real estate taxes, the Christian honey tax, the Jewish option to hire substitute agricultural workers, and admonitions to Jews about liquor production were functions of traditional attitudes toward Jews and occupational differences between Christians and Jews. Conversely, the duties also show that in matters of town defense and maintenance the ethnicity of the householder was irrelevant. Members of both groups contributed and were expected to cooperate with each other. The communities were not so separate that they could not work together in matters of common concern. They were, actually, two boroughs of the same town, not two separate towns.[40]

---

[39] EW 144 Sieniawa Inventories seventeenth-eighteenth centuries; BC 4045 BC 4047 BC 4078 Międzybóż Inventories 1725, 1730, 1740; Maciszewski, pp. 15–16; Ossolineum 2122/II Brzeżany Inventory 1698 (HM6653); cf. Goldberg, *Privileges*. It should be remembered that practice may have varied from written stipulations.

[40] Compare EW 525 Szkłów *Supl.* of the Jewish and Christian communities, undated, requesting the removal of the administrator Słobodzki; Puczyński, pp. 177–78. In Central Europe the Jews sometimes did constitute a separate township, complete with their own fire brigade; see J. Toury, "Jewish Townships in the German-Speaking Parts of the Austrian Empire—Before and After the Revolution of 1848/1849," *YBLBI* 26 (1981), pp. 55–72. Note his statement: "The existence of separate [i.e., Jewish and Christian] municipal precincts had not been the rule in Polish Galicia," p. 60.

The lists further imply that all individual citizens as well as the governing bodies of the two communities were ultimately subject to the same central authority. For the magnate, the communal governing bodies were not separate autonomous governments, but two extensions of his administrations. Each performed certain lower level governmental functions—tax collection, preservation of order, adjudication—with reference to a part of the town population. But their powers were delegated to them by the magnate. To remind them of this, their officials, budgets, and judiciary remained subject to magnate approval and review, and the magnate could impose his authority at any point.

The relationship between Jewish communal institutions and the magnates in governing the town's Jewish citizens can be illustrated by the judicial system. From the beginning of their settlement in Poland, in consonance with the medieval custom that every man had the right to be judged by his own law, Jews had the right to maintain their own rabbinic courts for deciding civil and petty criminal matters between Jews in the first instance. Appeals from these courts, serious criminal cases, and cases involving both Jews and non-Jews were to be heard by a special "court of the Jews" chaired by the regional deputy governor (*podwojewoda*) or his representative.[41]

The Sieniawskis and Czartoryskis, like other town owners, continued to allow their Jews to utilize Jewish courts within the traditional guidelines. They did not, however, sponsor any special "court of the Jews" parallel to the royally sponsored *podwojewoda* court. Rather, cases between Jews and Christians and cases concerning general welfare were either heard by joint commissions made up of representatives of both the Jewish *kahal* and the Christian town council or by the owner's representative or the owner himself. The latter also heard appeals of all sorts and cases involving serious criminal matters.[42]

---

[41] See the fifteenth-century confirmation of the 1264 Privilege of Bolesław of Kalisch in S. Bershadskii's *Russko-Evreiskii arhkiv*, vol. 3 (St. Petersburg, 1882), no. 1; Baron, *History*, vol. 16, p. 187; B. Cohen, "Hareshut Havoyevodit Vehakehilla Hayehudit Bameiot Ha-16–18," *Gal-Ed* 3 (1976), pp. 11–23; Z. Pazdro, *Organizacya i praktyka żydowskich sądów podwojewodzińskich w okresie 1740–1772* (Lviv, 1903); M. Schorr, *Organizacja Żydów w Polsce* (Lviv, 1899), pp. 45–51.

[42] Staszów Privilege, pt. 6, Gelber, "Letoldot Hayehudim Bestaszów," pp. 34–35; BC 2581 no. 16 Rohatyn; Maciszewski, pp. 133–41; cf. Goldberg, *Privileges*, pp. 22–25. Evidently these procedures were not always followed in practice; e.g., Rapo-

Thus the Jewish courts in the Sieniawski-Czartoryski towns were an integral part of the Sieniawski-Czartoryski court system. In particular, the provisions that criminal matters and appeals between Jews be directed to the owner's court put the Jewish courts in the position of being essentially one of Sieniawski's courts and not a separate judicial authority. Sieniawski agreed, in effect, that for cases within their competence, he would adopt Jewish criteria for selecting judges and deciding points of law; but once that competence was exceeded, the judge and to some extent the law were changed. Moreover, the magnates were not above trying to influence the deliberations of the rabbinic courts.[43]

That the Jewish courts were part of the overall Sieniawski court system can also be seen in the ways in which the Jewish and other courts cooperated with each other. When the Jewish court wanted to lend more force to a decision, it published it in the official municipal record books.[44] When a Jew was required by the *zamek* court to take an oath, it was likely that the rabbinic court would be directed to administer it.[45]

There were also cases of mutual interest to the Jewish and Christian communities. In 1708, for example, when the estate of Tomasz Markiewicz was settled, Bracławski, the *ekonom* of Sieniawa, directed representatives of both the Christian and Jewish communities to sign the decree.[46] When the dispute between Ajzyk Jachimowicz and the communal leader, Lejba Anklewicz Sukiennik, was being heard, the Christian community filed a brief on Lejba's behalf.[47]

The municipal record books from the towns reveal that appeals from the rabbinic court to the *zamek* court usually occurred in cases of monetary matters, particularly where the owner had a stake. There are several cases when Adam Mikołaj Sieniawski instructed his administrator to reach a final determination in disputes between Jewish

---

port, Orah Haim, nos. 17, 19 where Rapoport rendered decisions with regard to punishments in two cases of accidental killings without reference to the Polish courts.

[43] See Chapter 7.

[44] Maciszewski, pp. 143–44; BC 3826 no. 162, 4/12/1714.

[45] BC 2702 7/24/1730, pp. 607–609; note also translations of Jewish court documents into Polish that were kept on file in the municipal record books: BC 3823 no. 52, BC 3826 nos. 37, 44.

[46] BC 3826 no. 57.

[47] BC 3826 no. 59 5/30/1718. For details on this case see below.

freighters who participated in the river trade he sponsored.[48]

Sometimes an appeal to the *zamek* was based on the need to enlist its enforcement capabilities. The case of Michel Abusiewicz of Satanów, which was heard by the *zamek* court there on February 5, 1730, is one such instance. Michel owed several hundred *złoty* to creditors, who were pressing him for repayment. A fellow Jew, Melech Markowicz, offered Michel 800 *zł*. for the rights to Michel's home and store. Out of desperation, Michel jumped at the proposal "in one moment" without seeking other offers or even conferring with his wife. Michel and Melech went to the rabbi and concluded the deal. Meanwhile, "at almost the same time," Michel's wife was working on a deal of her own. Their neighbor Naftuly, who had long desired to expand his home by annexing Michel's, offered Michel's wife 2,000 *zł*. for their home. This would cover their debts and leave them enough money to buy a smaller place. Clearly Naftuly's offer was more attractive than Melech's. As soon as Michel's wife informed him of her agreement with Naftuly, he took Naftuly to the rabbinic court, 800 *zł*. in hand, and sought to repay Melech, annulling his deal with the latter. Melech refused, however, and Michel appealed to the *zamek*.

The *zamek* court considered Michel's hasty actions and his failure to confer with his wife, which, according to the *zamek,* was required by Jewish law. In addition Naftuly's offer was clearly advantageous and Melech had not yet taken possession of the house. In view of all this the *zamek* court decided in Michel's and Naftuly's favor, forcing Melech to accept his 800 *zł*. in return.[49]

This case is instructive as to the way in which the *zamek* court functioned and how it could be utilized. Strictly speaking, this case was not an appeal. Michel had not filed a suit against Melech in the rabbinic court. He had attempted to annul a contract that was signed there. As the decision of the *zamek* court implies, the problem was not the rabbinic court's ruling against Michel. There is no reference to a previous rabbinic court ruling being appealed, and the decision of the *zamek* court itself was based at least partially on a point of Jewish

---

[48] BC 3814 no. 4, BC 3826 nos. 36–37, 39–40, 46–48, 54; on this river trade see Chapter 4.

[49] BC 2702 pp. 114–19, 373, 413.

law.[50] It is almost certain that such a ruling was taken in consultation with the rabbi, it being highly unlikely that the administrator judging the case could have cultivated such familiarity with Jewish law. Hence the reason for the appeal seems to have been Melech's staunch refusal even to consider the annulment and the need to enlist coercive power against him.[51] So Michel did not even bother with the Jewish court but went directly to the *zamek* court, which would decide the case on the basis of Jewish law and equity *and* be able to enforce its decision. These two characteristics must have made the *zamek* court an attractive option for potential litigants.

In the first instance, the *zamek* court heard civil cases involving both Jews and non-Jews. These ranged from cases of simple disputes over debts, to complaints by or about Jewish arrendators or by Jews about the behavior of administrators, to disputes between Jewish and Christian individuals or communities over housing or trade issues.[52]

Sometimes a case was brought before the *zamek* court even when non-Jews were involved only obliquely. The court of Sataniv was treated to the following chain of events on July 24, 1730:

Two years previously Benia Ickowicz of Sataniv had traded a brown horse for a black one with Szlomka of Khodoriv. Szlomka then sold the brown horse to a Polish nobleman named Pan Jaworski. Jaworski proceeded to ride the horse to Sharhorod where a peasant recognized it as having recently been stolen from him. He registered a complaint, took his horse, and the nobleman was arrested for horse stealing. After some explaining, Jaworski convinced the authorities in Sharhorod to send to Khodoriv for confirmation that he had purchased the horse from Szlomka. This was done, the nobleman was released, and Szlomka reimbursed him the 85 *złoty* he had paid for the horse. Now it was Szlomka's turn to insist that he had received the horse in good faith from Benia. Benia was sent for and arrived in Khodoriv

---

[50] The note about Jewish law requiring consultation with one's wife probably refers to the provision that one may not sell property that was part of a wife's dowry without her consent: J. Karo, *Shulkhan Arukh,* (New York, 1967), Even Haezer, 85:4.

[51] Melech was a rich man, arrendator of the local copper mine; see below.

[52] Debt disputes: BC 3826 nos. 50, 51, 58, 74, 98; BC 2581 pp. 80–81, January 1738. Complaints about administrators: BC 3826 nos. 64, 92. Jewish-Christian disputes: BC 3826 nos. 95, 97, 99; BC 2702 pp. 479–80 Satanów 1730. Cf. Y Sosis, "Tsu der Sotsialer Geshikhte fun Yidn in Vaysrusland," *Tsaytshrift* 1 (1926), pp. 5–7.

riding on the wagon of Melech Markowicz.[53] Melech, arrendator of the Sataniv copper mine, happened to be bringing some copper to market. Not pausing to make fine distinctions, the Khodoriv authorities impounded Melech's copper until either he or Benia repaid Szlomka the 85 *złoty*. Melech paid the money.

Back in Sataniv (Benia having died in the meantime), Melech filed a case in the *zamek* court against Benia's widow, Yenta. At the *zamek,* Yenta claimed that Benia had purchased the horse from the arrendator Gdal. Gdal admitted this but asserted that he, too, had bought the horse—from a passing nobleman whom, he insisted, Benia had vouched for as honest and not to be suspected of selling stolen horses. A witness to Benia's assurance, Eyl Barysznik, swore to this effect, and the *zamek* court ordered Yenta to reimburse Melech, the copper mine arrendator, for his losses.[54]

Depending on their severity, criminal cases were heard by either the Jewish or Polish court. For example, between April 1731 and April 1732, 124 criminal cases were heard in the Medzhybizh court resulting in 847 *zł.* in fines being paid to the Czartoryskis' treasury. Of these, twenty-two involved at least one Jew (see Table 3.7). The most frequent cause for criminal suits was assault, with Jews alternating in the role of perpetrator and victim and sometimes serving as both. Theft, disturbing the peace, fire carelessness, and contempt of authority were other crimes of which Jews were convicted.[55]

Another area of adjudication in which the *zamek* court was active was in cases where the *kahal* could not be both the sponsor of the

[53] This is the same Melech who appeared in the case of the sale of Michel's house, cited above.

[54] BC 2702 pp. 607–609; see also BC 3826 nos. 44–45.

[55] GOSP 1566; cf. Baranowski, *Życie,* pp. 78–79. GOSP 1566 does not include more serious crimes such as robbery or murder. Other sources imply that Jews were usually the victims in these cases, while crimes of which they were often accused include smuggling, fraud, coin clipping, falsifying weights and measures, and dealing in stolen goods. See: BC 2702, pp. 700–701; BC 5897 Morzycki to ES 5/6/1719, EW 255 8/24/1715 pt. 8; *AGZ*, vol. 22, nos. 208:11, 244:39; Gierowski, *Rzeczpospolita,* p. 52; Prochaska, *Historja,* pp. 110, 137; cf. Maciszewski, pp. 155–56; Nadav, pp. 124–25. Note that in three of the cases listed on the Medzhybizh list, the source specified that the Jewish court levied the fine, which was later collected by the *zamek.* This is another example of the Jewish courts serving as part of the overall administrative system of the latifundium.

TABLE 3.7
PETTY CRIMINAL CASES INVOLVING JEWS
IN MEDZHYBIZH, 1732

Cases with Christian Defendants

Name	Crime	Fine (zł. / gr.)
(one defendant)	unspecified	1/18
(three defendants)	beating Jews	4/25
Roman Szwabski	beating a Jewess after a trial	16
(one defendant)	insulting a Jew	1/18
Iwan	beating the arrendator's wife	unspecified
unspecified	stealing Jewish books	1/18

Cases with Jewish Defendants

Name	Crime	Fine
Polak	overturning a grain basket	3/24
Jos Nochymowicz	beating a Jew	3/6
Oszer	beating a woman	14/18
(two defendants)	causing a tumult at the fair	12/24
Mordy Rzeźnik	damaging church and *zamek* property	3/6
Szmuyło Kuźnierz	unspecified	unspecified*
Judka Arendarz	disturbing Jewish court session	8
Aron Winnik	insulting a Jew	6/12
Icko	causing a fire	2/16
Aron Winnik	unspecified	3/6*
Abram Winnik	beating a woman	1/18
Majer	beating a Christian	1/18
Ickowa	ordering her son to beat a Jew	2/6
Chaim Szmuklerz	beating a Jewess	9/18*
(five defendants)	misappropriating mash	8
Zelik Zelmanowicz	disobeying the *zamek*	1/18

* Paid in Jewish court
Source: GOSP 1566

court and judged by it. Moreover, since the magnate had a direct interest in cases affecting taxation and community leadership, it was common for the magnate's court to hear cases of this nature. The best documented of these is the 1718 case of Ajzyk Jachimowicz versus Lejba Anklewicz Sukiennik and the rest of the *kahal*. Ajzyk claimed that the *kahal*, under Lejba's leadership, refused to hold elections for three years running, that Lejba himself misappropriated tax money and other resources, and that he illegally monopolized the city *arenda*. These were very serious charges, and the *zamek* court investigated the case for almost five months, between May and October 1718. In the final decree, issued in October 1718, it was stated that Lejba was innocent and that Ajzyk was to be punished.[56]

Rabbinic authorities traditionally disapproved of involvement of this type by a non-Jewish power in Jewish affairs, viewing it as interference. Ideally, Jewish institutions, including courts, were to be sovereign. Appeal to outside forces was a prerogative reserved to the official leadership as a sanction to be invoked against recalcitrant individuals. People who approached non-Jewish authorities on their own were usually considered treacherous.[57] The frequency and variety of cases that came before the *zamek* court show that the magnate did not share this view. As far as he was concerned, by ordaining Jewish courts he divided the judicial labor. He delegated, but did not relinquish, his authority. He remained basically responsible for the maintenance of law and order among all the citizens of his town and stood ready to step into the breach whenever he deemed Jewish courts or other institutions unqualified or unable to control the situation.

The rights and obligations specified in the privileges and lists of duties were not the only ones that applied to the latifundium's Jews. There were some important traditional rights and obligations that were never explicitly stated in the privileges or duties lists, but which are clearly implied by the contents of the correspondence and the petitions.

The Jews' most essential obligation, the premise for their ready admission into the magnate's town, was to develop a commercial infrastructure to benefit the lord's treasury. Eloquent testimony to the

---

[56] BC 3826 nos. 59, 66, 69–72; cf. BC 3826 no. 73, Skole *Kahal* vs. Taxpayers. For more cases involving Jews reaching the *zamek* court see BC 3813–28.

[57] *PVAA* and *PML* Index s.v. "Arkaot" (non-Jewish courts).

centrality of this obligation is contained in the petitions addressed to the owners by Jewish subjects. Whether requesting a loan to rebuild after some destructive event, tax relief, or food to prevent starvation, the most common justifying theme is: "So that I may be able to generate revenue for the treasury."[58]

It is clear that the Jews were among the best taxpayers in the towns. They usually owned the most valuable property and paid taxes at a higher rate. In Sieniawa, in 1718, the total amount of taxes collected from 175 householders was 1,613 *zł*. Of this, 1,404 *zł*. came from 103 Jews (see Table 3.3). In Shkłoŭ proper, in 1727, the Jews, numbering about 20 percent of the population, paid about 60 percent of the property taxes (Table 3.5). In Medzhybizh in 1717, 155 Jewish property owners paid more tax than 508 Christian ones (Table 3.1).

In order to keep paying high taxes and to be commercially successful, the Jews had to be secure. Once having been granted basic communal rights and economic freedom in the town, they had to be confident that, like other citizens, they were entitled to the protection of an unwritten bill of rights.

Foremost among these traditional, assumed rights was the obligation of the owner to live up to commitments and to enforce agreements. As the institution of petitions demonstrates, the inhabitants of the latifundium—including Jews—were convinced that the magnates had the responsibility to correct injustice where it existed. The owners themselves, who often answered these petitions personally, evidently accepted this obligation, at least in principle.[59] All petitions shared the assumption that if only the lord's attention could be drawn to the problem, he would do the right thing and redress the grievance.

---

[58] EW 189 *passim;* cf. Yaakov Yisrael of Kremenets, *Shevet Miyisrael* (Zhovkva, 1772), chapter 44, verse 12, p. 4c:

> For in this bitter Exile in which we are destined to be plundered and to bear the terrible yoke of taxes and assessments from the nations in whose lands we are located, God makes the money of Israel dear in the eyes of the nations ... this is a great good for us, for due to this we can exist among the nations and live in their lands.

[59] See the following petitions: EW 189 *Gromada* Rudecki 1714, Matwiej et al. 1714, Jakub Cieplicki 1732; EW 255 Jarosław Jews vs. Łukszyński undated, Burmistrz Jarosław 1718; BC 3826 no. 81 R to MZSC; BC 5870 J. Lejbowicz to ES 1.21173 undated; BC 5881 Łukszyński to ES 1.23428; BC 5934 R to ES 1.34633 4/16/1714, 1.34686 7/03/1719; cf. *SB*, p. 101.

Thus in 1715 the Stryi administrator, Michał Czaplic, tried to prevent the Jews of the town from sending representatives directly to Elżbieta Sieniawska to gain a ruling from her with regard to a dispute over taxes. In order to foil him, the Jews rode off during the night.[60]

Another, closely related right claimed by latifundium citizens—especially Jews—was protection from violence. In July of 1717, the three leading Jews of Stryi, Chaim Tywłowicz, Szawel Markiewicz, and Zelik Józefowicz, all of whom were arrendators or administrators for the Sieniawskis, wrote a letter demanding that Elżbieta Sieniawska order the nearby garrison to dispatch troops to defend the town. They informed her that a band of several hundred brigands had been terrorizing the region, having already plundered other localities, and were encamped in the woods, a mile and a half from Stryi, ready to attack.[61]

Jewish merchants who traveled frequently were particularly vulnerable to violent attacks, and when these occurred the Jewish communities demanded that the perpetrators be brought to justice.[62] Magnates accepted the responsibility for ensuring physical safety, and administrators, at least sometimes, came to the rescue of threatened Jewish citizens or captured the criminals who had victimized them.[63]

As the primary source of authority for his subjects, the magnate was also looked to as the primary source of benefit. In time of disaster the lord was expected to make things right. The peasant's attitude

---

[60] BC 5782 Czaplic to ES 1.5902 6/14/1715.

[61] BC 5886 Chaim Tywlowicz et al. to ES 1.24374 7/11?/1717; cf. *SB*, p. 211.

[62] BC 5972 Chaim Tywlowicz and the Stryj *Kahal* to ES (?) 1.45318 undated; see also: BC 5887 Damazki to ES 1.6804 8/18/1726; BC 5934 R to ES 1.34657 2/8/1715; Meir b. Zvi Hersh Margoliot, *Meir Netivim,* (Polonne, 1791–92), part 1, no. 37; *SB*, pp. 165–66.

[63] BC 5897 Morzycki to ES 1.26531 5/6/1719: capturing robbers; EW 176 Punkta *Gromada* Głuszkowskiej: saving Jews from peasant attack; BC 3814 nos. 57, 110, 141, Rapoport, Even Heazer no. 27: prosecuting perpetrators of criminal actions against Jews; Yaakov Yisrael, chapter 56, verses 1–2, p. 9a: expressing the opinion that Polish authorities generally protected Jews physically. See also note 61; cf. J. Goldberg, "Poles and Jews," p. 262; Bergerówna, p. 318. Sometimes this responsibility remained "in principle" only, as exemplified in S. Maimon's *Autobiography,* J. Clark Murray, ed. and trans. (London, 1954), pp. 15–16.

was, "I belong to your Lordship, let your Lordship feed me."[64] If
there was a flood, drought, plague, or poor harvest the serfs demanded
grain from their lord. If a serf's cow died or his plow broke, he could
borrow one from the manor.[65] Magnate town residents—Jews as well
as Christians—also expected the owner to come to their aid when
catastrophe struck. A list of requests from an unnamed Jewish community of Sieniawska's that had suffered a fire included requests for a
debt moratorium and for exemptions from tax and from obligations to
quarter passing troops.[66]

In 1699, the Vyshnia *sejmik,* undoubtedly in response to
Sieniawski's urging, instructed its delegates to the *Sejm* to procure
exemptions from royal customs and tolls for all residents of Berezhany because of the havoc wreaked there by the Saxon army.[67] In
1716, when many Shkłoŭ residents were flooded out, Sieniawski
directed his administrators to grant them a blanket tax exemption.[68]
Individuals also felt entitled to request aid from the owner when faced
with personal catastrophe. If a fire or an invading army destroyed a
home or store, or if personal tragedy such as the death of the family
breadwinner occurred, the victims would often request and receive tax
relief, a loan to rebuild, or grain to prevent starvation.[69]

One of the most important benefits that a lord owed his subjects
was a measure of *protekcja.* This meant that the magnate would bring
his influence and power to bear whenever one of his subjects was
involved with some other force or authority and that in general he
would favor his own subjects over other people.

There were at least three reasons that a magnate was inclined to
protect his subjects. First, the threat of harm to the individual or
group concerned would often result in harm to the magnate's

[64] Kula, *Economic Theory,* p. 65 (n. 58).

[65] BC 5934 R to ES 1.34569 1/16/1705; BC 4495 Szkłów 1765 *Instrukcja,* p. 6;
Majewski, *Gospodarstwo folwarczne,* pp. 217–22; Wiatrowski, pp. 142–46.

[66] BC 3822 no. 68, cf. Eliyahu ben Yehezkeil of Bilgoray, *Har Hakarmel* (Frankfurt a.d. Oder, 1782 [Jerusalem, 1973]), no. 6.

[67] *AGZ,* vol. 22 no. 120.32; cf. *AGZ* vol. 22 nos. 51.79, 42.74, 2.19; Prochaska, *Historja,* pp. 22–24; Weinryb, *Jews,* p. 122.

[68] EW 525 Szkłów 1717 *Informacja.*

[69] EW 189 *Supliki,* passim; EW 179 *Supliki,* passim; BC 2581/2 no. 46 7/22/1711;
BC 5757 Aron Szmuklerz to ES 1.265–66 9/13/1719 10/3?/1719; BC 5806 Fejga to
ES 1.10146 1/10/1723.

economic interests. If a community's tax burden was raised by some outside authority, the ability of its members to pay their obligations to the magnate would be diminished. If a merchant's goods were confiscated, he would not be able to make his contribution to latifundium commerce and would probably petition the lord for a tax exemption or a loan. If arrendators could not collect the revenues they had leased, the magnates would not be able to continue raising the price of the lease.

Second, for the magnate, a situation requiring his *protekcja* offered the opportunity to demonstrate his power. If he prevailed over rival authorities, his prestige was enhanced. Such enhancement did not have mere symbolic value. The more successful a magnate in enforcing his will, the less he would be challenged and the easier it would become for him to have his way without a fight. Moreover, magnates who acquired a reputation for effectively protecting their subjects could attract as latifundium settlers talented people with money to invest who would develop the towns into commercial centers and generators of revenue. An example of this process is contained in a letter of the Tenczyn administrator, Morzycki, to Elżbieta Sieniawska in 1715. Morzycki recommended granting settlement rights in Nowa Góra to a Jew, Icek, who was running away from "oppression" in his own town. Icek, Morzycki emphasized, had the recommendation of two noblemen and was wealthy (*tanti*).[70] Icek was confident that he could find refuge under the *protekcja* of Sieniawska. She thereby gained a useful subject.

Third, while staunchly opposed to even the hint of absolutist pretensions on the part of the Polish king, each Polish magnate was determined to be the sole source of authority in his own latifundium. As such he would not brook any challenge. In his drive to control every aspect of latifundium polity, economy, and society, he welcomed the chance to blunt competing forces.[71]

In the Sieniawski latifundium, the tradition of invoking *protekcja* went back at least as far as 1507, when Mikołaj Sieniawski requested from King Zygmunt I that the Jews of Medzhybizh be freed from pay-

[70] BC 5897 Morzycki to ES 1.26450 11/16/1715.
[71] Bergerówna, pp. 174–75; Czapliński and Długosz, pp. 176–97; Goldberg, "Poles and Jews," p. 262.

ing royal customs duties.[72] The heirs to the Sieniawski fortune continued to provide *protekcja* for their subjects, including their Jews, in the eighteenth century.[73] The challenge to their authority came from several quarters.

The most common circumstances in which a magnate was called upon to assert his power on behalf of his Jews concerned other magnates or noblemen. A typical problem was indebtedness: a nobleman or a Jewish subject of a magnate owed money to a Jew living under a second magnate. The debtor, however, was resisting collection of the debt. In such cases the creditor would write to his lord or lady asking for intervention. In one case, in the Sieniawski territories, Józef Markiewicz claimed that a certain *Imci Pan* Missuny owed and refused to pay him 3,700 zł. that was lent in September 1712 and was due to be repaid on October 31 of the same year. Finally, in 1716, after strenuous efforts to collect, Markiewicz wrote, "Thus I have no other means besides the singular *protekcja* of My Lady whom I supplicate. . . . It is hard for me for I live by credit and absolutely must do right by each of my own creditors."[74]

The chances that Sieniawska would respond to such a request were apparently good. About 1722, in reaction to a request similar to Markiewicz's from the Jew Moszko Mordyński of Międzyrzec Podlaski, Sieniawska went so far as to write to her sister magnate, the Princess Radziwiłł, wife of the chancellor of Lithuania:[75]

[72] Maciszewski, p. 59; see also M. Horn, "Żydzi województwa bełskiego w pierwszej połowie XVII w.," *BZIH* 27 (1958), p. 32; *Słownik geograficzny królestwa polskiego*, vol. 7 (Warsaw, 1886), p. 478. *Pinkas Hakehillot: Poland*, vol. 2 (Jerusalem, 1980), p. 57. Of course there were also times when the Sieniawskis dealt harshly with their Jews; e.g., Adam Mikołaj Sieniawski's grandmother, Elżbieta z Potockich Sieniawska, ordered the expulsion of the Jews from Shkłoŭ in 1650, hoping thereby to appease the Cossacks; see M. Hrushevs'kyi, *Istoriia Ukrainy-Rusy*, vol. 9 (New York, 1957), p. 220, n. 4.

[73] For example, BC 4495 Szkłów *Instrukcja* Appendix, pt. 5 which, in response to a complaint by Christians that Jews have been overprotected, stresses that *protekcja* must be provided to Christians and Jews in equal measures.

[74] EW 255 *Supl.* Józef Markiewicz; BC 5886 Józef Markiewicz to Lubiszewski, secretary to ES 1.24356 3/16/1716. See, similarly, EW 255 *Supl.* Lewko Szajewicz.

[75] AR V 14275 ES to JOMXKanclerzyna WKL ca. 1722; cf. *PVAA* no. 503, p. 235, 1695 letter of R. Leszczyński on behalf of his Jew, Michael Abraham.

My Great, Powerful, Lady and Sister,

In hope of being favored throughout my life with the grace and respect of your Highness whom I so esteem, I implore you with my brief on behalf of the Jew Moszko Mordyński, a townsman of mine in Międzyrzec, who according to a signed note is owed a debt by Josef, a Jewish citizen of Biała. I most humbly request Your Highness to order that repayment be made . . .

By the same token, magnates could be depended upon to provide *protekcja* for their Jews who owed money but could not pay because of business reverses or adverse circumstances. The co-arrendator of Końskowola once wrote to Sieniawska requesting a written brief to be sent to the nobleman, Fujszpan, asking for a postponement of the debt due to him.[76] Sometimes, according to August Aleksander Czartoryski, Jews took advantage of the lord's willingness to grant this type of *protekcja*. He complained, in 1765, that whenever a foreigner attempted to sue any Jew of Shkłoŭ the Jew automatically asserted that to allow such a suit would be a breach of *protekcja*.[77]

The magnate was probably even more cooperative with Jews who were faced with noblemen, or their subjects, who defied *arenda* contracts. In 1705, the arrendator Abram Irszowicz complained that he did not succeed in collecting any of the expected revenue he had leased from the tax on passing cattle herds "since [the cowhandlers] were protected by the great lords and I really had to struggle with them, because they didn't want to pay anything."[78] Such defiance of an arrendator ultimately meant reduced revenues for the magnate's treasury, and so Abram was confident that Sieniawska would command the local administrator to be more conscientious about backing up Abram's authority.

Sometimes Jews were the victims of criminal actions committed by noblemen. Here, too, whether it was false accusation, robbery,

---

[76] BC 5870 J. Lejbowicz to ES 1.21173 undated; see also BC 5886 Chaim Tywlowicz and Szawel Markiewicz to Lubiszewski 1.24375 8/4/1717; cf. *ABK* no. 48; *PVAA* nos. 375 p. 166, 383 pp. 167–68, 483 p. 227, 544–46 p. 263.

[77] BC 4495 Szkłów 1765 *Instrukcja* Appendix, pt. 5.

[78] EW 189 *Supl.* Abram Irszowicz. See, similarly, EW 189 *Supl.* Sieniawa Targownicy 1733; BC 5934 R to ES 1.34661 7/16/1715; AR V 14275 ES to Krogulecki 7/11/1702.

murder, or forced conversion, the Sieniawski-Czartoryski sources show Jews turning to the magnate for justice even when their antagonists were noblemen—ostensibly the magnate's brothers.[79]

Another group in Polish society whose members desired to share control of the Jewish population was the clergy. Although their power was attenuated in the mid-sixteenth century, ecclesiastical courts existed in Poland and, when run by a powerful cleric, they could constitute a force to be reckoned with.[80] When Jews were perceived as committing crimes of a religious nature or against the church, the ecclesiastical courts often claimed jurisdiction. In 1724, Lewek, the arrendator of Tenczyn, wrote to Elżbieta Sieniawska requesting *protekcja* against the local vicar. Lewek, who had been arrendator for only two months, had been fortunate enough to marry off his daughter. But during the wedding, a group of peasants held a gambling session in the brewery that Lewek controlled. Since gambling was sinful and Lewek was responsible for seeing to it that no sins were committed on the premises of his leasehold, the vicar's court fined him the rather large sum of 300 *grzywny*. Lewek asserted that not only had he been ignorant of the gambling, but that the vicar had given it his blessing. The implication was that the trial was only a pretext to extract money from the Jew. Lewek asked Sieniawska to write a brief on his behalf to the vicar's superior canceling the fine.[81]

As implied by the privileges granting Jewish communities the right to conduct organized religious life, even in nobility-owned lands, the Polish clergy was, in theory, opposed to any strengthening of Jewish institutions. In 1722 when the Jews of Staszów sought to build a synagogue, it was necessary to obtain the consent of no less a personage than the bishop of Cracow. This consent was not automatic and required personal negotiations between the bishop and a representative of the community as well as at least one letter to the bishop

[79] BC 5809 F to ES 1.10747–10753 ca. 1724–26; BC 5935 R to AAC 1.34934, 1.34936, 7/7, 8/22/1736; EW 179 *Supl.* Satanów Jewish merchants and teamsters 1732; cf. *ABK* no. 218; Prochaska, *Historja*, p. 113.

[80] Kaczmarczyk and Leśnodorski, *Historia*, p. 157; Mahler, *Toldot*, pp. 333–34, 340; cf. Goldberg, "Poles and Jews," pp. 253–55.

[81] BC 5870 Lewek to ES 1.21191 1724; cf. EW 189 *Supl.* Marek Lajzerowicz et al., 1735; BC 3826 no. 92.

from Sieniawska expressing her desire that the synagogue be built.[82]

Despite having relinquished control over Jews resident in private lands, the king and the institutions of the central government still made claims, especially monetary ones, on all Jews. The Jewish head tax and the excise tax (*czopowy*) on liquor as well as various extraordinary levies continued to be owed to the central treasury. Obviously, high tax obligations to the central government impaired the ability of the taxpayers to contribute revenue to the magnate's coffers.

Thus it is interesting that, for the record, Adam Mikołaj Sieniawski issued a decree on December 20, 1711, exhorting private owners not to assist their Jews in avoiding tax obligations to the royal treasury. Yet, in the same year, when the *sejmik* of Halych voted a special levy of 20,000 *zł.* on the Jews of the region, Sieniawski's Jews were exempted.[83]

In 1712, Elżbieta Sieniawska was instrumental in gaining an eight-year exemption from liquor taxes for her Jews in Stryi. She also insisted that the royal governor (*wojewoda*) of Rus', Jabłonowski, had no right to demand direct taxes from the Jews of Stryi.[84]

King and magnate also came into conflict over the question of jurisdiction. Sieniawski-Czartoryski Jews who had been arrested or sued by royal officials appealed to Sieniawska to get them released from royal jails or to intervene in their trials in royal courts.[85]

The area in which magnate and royal interests were most consistently opposed was commerce. For the king and central government, long-distance trade was a taxable activity that produced a large

---

[82] BC 5934 R to ES 1.34749 9/9/1722. The representative of the community was Rubinowicz, see Chapter 6. See also Goldberg, *Privileges,* pp. 17–18; Weinryb, *Jews,* p. 123; Mahler, *Toldot,* p. 333. The clergy themselves—monasteries and individuals—often owned or controlled towns with Jewish inhabitants. In such cases, when their own interests were at stake, their attitudes toward "their" Jews were more positive.

[83] A. Leszczyński, "Żydzi ziemi bielskiej od połowy XVII wieku do 1705 r.," doctoral dissertation, Wyższa Szkoła Pedagogiczna im. Powstańców Śląskich w Opolu (Opole, 1977), p. 66; *AGZ,* vol. 25, no. 102.6; cf. vol. 22, nos. 120.32, 125.65; vol. 25, nos. 135.12, 227.3–4.

[84] *AGZ,* vol. 22, no. 195.35; BC 2706 Jabłonowski to ES 6/21/1719; BC 2707 Jabłonowski to the Jews of Stryj 1/23/1712 (?); cf. Baron, *History,* vol. 16, p. 204.

[85] EW 255 *Supl.* Izak Jakubowicz; BC 5899 Nahaczowski to AAC (?) 1.26948 10/22/1738; BC 5997 A. Zelmanowicz to ES 1.50304 5/5/1724; cf. Baron, *History,* vol. 16, pp. 403–404, n. 27.

amount of revenue through customs duties and tolls. For the magnate, commerce was a means of procuring goods and generating wealth in the latifundium. Part of this wealth, he believed, would find its way to his treasury. Since Jews composed a large percentage of the high-volume, long-distance merchants, the conflict between royal and magnate commercial interests was largely played out in relationship to them. The king's agents sought to increase the duties paid by Jewish merchants. The magnates helped the Jews to decrease these payments or to avoid them altogether.[86]

The magnate's fourth competitor for authority over his Jews was the Jewish community and its institutions. While king, clergy, and other noblemen may have had the legitimate right to exercise control over the behavior of Jews when it touched upon areas of their respective legal competence, the *kehilla* organization had a legitimate claim, by law and by tradition, to command the loyalty of its members. The *kehilla*'s governing body, the *kahal,* operated over a broad range of activities and had a constant, direct, personal effect upon the individual Jew. This made the *kehilla* the magnate's most formidable rival when it came to ruling his Jews. The *kehilla*'s rights—both on the local and the supralocal levels—to legislate, tax, judge, and administer always held the potential for subverting the parallel powers of the magnate. The magnate could not consolidate his rule completely so long as the *kehilla* stood between him and his Jewish subjects.

Consequently, as is clear from the Sieniawski-Czartoryski sources, the magnates attempted to dislodge the *kehilla* from its powerful position and to relegate it to the function of serving as agent of the magnate's interests. One of the key tactics in this effort was to invoke *protekcja.* This meant giving an individual the right to disobey his community or allowing an individual community to defy higher authority.[87]

The demographic, economic, legal, and political factors discussed so far played a large role in determining the position of the Jews in the latifundium towns. They were not, however, the sole determinants. In order to fully understand the Jews' situation in these towns, it is also necessary to consider the attitudes of their non-Jewish neighbors. What was the town climate *vis-à-vis* the Jews?

---

[86] Dinur, p. 118 (n. 38); see Chapter 4.
[87] See Chapter 7.

For several reasons, the situation of Jews resident in privately owned towns was usually more felicitous than that of their counterparts in the royal towns.[88] The fact that Jews were usually invited, and almost always welcomed, to the private towns by the owners meant that the basic perception of their right to be there was different from that in the royal towns where the *modus vivendi* for Jews was often formalized only after creating a *fait accompli.* Since the highest authority, the town owner, desired the Jews to live in the town, the likelihood that other residents would tolerate the Jews' presence was greater than in royal towns. In the latter, Christian townsmen often pressured the king and *Sejm* to abolish or limit rights that the Jews had gained through lobbying or in a *de facto* manner.[89] Moreover, in many cases, private towns were established in the new territories in the Southeast. In these towns, Jewish settlers were often included in the founding group. Having worked hand in hand with the Christians in developing the town, they would be less likely to bear the stigma of newcomers reaping the benefits of the toil of the founders.[90]

In addition, in newly established towns it was likely that a division of economic labor emerged among the various ethnic groups from the beginning. This meant that economic competition would be held at a lower level than in the older royal towns, where Jews often attempted to enter economic fields by competing with and eventually displacing the established artisans and merchants.[91]

The town's size probably also played a role in determining attitudes toward the Jews. In the large royal centers, the Jews were a visible but relatively small minority. They were frequently regarded as a disruptive force whose departure would be beneficial. In the smaller, private towns, where the Jews usually constituted a large percentage

---

[88] Baron, *History,* vol. 16, pp. 119–20; H. Hekker, "Evrei v polskikh gorodakh vo vtoroi polovinie XVIII veka," *EvS* 6 (1913), pp. 184–200, 325–32; Rutkowski, *Historia,* pp. 176–86; Ettinger, "Maamadam Hamishpati," pp. 132–33; Weinryb, *Jews,* pp. 120, 352 (n. 1); cf. Bogucka and Samsonowicz, p. 75.

[89] A. Y. Brawer, *Galicia Veyehudeha* (Jerusalem, 1965), p. 33; Hundert, "Security and Dependence," pp. 194–96.

[90] Compare how the Christians of Sieniawa expressed their appreciation for Lejba Sukiennik's efforts on behalf of the town during the Swedish occupation, BC 3826 no. 59 5/31/1718.

[91] Kremer, pp. 302–307; cf. S. M. Dubnov, *Toldot Hahasidut* (Tel Aviv, 1931 [1975]), p. 312.

of the population, the significance of their contribution to the town's economic life could be more readily appreciated.[92]

To say that attitudes toward Jews in private towns were generally more positive than in royal towns, however, means that the Jews' presence in the town and their rights were usually not called into question. It does not mean that antagonisms never arose between the two communities.[93] In discussing the court system it was alluded that disputes over housing and trade did arise. There are also several petitions indicating that Christians sometimes felt that the Jewish community or its members flouted the law or were given preferential treatment with regard to taxation and business opportunity.[94]

A good example of this phenomenon is the 1731 complaint of the Jarosław administrator, Daniel Borgolt. He charged that the Jews did not honor the *arenda* monopoly of the municipality and that they refused to appear in court when sued by Christian creditors. He alleged that the power of the Jews in the town was such that the only means of forcing them to observe the law was through direct appeal to the owner—a costly and time-consuming process. He concluded that "Jews are entitled to justice from Christians, but Christians cannot make a case against a Jew. Who is able to travel to My Lady to complain about every single matter?... As the Jews were enslaved in Egypt soon the Jarosławians will be enslaved to the Jews."[95]

It is interesting that, despite his frustration, Borgolt requested only that Jews be made to observe the law and cooperate with the authori-

---

[92] Goldberg, "De Non," pp. 40–41; *AGZ*, vol. 23, no. 168.6; EW 189 *Supl.* Gotel, who offers certification from the authorities in his hometown, Szydłów, as to his salutary economic activities. There are letters of the administrator Borgolt regarding the desirability of having the Council of Four Lands meet in Jarosław: BC 5767 Borgolt to ES 1.2670, 1.2687, 1.2691, 1.2692 June-August, 1717. Cf. Hundert, "Security and Dependence," pp. 240–42.

[93] It also does not mean that traditional prejudices disappeared, see: GOSP 1566 Międzybóż 1732, pp. 33–44; EW 525 Szkłów *Supl.* undated; EW 255 *Supl.* Burmistrz Jarosław, undated; cf. Baranowski, *Życie,* pp. 78–79, 245; Kremer, pp. 307–308.

[94] EW 179 *Supl.* Satanów 1743; EW 255 *Punkta Pospólstwa* M. Jarosławia undated; EW 525 *Supl.* Szkłów undated, 1715 *Informacja* pt. 11; BC 2574 no. 48; BC 4495 Szkłów 1765 *Instrukcja* Appendix, pt. 5; BC 5767 Borgolt to MZSC 1.2902 7/4/1731; BC 5782 Czaplic to ES 1.5900 9/7/1712; cf. Prochaska, *Historja,* pp. 114–17; Sosis, pp. 5–7.

[95] BC 5767 Borgolt to MZSC 1.2902 7/4/1731.

ties. He demanded neither expulsion nor economic limitations for them. Apparently he realized that such measures would be counter-productive or simply unacceptable to Maria Zofia Czartoryska.[96]

For their part, the Jews resented their unequal tax burden and asserted that alleged favoritism was in reality only enlightened self-interest on the part of the magnate. This attitude is clearly expressed in a petition of the Shkłoŭ *kahal* written in rebuttal to demands of the Christian townsmen that the Jews be made to pay a special extra tax because of the huge capital wealth represented by their large homes. The Jews claimed that they were already paying higher real estate tax rates than the Christians; that they had to pay special levies voted by the *Sejm* from which Christians were exempt; that the large houses were essential to commerce because they served as security for loans the Jewish merchants had to take in order to conduct trade and pro-duce income for the magnate's treasury; and that the large houses made the town look good, reflecting well upon its owner. The *kahal*'s brief concluded by adding to the rejection of any new tax a demand for relief from current taxes. Moreover, the *kahal* insisted that the municipal authorities not be allowed to impose any financial obliga-tions on the Jews, lest additional financial burdens force them to leave the town.[97]

Conclusion

The dissatisfaction expressed in complaints like that of Borgolt and the tone of petitions similar to that of the Shkłoŭ *kahal* are testimony to the confidence and security of the Jewish communities in the lati-fundium towns. If it is true that at times the Jews behaved high-handedly or defiantly, then such behavior must have been based on the conviction that there was little to fear.

In light of the material analyzed in this chapter, it is not surprising that Jews in the towns could be confident of their position. Demo-graphically, they constituted a significant enough proportion of the population that their exodus would have seriously undermined the

---

[96] Borgolt himself appreciated the commercial value of the Council of Four Lands meeting in Jarosław; see note 92.

[97] EW 525 Szkłów *Supl. Kahal* to AAC undated.

population base of many, if not most, magnate-owned towns. Geographically, the Jews were concentrated in and around the marketplace, the hub of political, economic, and social activity in the town. By being close to this activity, they were in a position to control much of it. In economic terms, the Jews' high contribution to town commerce and tax revenues made their presence indispensable to the owner, and the other residents benefited from the commercial services provided by the Jews.

As to the political conditions, Jews were granted in writing or by tradition religious and economic freedoms and the promise of physical security, justice, and *protekcja*. On this basis, they could develop a stable community and fruitful personal lives.

The two terms commonly employed by the Sieniawski-Czartoryski magnates when referring to Jewish inhabitants of their towns were "townsman" (*mieszczanin*) and "citizen" (*obywatel*). These are the same terms used in referring to Christians.[98] It may be that these terms are not to be understood as technical legal descriptions of Jewish status.[99] Even so, the fact that they were applied as easily to Jews as to others, even in a nontechnical way, is significant. It implies that in the minds of the magnates, the Jews resident in their latifundium were, in all but perhaps the narrow legal sense, full-fledged members of the town bodies.[100] Their importance to the private towns put them on a par with the other inhabitants. The Jews were aware of the weight of their contribution and were not timid about demanding treatment commensurate with their standing.

---

[98] For example, EW 255 *Supl.* Jozef Markiewicz; BC 3826 nos. 58, 62; BC 5886 Markiewicz to Lubiszewski 1.24367 3/12/1716; AR V 14275 ES to JOMXKanclerzyna WKL ca. 1722. Archiwum PAN Kraków 3795 (HM 6739) 9/18/1754. Sometimes Jews were even referred to as "*Pan.*"

[99] Goldberg, *Privileges,* pp. 26–28, states that Jews were officially classified as *incolati* (residents) rather than citizens; i.e., they lacked political rights. For a detailed discussion of Jewish status in the Commonwealth, particularly in the Ukraine in the pre-1648 period, see Ettinger, "Maamadam Hamishpati," pp. 134–45.

[100] Compare Jacob Toury, "Types of Municipal Rights in German Townships—The Problem of Local Emancipation," *YBLBI* 22 (1977), pp. 55–80; see especially p. 56: "... already before the onset of modern times it was conceivable that Jews might achieve—in one form or another—civic status in German townships."

CHAPTER FOUR

The Jews, the Magnates, and Commerce

The central role of the Jews in Polish commerce and of commerce in the life of Polish Jewry is an axiom of Polish-Jewish historiography.[1] From the poor peddler who sold notions out of a pack door-to-door, to the rich interurban merchant who transported thousands of *złoty* worth of merchandise, Jews were involved on all levels of commercial trade as retailers, wholesalers, and brokers.[2]

---

[1] The classic survey of Jewish commerce in Poland is: I. Schiper, *Dzieje handlu żydowskiego na ziemiach polskich* (Warsaw, 1937). Other Jewish historians who have characterized the Jewish commercial role are: M. Bałaban in his many works on the history of the Jews in Poland, see especially *Historja Żydów w Krakowie i na Kazimierzu*, 2 vols. (Cracow, 1931–36); *Żydzi lwowscy na przełomie XVI i XVII w.* (Lviv, 1906); Baron, *History,* vol. 16; H. H. Ben-Sasson, *Hagut Vehanhagah* (Jerusalem, 1959), pp. 55–65; I. Halpern, "The Jews in Eastern Europe," *The Jews,* vol. 1, L. Finkelstein, ed. (New York, 1960), especially pp. 298ff.; M. Kossower, "Der Inlendisher Handel fun Poilishe Yidn in 16ten un 17ten Yarhundert," *Yivo Bleter* 12 (1939) pp. 533–45; Mahler, *Toldot;* B. D. Weinryb, *Jews.* Polish historians have for the most part taken the Jewish commercial role for granted and devoted only passing attention to it. See *Historia Polski,* vol. 2, pt. 2, (Warsaw, 1958), pp. 138–40; Baranowski, *Życie,* Index, s.v., Żydzi (Jews); J. Burszta, "Handel magnacki i kupiecki między Sieniawą nad Sanem a Gdańskiem od końca XVII do połowy XVIII wieku," *RDSG* 16 (1954), pp. 183, 218; Guldon, p. 20; Homecki, p. 37; M. Wolański, *Związki handlowe Śląska z Rzeczpospolitą w XVII wieku* (Wrocław, 1961), pp. 238, 267ff., 278ff., 300–301; A. Wyrobisz, "Materiały do dziejów handlu w miasteczkach polskich na początku XVII wieku," *PH* 62 (1971), p. 715.

[2] Schiper, *Dzieje handlu,* pp. 261–63, estimated that 50 to 65 percent of Polish Jews in the mid-eighteenth century derived their primary livelihood from commerce, including liquor production. Mahler, *Yidn,* vol. 1, p. 84: "Commerce was the most popular and most traditional Jewish occupation." The census sources he analyzed did not usually specify commerce as an occupation, however; see also Kossower, pp. 533–34; Sosis, p. 5; Bogucka and Samsonowicz, p. 470. Whatever the precise percentage of the Jewish population involved in commerce was, it is unquestionable

Although other groups—Germans, Armenians, Scots, and Italians—
were, in fact, equally commercially oriented, or even more so, Jews
were so visible in trade that Poles and foreigners alike were convinced that they dominated the commercial life of Poland. Pam-
phleteers railed against Jewish monopolization of the marketplace
gained through the introduction of nontraditional modes of trade and
credit. Townsmen continually petitioned for legal measures to roll
back what they viewed as the Jewish commercial juggernaut.[3] Complaints of this type, especially in large royal towns, contained much
exaggeration, but it is evident from the Sieniawski-Czartoryski
sources that Jews were the mainspring of local commerce in smaller,
private towns in the southeastern portions of the country. In Jarosław,
in 1723, the townspeople contended that "there are no longer any
Christian merchants among us in Jarosław . . . Jews divert and handle
all commerce."[4] Comments of this nature are confirmed by the fact
that Jews owned most of the stores and, in general, were concentrated
on the marketplace in private towns.[5]

---

that commerce was an essential element in Polish-Jewish economic life. Jewish
economic innovations designed to facilitate commerce such as the *Heter Iska* (circum-
vention of the biblical prohibition on loaning on interest) and the *Mamram* (letter of
credit) developed in Poland. Moreover, sixteenth-, seventeenth-, and eighteenth-
century rabbinic literature is replete with problems, examples, and references based on
commercial experiences. Jewish communal record books (*Pinkasim*) also contain
many enactments designed to regulate commercial life. For anecdotes about Jewish
merchants, see *SB* Index s.v. Merchants.

[3] Goldberg, "De Non Tolerandis Iudaeis," p. 41 (n. 5). Smoleński, p. 9; Schiper,
Dzieje handlu, pp. 195–210; *AGZ*, vol. 22, nos. 31.62, 94.23–26, 101.19, 119.18,
122.18; vol. 23, nos. 157.34, 162.10, 168.6, 174.29 203.8, 270.13; Gierowski,
Rzeczpospolita, pp. 31–33. For observations of foreigners about Jewish domination
of Polish commerce, see G. D. Hundert, "Security and Dependence," p. 117 and
bibliography cited there.

[4] EW 255 Jarosław 6/16/1723 *Supl.* Mieszczanie. For similar comments see: EW
525 Szkłów undated *Supliki* concerning Jews in commerce; one from Christians, one
from Jews. EW 255 Jarosław undated *Supl.* Burmistrz et al.; cf. Nadav, pp. 122–24;
Brawer, *Galicia Veyehudeha*, pp. 104–105; Prochaska, *Historja*, pp. 47, 109–10.

[5] See Chapter 3. See also: Baranowski, *Życie*, pp. 69–71, 80–81; Homecki,
p. 37; Hundert, "Security and Dependence," pp. 207–209; Maciszewski, p. 164;
Prochaska, *Historja*, pp. 109–10; Schiper, *Dzieje handlu*, pp. 159–69, 264–69;
Wyrobisz, "Materiały," p. 715.

Noble and Magnate Support

To a large extent, the success of the Jews in commerce in Poland was due to the support and encouragement that the Polish nobility lent to their activities. Jews dealt in luxury goods desired by the nobility. Gold, silver, silks, furs, and pearls could be obtained from Jewish merchants at reasonable prices. Jews also provided important commercial services like moneychanging and petty moneylending.[6]

The nobility were generally willing to encourage Jewish commerce by patronizing Jewish merchants and advocating the easing of legal restrictions on Jewish commercial activity.[7] The magnates were also interested in furthering Jewish commerce, but for different reasons and in different ways from their brethren of lower rank and lesser means.

The main problems faced by Jewish merchants in Poland were:

* legal restrictions on the right to do business in certain locales or to trade in certain goods;
* difficulty in obtaining capital;
* numerous and high customs and toll charges;
* inefficiency of the central government in enforcing the rule of law, making travel dangerous and the redress of injury difficult.

The Jewish merchants' greatest allies in overcoming these obstacles were the magnates. Unlike the majority of the noblemen, the magnates had an interest in Jewish commerce that was only secondarily motivated by the desire to take advantage of Jewish commercial services. Magnates, like the Sieniawskis and Czartoryskis, had little need to patronize the weekly markets and periodic fairs—dominated by the Jews—held in the towns they owned. Rather than deal with independent Jewish merchants, they marketed most bulk products such as grain, linen, salt, wood, and potash through their own private commercial network consisting of their—mainly non-Jewish—admin-

---

[6] S. Dubnov, *Weltgeschichte des Jüdischen Volkes*, vol. 7 (Berlin, 1928), p. 131.

[7] Baron, *History*, vol. 16, pp. 131–32, 234, 432, n. 37; Guldon, p. 20; Homecki, p. 37; Hundert, "Security and Dependence," pp. 88, 112, 120, 192–94, 204, 215; Mahler, *Toldot*, pp. 261–62; Schiper, *Dzieje handlu*, pp. 64–66 and passim: Weinryb, *Mehkarim*, pp. 27–28.

istrators.[8] Required items that were not produced on the latifundium were purchased by dispatching employees directly to Gdańsk, Lviv, Wrocław, or Leipzig. In these large cities the magnates' agents bought products directly from the large-scale import concerns.[9] The only way in which local merchants and tradesmen provided commercial service to these magnates was by supplementing the day-to-day food, cloth, and repair needs of the local latifundium complex.

In the sphere of finance and credit, Jews were moneylenders of the last resort for the magnates. They apparently turned to Jews only in the rare case when other magnates or the monasteries failed them.[10]

[8] For examples of latifundium administrators purchasing goods and marketing latifundium produce directly, see Elżbieta Sieniawska's correspondence with the administrators of the Sandomierz holdings, Morzycki, Zabagłowicz, and Rubinowicz in BC 5945–46, BC 5897, and BC 5934–35. On the role of Jews, especially Rubinowicz, in the administration, see Chapter 6. Apparently, the situation was somewhat different in the sixteenth and early seventeenth centuries when the marketing of major produce was typically in the hands of Jewish brokers; see Schiper, *Dzieje handlu,* pp. 59–60, 64–66, and R. Yoel Sirkes *(Old) Responsa* (Frankfurt/Main, 1697), no. 27. The Sieniawski-Czartoryski material does not support Dinur's assertion, *Bemifne Hadorot,* p. 104, that in the eighteenth century the Jews' role in organizing the export of latifundium produce was growing.

[9] BC 2527 11/13/1713 Imp Winnicki brought different types of cloth back from Gdańsk; BC 2900, no. 18 7/1/1720 Nahaczowski bought Turkish, Dutch, and French cloth from DeSmeling's in Lviv. Similarly, BC 2904, no. 51; BC 2901, p. 153, 2/28/1717; BC 3502, pp. 161–90, 1701–1702. See also the extensive shopping orders filled by the *spław* skippers in Gdańsk; e.g., BC 2526 Sept. 1720 P. Grodzicki skipper and BC 4818–19 passim. Kula, *Economic Theory,* p. 122. Apparently, none of the big import-export concerns were Jewish. In the lists of twenty-eight such firms in Gdańsk presented by Homecki, p. 117, and fifty Gdańsk merchants enumerated by E. Cieślak, "Z dziejów żeglugi i handlu gdańskiego w połowie XVIII wieku," *Rocznik Gdański* 24 (1965), p. 86, none seems to have been Jewish. Elżbieta Sieniawska dealt with, among others, the firms of Tarone and Bordalo, and Taylor in Wrocław; cf. S. Echt, *Geschichte der Juden in Danzig* (Leer/Ostfriesland, 1972), pp. 27–30.

[10] M. Wąsowicz and S. Siegel, *Kontrakty Lwowskie, 1678–1724* (Lviv, 1935), pp. 193–96, indicates that out of 409 cases of magnate borrowing in the Lviv area in the 1720s, the Jews were creditors in only 0.6 percent of the cases. The secondary nature of Jewish moneylending to the magnates is exemplified by BC 5934 R to ES 1.34752 9/30/1722, where R noted that in order to pay a pressing debt that ES owed to a monastery he would borrow from the "Jews, or from somebody." This implies that the relationship between the monasteries and the Jews was roughly analogous to the relationship between banks and finance companies today; cf. J. Morgensztern,

Thus, of all noblemen, magnates were least in need of the Jewish commercial network. Still, the magnates strongly supported Jewish commerce by encouraging Jews to develop magnate-owned towns as commercial centers. The reason for this was expressed succinctly by August Aleksander Czartoryski: "All towns are established primarily for commerce and through it they generate profit and wealth."[11] In order to generate such wealth, magnates like the Sieniawskis and Czartoryskis sought to induce Jews to settle in their towns and to set up stores. In royal towns, Jews were often restricted in their commercial development. In the newer, magnate-owned towns, Jews were usually welcome settlers. They were granted material assistance in building homes and stores, tax concessions, and the right to conduct trade freely.[12]

The privileges granted by Elżbieta Sieniawska specifically allowed Jews in her towns to deal in all types of merchandise and liquor and to sell both from their homes and their shops.[13] This is a prime example of a magnate providing the essential element of commercial life: a field in which to operate. Consequently, Jews flocked to the private towns and established a flourishing commercial presence.[14]

Magnate assistance to Jewish merchants did not end with settlement policy. The magnates also sought to promote the fairs and markets where these Jews conducted their business. They issued privileges allowing fairs and markets to be held and stores to be built, granted concessions to the merchants who attended, built new market-

---

"Operacje kredytowe Żydów w Zamościu w XVII w.," *BZIH* 64 (1967), pp. 3–32.

[11] EW 402, 1742; cf. Bergerówna, p. 270.

[12] On resistance to Jewish commercial activity, see: Goldberg, "De non Tolerandis Iudaeis," pp. 39–41, 51; Schiper, *Dzieje handlu*, pp. 195–210, 225–88; *AGZ* as cited in note 3. On magnate encouragement of town commercial development, see Rychlikowa, *Produkcja*, pp. 127–39. On magnate assistance to Jewish settlement and commerce, see Schiper, *Dzieje handlu*, pp. 159–69; Weinryb, *Jews*, pp. 10–11, 119–20. Sometimes magnates were so eager to have Jews settle in their towns that they forced them to do so; see Ber of Bolechow, pp. 132–34.

[13] AGAD *Akta komisji rządowej spraw wewnętrznych i duchownych*, no. 185, par. 3; Gelber, pp. 34–35; cf. Weinryb, *Jews*, pp. 10–11, 41–42, 120; Baron, *History*, vol. 16, pp. 28, 119–20, 122–24; Leszczyński, *Żydzi*, p. 64.

[14] Leszczyński, *Żydzi*, p. 187; Weinryb, *Jews*, pp. 112, 117–18, 120.

places, and provided *protekcja* from violence and certain taxes.[15] They also tried to protect their towns from competitors. Czartoryski, for example, fought the royal town of Łuków for twenty years, insisting that the date of its fair be changed so as not to detract from that of his town, Siedlce. He carried on a similar dispute with the Radziwiłł family concerning the market in their town of Olyka. Czartoryski felt that this market posed intolerable competition to his own town, Klevan'. As part of his campaign to drive it out of business, he ordered his peasants not to sell any grain in Olyka. He also demanded that the Jews in Klevan' guarantee that they would buy all available grain from his peasants.[16]

In addition to encouraging settlement and protecting markets, magnates advanced Jewish commerce by providing financial aid. They lent the Jewish merchants capital with which to build the stores and buy the stock necessary to attract commerce to their towns. It was, for example, a loan of one million *złoty* from Józef and Stanisław Potocki that enabled the Jews of Brody to rebuild their town after a series of fires and to make it a first-rank commercial center.[17] Likewise, the Sieniawskis gave loans for the purpose of establishing, developing, or rebuilding businesses and financing trade.[18] Such loans provided an additional strong motive for the fostering and protection of Jewish commerce. Once a magnate's money had been invested in Jewish enterprises, it was only prudent for him to do his best to ensure the success of the Jews' endeavors.[19]

Another way in which magnate owners helped Jewish merchants

---

[15] Bergerówna, pp. 316–19; Rychlikowa, *Produkcja*, pp. 129–30; Powidaj, p. 52; Leszczyński, *Żydzi*, pp. 166–70; BC 2581/1 no. 44, Szkłów ca. 1740; GOSP 537 Międzybóż 1727.

[16] On these disputes, see EW 11, 402, 506; Rychlikowa, *Produkcja*, pp. 129–30. Sometimes local Jewish merchants were protected from "foreign" Jewish competitors by being granted special trading rights. See Goldberg, *Privileges*, pp. 33–34.

[17] Ber of Bolechow, p. 85; N. M. Gelber, *Toldot Yehudei Brody* (Jerusalem, 1956), pp. 31–32. A similar type of loan is recorded in PHo, nos. 196, 198, 199; cf. Leszczyński, *Żydzi*, pp. 194–202.

[18] BC 2702, pp. 308–309, 363–66; BC 2693 1699; EW 133 ca. 1717; GOSP 597, pp. 221–27, 1738; GOSP 1576 Szkłów 1714; *PVAA* nos. 378, p. 167, 495, p. 215. EW 189 contains several *Supliki* from Jewish merchants requesting aid in reestablishing their businesses after various catastrophes.

[19] Schiper, *Dzieje handlu*, pp. 213–15, 225–28; Weinryb, *Jews*, p. 11.

was by offering them their *protekcja*. In the Sieniawski-Czartoryski documents, two forms of *protekcja* for merchants stand out: protection against molestation, official or otherwise, and help in avoiding or reducing customs and toll charges.

One of the characteristics of the weak Polish central administration was its inability to enforce the law. As a result, traveling merchants were at the mercy of army units in search of supplies, larcenous peasants, extortionary officials, and unscrupulous fellow merchants.[20]

One defense against such menaces was the backing of a magnate willing to guarantee the safety of his clients. In May 1710, for example, Adam Mikołaj Sieniawski issued an order, directed to commanders of the Saxon and Polish armies and to customs and treasury officials, stating that his boats, carrying his own cargo as well as that of private merchants, "should be allowed to pass freely and safely. They are not to be harmed in any way or on any pretext. Of course, whatever aid may be required should be rendered. I wholeheartedly request and order this. Signed by my own hand for greater credibility."[21]

Presumably such decrees reassured merchants that they could travel safely and gave pause to potential tormentors, particularly when these were government officials, soldiers, peasants, or townsmen who could easily fall into Sieniawski's grasp. Sometimes, however—especially when not traveling under the auspices of their own magnate— merchants did come into harm's way. On such occasions they appealed to their lord to intervene, after the fact. The case of Izak Jakubowicz, a merchant from the section of Jarosław owned by Elżbieta Sieniawska, is an example.

Izak was arrested at the Fordon customs house because of back fees allegedly owed by his brother, Zelman. After fifteen weeks' imprisonment he wrote to Sieniawska describing his plight, pleading: "Falling at the feet of My Especial Lady, I, your unworthy servant, beg My

---

[20] For examples of each of these, see: Wyrobisz, "Materiały," pp. 704–13; BC 5934 R to ES 1.34657 2/8/1715; AR V 14275 ES to Kerner 4/19/1724; EW 189; *AGZ*, vol. 22, no. 21.74; cf. J. Goldberg, "Społeczność żydowska w szlacheckim miasteczku," *BZIH* 59 (1966), p. 5; *SB* pp. 165–66 (see n. 23).

[21] BC 4818 p. 104; cf. BC 2581/1, no. 21 6/25/1736, and Archiwum PAN Kraków 3795 (HM 6739) 9/8/1754 which are similar decrees from A. A. Czartoryski.

Lady's kindness and protection to free me from this prison.''[22] Having no reliable court system to invoke a writ of *habeas corpus*, Izak's best hope of challenging what he viewed as an arbitrary action by the customs authorities was intervention by his magnate.

In a similar situation, Fiszel Idzkowicz, merchant of Sieniawa, once turned to Maria Zofia Sieniawska Czartoryska to bring his nemeses to justice. Fiszel had hired a boat to take him and his goods to Gdańsk. In the middle of the voyage he met three boats hired by Moszko Jaworowski. For some reason, the latter ordered the merchants and crew accompanying him to board Fiszel's boat and confiscate part of the shipment of saltpeter he was transporting. Later, in Gdańsk, Fiszel gave goods on consignment to some Jewish merchants from Krzeszów who, he claimed, sold the merchandise but did not pay him. In his petition Fiszel noted that Moszko was the subject of the Marshal of Crown Poland and that the Krzeszów merchants enjoyed the protection of the powerful Zamojski family, but "I, having no one else to grant succor other than My Gracious Lady, humbly petition that I be consoled and my harm rectified, for my damages are great.''[23]

As these cases demonstrate, it was understood that every magnate was responsible for the protection of the merchants who lived in his territories, no matter where they traveled. Whenever they were harmed they considered it their right to petition their magnate to bring the perpetrators to justice or to see that restitution was made. Since such problems involved royal officials or troops or subjects of other magnates, the likelihood of the Jew being vindicated depended on the power of the magnate. Hence, the more powerful the magnate, the stronger his attraction for Jewish merchants.

The sphere in which magnate *protekcja* was most necessary and most frequently exercised was that of customs and tolls. In Poland customs and tolls were regarded as tools of fiscal policy. The key question was how much revenue these exactions supplied directly; their effect on trade was rarely considered. Consequently, customs

---

[22] EW 255 undated *Supliki* of Izak Jakubowicz of Jarosław.

[23] EW 189 undated *Suplika* of Fiszel Idzkowicz of Sieniawa to Maria Zofia Sieniawska Czartoryska. The Marshal was probably Józef Mniszech (1670–1747). Similar cases are recorded in: BC 5866 Józef Moskowicz to Józef Lubiszewski, secretary to ES 1.24367 3/12/1716; BC 5972 Chaim Tywlowicz and Zelik Józefowicz to ES 1.45326 11/20/1714. See also n. 20; cf. Rapoport, Even Haezer no. 27.

and tolls were high and numerous. The five different components of the Crown customs duty added 10 to 12 percent to the price of all merchandise. Besides duty, there were charges per driver, per wagon, per horse, per boat, and per crew member. Even after paying all of these, the merchant had to contend with additional duties and tolls in each of the administrative districts, towns, and private territories he passed through. Paying all of these tolls and duties would have made the cost of commerce prohibitive and brought trade to a standstill. Rather than face such a consequence, the merchants in Poland developed a tradition of evading payments whenever possible. This evasion took several forms: circumventing customs and toll houses, lying, bribing officials, and invoking *protekcja*.[24]

Evasion was so common that when a boat or flotilla came to a customs house, the official customs schedule was only a point of departure for negotiations between the merchants and the officials as to how much merchandise would be declared, how much customs duty would be paid, and how much of a "gift" the customs employees would demand.[25] The outcome of these negotiations depended in no small measure on the social status of the merchants involved. Jewish merchants were at a distinct advantage when dealing with the many Jewish lessees of private customs and tolls.[26] On the other hand, when the official was a townsman or a nobleman, Jews apparently did not fare as well. This is indicated by a remark Sieniawska made in a complaint to *Pan* Kerner, the Crown customs commissioner at Fordon. Insisting that her boat and cargo had been wrongfully charged, she

[24] M. Nycz, *Geneza reform skarbowych Sejmu Niemego* (Poznań, 1938), pp. 63–70; Gierowski, *Rzeczpospolita*, pp. xvi–xviii; idem, *Między*, pp. 72–75; R. Rybarski, *Skarb i pieniądz za Jana Kazimierza, Michała Korybuta i Jana III* (Warsaw, 1939), pp. 284–311. In EW 189 *Suplika* Jan Szczur mentioned that he concealed seventeen out of twenty casks of salt from the customs inspector at Fordon. The expense accounts for the *spław* voyages in BC 4818–35 include itemizations of bribes paid to customs officials.

[25] BC 4818 *Inkwizycja* . . . 9/13/1716, 11/3/1717; cf. Burszta, "Handel," pp. 206–207.

[26] *PML*, no. 213, p. 44: Jews are exhorted to make truthful customs declarations in reciprocity for the 50 percent discount granted them by Jewish customs collectors.

said that they had been treated "with no more respect or discretion than if they had belonged to a Jew."[27]

Given the need to elicit "respect and discretion" from customs officials, one effective tool a merchant could employ was the *protekcja* of a magnate. From the turn of the sixteenth century, all noblemen were exempt from customs on the export of their produce and on the import of goods for their own use. Abuse of this privilege was commonplace. Typically, a nobleman would give a merchant a "passport" testifying that he was transporting the merchandise on the nobleman's behalf. In reality, the nobleman and the Jew were partners, or the Jew had paid for the passport.[28]

The Sieniawskis also participated in these ruses. For example, in 1714 an alert customs inspector discovered over 19,300 *zł.* worth of undeclared merchants' goods hidden on Sieniawski's boats.[29]

It was not unusual for customs officials to attempt to stymie such practices. In September 1713, an apostate Jew named Izrael, serving as a functionary at Fordon, charged that Izak of Staszów was carrying salt that was really his own and not Sieniawska's, as he had claimed. *Pan* Kerner imprisoned Izak, and Sieniawska's skipper appealed to her to get the Jew freed.[30] According to Sieniawski's clerk (*pisarz*), Hersz Moszkowicz, Kerner was totally exasperated by the pervasiveness of cheating and once remarked that the Sieniawskis and other noblemen "use their protected liberties only to rob."[31]

Sometimes Sieniawski's officials did not even bother to lie. Some of the skippers, supremely confident of their magnates' power and immunity, refused to pay or simply neglected to stop at customs and toll houses.[32] Even when skippers did observe the rules, and they and the merchants did enter into negotiations with the customs officials, the magnates' authority and prestige were behind them. In June 1736, for example, Czartoryski issued a decree in which he commanded that

[27] AR V 14275 ES to Kerner 4/19/1724.

[28] *AGZ*, vol. 23, no. 92.8; Dinur, p. 118; Gierowski, *Między*, pp. 72–74; idem, *Rzeczpospolita*, pp. xvi–xviii, 41; Nycz, pp. 65–70; Rybarski, pp. 307–11.

[29] Gierowski, *Rzeczpospolita*, p. xvii; BC 5925 Przebendowski to AMS 1.32624 6/10/1714; cf. AR V 14275 ES to *Podskarbi* WKL 3/18/1711.

[30] BC 5934 R to ES 1.34627 9/10/1713; cf. AR V 14275 ES to *Podskarbi* WKL 1/2/1715; also, BC 5972 Chaim Tywlowicz et al., to ES 1.45328 7/19/1717.

[31] BC 4819 11/13/1717 Testimony of Hersz Moszkowicz.

[32] BC 4818 *Inkwizycja* . . . 9/13/1716; BC 4819 *Inkwizycja* . . . 11/3/1717.

"improper customs payments should not be charged."[33] Once, in arguing with a customs official, *Pan* Geza, Hersz Moszkowicz threatened that if more consideration were not shown, the Sieniawskis would transport only their own grain and no merchants' goods. Then, of course, both customs fees and bribes would be forfeited.[34]

Magnate Motives

Magnate support for Jewish commercial ventures was not altruistically motivated. As implied by Czartoryski's opinion that the *raison d'etre* of towns was to generate revenue, successful markets and fairs were a prime source of wealth: richer townsmen paid higher taxes; peasants, whose agricultural products were purchased by the local Jewish merchants, obtained cash to spend on the lord's liquor; market-tax and toll leases remunerated the magnate handsomely; prosperity attracted more taxpaying residents. In short, Jewish commerce in the towns brought considerable revenue into the magnate's treasury.[35]

Thus there were good reasons for the magnate to foster the success of Jewish commercial ventures. But, while to the magnate the primary function of Jewish entrepreneurs was to lay an infrastructure for the generation of revenue and wealth on the latifundium, there were other ways in which Jewish commerce benefited the magnate, if only secondarily.

As already indicated, the magnates or their representatives did not usually buy and sell at the markets or fairs in their small towns. Their suppliers and customers were primarily the large-scale importers and exporters in the large cities. Typically, they transported goods to and from market through their own administrative networks, not via independent Jewish middlemen. Still, Jews did constitute a secondary source of supplies and an alternative market for produce.

The account books for the various administrative centers of the Sieniawski-Czartoryski latifundium list many small purchases of

---

[33] BC 2581/1 no. 21; cf. BC 2581/2 no. 14 11/1/1687.

[34] BC 4819 *Inkwizycja* . . . 1718, testimony of Jan Krasiński.

[35] Baranowski, *Życie,* pp. 74–75; BC 5943 ES to Queen Marysieńka 1.37133 8/7/1703; EW 525 Szkłów *Supl. Kahal* ca. 1731; cf. Rychlikowa, *Produkcja*, p. 132.

cloth, clothing, food, building materials, and other needs of the latifundium staff as well as payments to artisans for construction and
repair work.[36] In the vast majority of instances the recipient of the
money is not identified. This makes it difficult to determine which
items were supplied by Jewish merchants and which services were
provided by Jewish artisans. Yet there is no evidence that the buying
habits of the administrators who made these purchases were any different from those of other noblemen in the area. If Jews controlled the
local cloth trade, or sectors of it, it is likely that cloth would be purchased from them. There is evidence that Jews were the main suppliers of *sukno na barwę*—woolen cloth for dyeing—and other fabrics
needed for the uniforms supplied to the members of the latifundium
staff. This was the item most frequently purchased by latifundium
administrators, and the largest recorded purchases of it were made
from Lejba Sukiennik of Sieniawa and several other Jews.[37]

Similarly, Sieniawski and his representatives had many dealings
with gold- and silversmiths—either commissioning work from them
or selling them silverware in order to raise cash. Since Jews predom-
inated in this field in eastern Poland, it is probable that the smiths in
question were Jews. Indeed, whenever specifically named, the smiths
are easily identified as Jewish.[38] Likewise, given Jewish prominence

[36] For examples of this type of account see BC 3502, pp. 161–68, pp. 209–11.

[37] Most of this *sukno* came from Leszno, where the cloth trade was controlled by
Jews; see: L. Lewin, *Geschichte der Juden in Lissa* (Pinne, 1904), pp. 28–30. In the
sources I have found eleven Jewish cloth merchants mentioned specifically as having
had dealings with the Sieniawskis. See: BC 2527, pp. 26, 47, 50–52; BC 2599
3/10/1713; BC 2647, p. 253; BC 2904, no. 51; BC 5757 1.265–66; BC 5881
1.23581–83; EW 133; EW 255; GOSP 51, p. 45. These Jews did not normally supply the Sieniawskis with the more expensive fabrics that they used for their personal
clothing. For example, for the funeral of Adam Mikołaj Sieniawski in 1726, thirteen
hundred ells of black crepe were purchased from the Jews of Chmielnik, while the
velvet came directly from Wrocław; see Gierowski, "Wrocławskie interesy," p. 242.
BC 2599, 1722, pp. 297ff. shows that Jews supplied *sukno* and nobles or non-Jewish
merchants supplied silk and taffeta. On the general question of Jews in the cloth
trade, see: Hundert, "Security and Dependence," pp. 179ff.; Prochaska, *Historja*, pp.
109–10, Schiper, *Dzieje handlu*, pp. 232–33, 238, 249, 264–65.

[38] Kremer, pp. 303–304, 307, n. 29; BC 2903 no. 54 7/15/1726. For examples of
Sieniawski buying gold from Jews, see: BC 2626, p. 115 8/29/1722; BC 2599, p. 167
6/30/1715 and passim: GOSP 51 passim; BC 221 no. 57 5/15/1720. See EW 282
March, May, and July, 1718, for examples of selling silverware to Jews in order to

in the spice, grocery, fur, wine, horse, and glass trades, the many suppliers of these items to the different latifundium centers were, as the sources indicate, likely to be Jews.[39]

Jews also represented a secondary market for latifundium products. Depending on conditions, there was frequently some surplus of latifundium products—such as salt, lime, poultry, mead, fish, livestock, cloth, or saltpeter—neither required for consumption nor exported to one of the large cities. In addition, in Gdańsk, the magnate purchased large quantities of herring, which was intended for resale locally—at up to 300 percent profit. The commerce-oriented Jews, who did not produce such commodities, bought them either for personal use or for resale.[40]

They were not, however, always willing customers. Often the magnate would force the *kahal* and arrendators to buy these surpluses. In an undated petition of the Sataniv *kahal*, for example, the Jews protested against being forced to buy unsaleable mead. In 1716 Jews had to buy the surplus fish of the Medzhybizh ponds, and reference has already been made to Czartoryski's order to the Klevan' Jewish merchants to guarantee the purchase of all peasant grain in the region.[41]

Probably the best example of the Jew serving as an alternative market for the magnate is in the grain trade. The Jews in eastern Poland were not very active in the most important grain export trade:

---

raise cash; cf. also, Ber of Bolechow, p. 138, and Leszczyński, *Żydzi,* p. 140.

[39] For examples of Jews supplying the commodities noted see: BC 2903 no. 13 1716; BC 5934 R to ES 1.34632 4/6/1714—horses. BC 5756 Abraham Amirowicz to ? 1.80 10/25/1719; BC 5828 M. Czaplic to ? 1.5892 1/30/1715; BC 5899 S. Nahaczowski to MZSC 1.26921 4/24/1731—wine. BC 2529 1705–10, pp. 24ff.; BC 2628 1701–12, pp. 1–85; BC 2904 no. 17, 1706–11; BC 3507 3/28/1721; BC 5934 R to ES 1.34638 6/20/1714; EW 133, 1733; EW 188; EW 282 1727–28; BC 5881 Łukszyński to ES 1.23520 6/28/1715—food and spices. EW 134; BC 2693/1, pp. 1–345—glass and furs.

[40] For examples of Jews purchasing surplus latifundium products and herring, see: BC 2626 12/1/1708, p. 115; BC 2905 no. 2 1693, no. 13 1698; BC 4041; BC 4046; BC 5935 R to MZSC 1.34912 6/25/1720. Occasionally Jews used the magnate's network to market their own merchandise; e.g., BC 4819, pp. 21–22, Registers of yarn sold by Jews and others to Sieniawski for shipment to Gdańsk, January 25 – March 18, 1715.

[41] EW 179; BC 2599 2/16/1716, p. 233; also, n. 16. On the phenomenon of forced sales, see: Guldon, pp. 123–24, 179 (n. 18); L. Żytkowicz, "Okres gospodarki," p. 253.

down the Vistula through Gdańsk. This market was dominated by magnates exporting grain grown on their latifundia.[42] The Jews were more prominent in the local and regional grain markets, purchasing grain from middle or petty noblemen and from peasants. They sold it in smaller towns or regional centers such as Jarosław, Brody, or Zhovkva; to distillers, army detachments, local officials, townspeople, and peasants who happened to have run short of grain.[43]

A significant share of the revenue generated by the Jewish-dominated local grain market eventually landed in the magnate's tax and propination coffers. Perhaps this was sufficient reason for the magnate to encourage the Jewish trade, but there were additional considerations as well. The grain market, particularly the export sector, was volatile. It depended on several factors:

- a sizable crop;
- the absorptive capacity of the external market;
- prices commensurate with the costs of production and transportation;
- the availability of transport; and
- the absence of political or military barriers to trade.[44]

Given these contingencies, it was advantageous for the magnate to have an alternative marketing option. This was especially true in periods like the early eighteenth century, when war and natural disasters sometimes combined to cripple agricultural production as well as

[42] Hundert, "Security and Dependence," pp. 124–30, 142ff., 177; Burszta, "Handel," pp. 202–204, Table IX showed that freighters (and mostly the nobles among them) transported only very small amounts of grain; cf. Wyrobisz, "Materiały," p. 714 (n. 56); Kremer, p. 303. Jews were more active in the overland grain export market through Silesia, which paralleled the cattle trade in which they were prominent, see Wolański, *Związki*, pp. 278ff.; Schiper, *Dzieje handlu*, pp. 238, 264.

[43] Homecki, pp. 36–40; Rychlikowa, *Produkcja*, pp. 132–38; Schiper, *Dzieje handlu*, pp. 264–65. Again, there is a similarity to the cattle trade, where the magnates had their employees drive their cattle to market while Jews were active in rounding up the small herds of middle and petty noblemen; see J. A. Gierowski, *Historia Śląska*, vol. 1, pt. 3, K. Maleczyński, ed. (Wrocław, 1963), pp. 267–68; BC 4495, 1765, pp. 3–6; BC 5934 R to MZSC 1.34920 1/8/1731; BC 5945 ES to Morzycki 1.37697–99, 1.37703, Sept.–Oct. 1720; Wolański, *Związki*, p. 238.

[44] Baron, *History*, vol. 16, p. 234; Rychlikowa, *Produkcja*, p. 201.

transportation. In such years the local grain market was utilized by the magnates to market manor grain.[45]

It is therefore understandable that in 1731 Rubinowicz, the *ekonom* of Rytwiany, recommended to Sieniawska-Czartoryska that grain should be sold to the Jews locally rather than being shipped to Gdańsk. In addition, Wideński, the administrator of Puławy, thought it best to sell the grain from his area to a local Jew. They both reasoned that falling prices in Gdańsk made the price offered by the Jews locally appear attractive, once transportation costs were subtracted. Moreover, there was an element of risk in traveling to Gdańsk, and there was no guarantee that the grain would be sold once it arrived there. In contrast, the local Jews made a *bona fide* offer and would arrange to pick up the grain themselves.[46]

In another case, in 1727, Łukszyński, an administrator from the Jarosław complex, reported having failed to conclude expected deals with a nobleman named Sawa and local bakers. He decided to try to sell all of the grain under his supervision to Rzeszów Jewish traders in a straight cash deal. Also, the account of the disposition of grain and other products for the Medzhybizh complex in the years 1724–27 shows that more than half of the latifundium grain sold locally was purchased by the Jewish arrendators and the *kehalim* (who probably used it for liquor manufacture).[47]

The Spław

The aspect of the commercial relationship between Jews and magnates best documented in the Sieniawski-Czartoryski archive is the

[45] Gierowski, *Między*, ch. 6; Homecki, pp. 58–59, 116; Rychlikowa, *Produkcja*, pp. 132–38; Topolska, p. 126. In the second half of the eighteenth century internal demand for grain—especially in the form of liquor—increased and grain was marketed more and more on the internal market. At times converting grain to liquor was so profitable that the magnates supplemented their own crop with purchases from noblemen and peasants in order to keep their distilleries running at capacity; see Rychlikowa, *Produkcja*, pp. 107, 126, 202–207.

[46] BC 2905 no. 122 A. Wideński to MZSC, 1731; BC 5935 R to MZSC 1.34918–20 Jan.–Feb. 1731.

[47] EW 134 3/14/1727; BC 4046. See also: BC 4820, pp. 47ff.; EW 188 where Jews are listed as grain customers.

so-called *spław*: the trade in goods between the Red Ruthenian region and Gdańsk via the San and Vistula rivers. The detailed *spław* records that have been preserved make it possible to analyze the role of Jews in this sphere of commerce in quantitative terms and to understand the extent of their significance.

Like other magnates whose holdings included port towns along major rivers, every spring the Sieniawskis would send one or more flotillas of boats from Sieniawa to Gdańsk loaded with grain, skins, linen, and forest and mineral products produced on the manors or received as taxes in kind. These were sold in Gdańsk, and the proceeds were used to purchase a large variety of goods required by the magnates for the maintenance of their property or for personal consumption.[48]

Often the long shopping lists required more cash than was raised by the sale of the products. Also, after unloading the bulk commodities, the boats and crews had to return, largely empty, upstream—an expensive proposition. Worst of all, the tremendous fluctuation in crop yields from year to year made it difficult to guarantee even the cost of transportation. In short, a source outside of latifundium produce was required—particularly in lean years—to ensure the profitability of these annual voyages.[49]

The magnates' capital resources made it possible for them to finance boat construction. This, combined with their customs and toll privileges, gave them an effective monopoly on the river trade. Besides magnates, only very rich merchants could afford to hire boats and pay the customs and tolls and still remain competitive. Even they had to pool their resources and hire their boats from the fleets of the magnates. If they had been forced to provide their own transportation,

---

[48] Burszta, "Handel," pp. 174–75, 180–88, 206–11; Guldon, pp. 20–22, 27, 30–31, 112–25; Homecki, pp. 8, 29–34, 41–44; H. Obuchowska-Pysiowa, *Handel wiślany w pierwszej połowie XVII w.* (Wrocław, 1964), pp. 69–117. For representative lists of what was purchased in Gdańsk, see BC 4818, pp. 25–28, 90–92. For mention of the *spław* (in Lithuania) in Jewish sources, see Maimon, *Autobiography*, pp. 24, 35; R. Shmuel ben Elkanah, *Mekom Shmuel* (Altona, 1738), no. 11; on the Vistula trade in general, see the bibliography listed by A. Kamiński, "Neo-Serfdom," p. 254 (n. 5).

[49] Burszta, "Handel," pp. 193–94; Gierowski, *Między*, pp. 71–72; Guldon, p. 113; Rychlikowa, *Produkcja*, pp. 158–62 estimated the transportation component as 40 percent of the price of grain in Gdańsk.

most merchants would have been hard pressed to participate in the *spław* due to prohibitive transportation and customs costs.[50] Their need for cheap transportation made small- to medium-size merchants a ripe source for augmenting *spław* revenues. For a price, the magnates offered these town merchants and their produce space on their boats as well as *protekcja* against marauders and excessive customs charges. This drastically reduced the merchants' costs and risks. By the same token, the freight fees paid by these merchants, called freighters,[51] served to bolster the *spław* receipts considerably. In the late seventeenth century this mutually beneficial arrangement was institutionalized, and it continued at least through the 1730s.[52]

Overall responsibility for the organization of the *spław* expeditions lay with the general commissioner of the Red Ruthenian region of the latifundium. His primary duties were to coordinate the serf teamsters' delivery of grain from the eastern manors to the warehouses in Sieniawa and to hire the skippers (*szyprowie*)—always noblemen— who handled the actual arrangements for the voyage to Gdańsk. Preparations included readying the boats, hiring the crew for the round trip, laying in supplies to feed them, recruiting freighters, and loading the latifundium products and freight. All of this had to be done in a coordinated manner and according to schedule. During the trip, the skipper's authority extended to both the crews and the freighters. He supervised everything en route, paid the tolls and customs, disposed of the lord's merchandise in Gdańsk, discharged the other tasks assigned to him there—paying bills, delivering messages, buying goods— reloaded, and brought the whole expedition back to Sieniawa.[53]

---

[50] Burszta, "Handel," pp. 176, 193–94; Guldon, pp. 84–88, 110–11; Rychlikowa, *Produkcja*, pp. 162–65. Cf. B. Wachowiak, "Ze Studiów nad spławem na Wiśle w XVI–XVIII w.," *Przegląd Zachodni* 7 (1951), pp. 122–36. For examples of Jewish merchants renting boats, see BC 3826 no. 38 7/8/1732, p. 165; GOSP 597 1731–42 under "*Statki Arendowane.*"

[51] The old Polish term is *froktarz*; the freight they carried was called *frokt*.

[52] As the century advanced, improved grain yields and stricter customs procedures had a dampening effect on the freight trade; see Burszta, "Handel," pp. 219–20; Guldon, pp. 107, 136–37; Rychlikowa, *Szkice,* pp. 73–75.

[53] Burszta, "Handel," pp. 188–90; cf. Obuchowska-Pysiowa, pp. 40–60; cf. Homecki, pp. 45–57; Rychlikowa, *Produkcja*, pp. 153–58; Topolska, p. 125. For technical descriptions and illustrations of the boats used in the *spław*, see J. Burszta, "Materiały do techniki spławu rzecznego na Sanie i średniej Wiśle z XVII i XVIII w.," *Kwartalnik Historii Kultury Materialnej* 3 (1955), pp. 752–82; and

In addition to the skipper and crew, the personnel also included a *pisarz* (clerk), who recorded the freighters, their merchandise, and payments; and a *szafarz* (steward), sometimes called factor, who served as purser, procuring and dispensing supplies en route. The two positions were sometimes combined and could be filled by Jews.[54]

The freighters who joined the Sieniawski-Czartoryski *spław* expeditions came from within a 200-mile radius of Sieniawa. After Sieniawa, which claimed more than twice as many freighters as any other place, the towns that supplied most of the freighters were Yavoriv, Oleszyce, Lubaczów, Nemyriv, and Jarosław.[55]

The people who assembled in Sieniawa ranged from peasants who decided to try their hand at selling a few ells of cloth or a round of butter in the big city, to petty merchants for whom an occasional trip to Gdańsk offered a means of improving their commercial standing, to established store owners and wholesalers whose regular trips to Gdańsk were an important source of stock and income.[56]

The freight tariffs were based on the value of the freight; one-half was payable upon embarkation and the remainder after the goods were sold in Gdańsk. The first payment was used by the skipper to pay expenses along the way. Anything left over, as well as the second payment, went toward the Sieniawskis' bills in Gdańsk and to the general treasury back in Sieniawa.[57]

Not surprisingly, the products taken to Gdańsk were (aside from a small quantity of transit goods—Moroccan leather, rice, coffee, cotton, and spices) forest, animal and agricultural products, and village

---

K. Waligórska, "Konstrukcja statków pływających po Sanie i Wiśle w XVIII w.," *Kwartalnik Historii Kultury Materialnej* 8 (1960), pp. 229 – 41.

[54] Burszta, "Handel," pp. 190 – 91, 214. See n. 69. The meaning of these terms could vary. For example, from Maimon, *Autobiography,* p. 24, it is clear that Radziwiłł's *szafarz* was equivalent to Sieniawski's *szyper*.

[55] Based on Burszta, "Handel," p. 197, Table IV; cf. Obuchowska-Pysiowa, pp. 76 – 92.

[56] Freight fees fluctuated from a few *tynf* to more than one thousand *tynf*. This wide range reflects the great variation in the types of people who participated as freighters; cf. Burszta, "Handel," pp. 199 – 201.

[57] Burszta, "Handel," pp. 192 – 95; BC 4819 7/17/1715, p. 28; BC 4827 4/6/1720; EW 189 undated dispute between Jan Szczur and the skipper concerning freight tariffs.

craftsmen's handiwork. The products carried on the return trip to Sieniawa can be divided into three main categories:[58]

- those needed to make garments: both expensive and inexpensive fabrics, dyes, sewing needs, and notions;
- those intended to enliven the bland country diet: food delicacies, wine, sugar, and spices;
- those required to improve the physical household: metals, utensils, and chemicals.

While there was pressure from Sieniawski for skippers to accept only freighters who would travel in both directions, in reality only an average of 51 percent, and never more than 80 percent, did so (see Table 4.1). In general, those less likely to make the return trip by boat were the poorer freighters who either could not afford to purchase merchandise in Gdańsk or were uninterested in doing so. On the other hand, several wealthy freighters, particularly noblemen, made the trip in the direction of Sieniawa only, perhaps after having arrived in Gdańsk via a different magnate's boats. Of course, the skippers were always open to accepting new passengers in Gdańsk.[59]

High profit from the *spław* expeditions depended upon the participation of a large number of freighters. To this end, great effort was expended on recruitment. Skippers made recruiting trips from town to town to sign up merchants and, in some years at least, attempted to attract "foreign" freighters, who lived on the lands of other magnates, by offering them a slight discount on the freight rates. Sieniawski himself issued circulars designed to attract freighters, and he was personally concerned with maximizing the profits and reducing the inefficiencies of the *spław*.[60]

---

[58] For a complete list of products see M. J. Rosman, "Helkam shel Hayehudim Bemishar Hashayit Midrom Mizrah Polin Legdansk," *Gal-Ed* 7–8 (1985), Tables 1–2. For quantities see Burszta, "Handel," pp. 202–204, Table IX and pp. 228–32, Appendix 4; cf. Obuchowska-Pysiowa, pp. 98–117.

[59] Burszta, "Handel," pp. 194–95, BC 4825 5/6/1716, p. 10; cf. BC 4820 5/9/1723, p. 88, fifteen Jewish and three "Catholic" freighters guarantee that if there is not enough freight going back upriver to Sieniawa they will pay up to five hundred *zł.b.m.* to cover the crew's expenses.

[60] BC 4818 5/20/1710, 1/25/1714, p. 158; BC 4819 1716, p. 39; BC 4820 1719, p. 6; BC 4824 8/17/1714; BC 4827 4/6/1720. BC 4820 1/3/1726, p. 150 contains a recruitment circular which reads:

TABLE 4.1

RATIO OF FREIGHTERS MAKING ROUND TRIPS BETWEEN SIENIAWA AND GDAŃSK TO THOSE WHO TRAVELLED TO GDAŃSK ONLY

Year	Ratio
1695	.21
1696	.73
1697	.32
1698	.59
1699	.54
1700	.63
1714	.60
1715	.63
1716	.57
1717	.63
1718	.68
1719	.80
1720	.74
1726	.49
Average for 14 years:	.51

Source: BC 4818–27

According to the available data, between 1695 and 1726 the freighters supplied a yearly average of more than 24,000 *tynf*. This usually exceeded the revenue raised by the sale of the lord's own products in Gdańsk—especially in the Northern War period when grain

---

I hereby inform all who should know and in particular merchants of every kind, both in my own territories and in those of other lords, who trade with Gdańsk, that I am specially ordering my man, *Pan* Orszulski, *pisarz* of my fleet, to announce that next spring my boats will voyage to Gdańsk. If any merchant wants to travel on my boats to Gdańsk, he has only to transport himself, together with his merchandise, as well as all letters of *protekcja*, early enough to the landing. I also guarantee that with respect to the freight there will be no violations of what is proper; rather I order that it will be treated with all discretion . . . signed by my own hand, 1/3/1726 in Lviv.

For the Polish text, see Burszta, "Handel," pp. 193–94 (n. 156).

yields were low. Thus the freight sector of the *spław* was clearly a significant element in the Sieniawski latifundium income.[61]

The Jewish Freighters

In light of the Polish Jews' propensity for commerce it is not surprising to find them highly involved in the *spław* trade. In a letter dated October 7, 1716, from Jarosław, Łukszyński mentioned that due to the Jewish holidays he was unable to settle accounts with "the freighters." Burszta, in his long article on the *spław*, noted that "the Jews predominate, particularly in the years 1714–1720."[62] Statements like Burszta's and comments like Łukszynski's contribute to the semblance of Jewish commercial dominance in Poland, but they do not illustrate such dominance nor even define the sense in which the Jews may have been in control. Were they the vast majority of merchants? Were they the richest merchants? Were they the most active merchants?

Analysis of the lists of freighters, their commodities, and the freight fees they paid[63] yields a quantified description of the importance of the Jews in the Sieniawa *spław* trade. This is a significant step in discovering the nature of the Jewish role in the general Vistula trade and in commerce as a whole. Unlike impressionistic literary sources and usually anonymous and inaccurate customs records, the freight lists allow for construction of a fairly accurate picture of how many Jews dealt in this area of commerce and how much their contribution was worth. Rather than rely on anecdotes about the relatively few wealthy Jewish lessees to illustrate Jewish commercial activities, we can actually come to an assessment of the "typical" Jewish merchants, what they dealt in, and how they operated. The first noteworthy conclusion to be drawn from the numbers is that during the years in question most

---

[61] According to available records, total income from product sales in Gdańsk never exceeded eighteen thousand *tynf* (BC 4818, 4820, 4823, 4824, 4827). Sometimes there was additional income from the sale of boats used to make the trip to Gdańsk. As noted in Chapter 2 average annual income from a latifundium complex was in the 30,000 *zł.* – 85,000 *zł.* range. Cf. Burszta, "Handel," pp. 181–83, 209–11; Homecki, pp. 16–29, 54–57.

[62] Łukszyński to ES 1.23561 10/7/1716; Burszta, "Handel," p. 199, cf. Guldon, p. 63; Obuchowska-Pysiowa, pp. 82–85.

[63] The lists of freighters are found in BC 4818–35.

freighters were not Jews. The ethnic breakdown of the freighters was as follows:

Poles, Ukrainians, miscellaneous:[64]	575
Jews:	285
Total:	860

The Jews, then, represented about one-third of the total number of freighters for whom records exist. As Figure 4.1 demonstrates, on a per year basis the percentage of Jewish participants matched the overall proportion in 1695–1716. Beginning in 1717, however, the proportion of Jews jumped to between 55 and 70 percent per year.

This implies that, at least in the latter years, Jewish freighters were likely to make the trip to Gdańsk more frequently than non-Jewish ones. In fact, the average Jew made 3.3 trips during the years listed, while the average non-Jew traveled 1.4 times. Of the twenty-six freighters who made the trip in at least one direction for eight years, sixteen were Jews.

Besides traveling more frequently, Jews carried a much larger variety of products and contributed a much larger share to the *spław* revenue than the Polish and Ukrainian freighters. Analysis of the lists of products carried by the freighters makes it clear that the more expensive or unusual the product, the greater the likelihood that a Jew would carry it. On the way to Gdańsk the few transit goods transported were handled almost exclusively by Jews. On the way back, besides carrying the common varieties of cloth, Jews specialized in the more expensive fabrics such as silk and Venetian cloth, and in exotic imports such as indigo, dried French plums, dried fruits from India, and Indian spices.[65]

---

[64] This category includes peasants, noblemen, and townsmen, as well as West Europeans and people whose ethnic origin is not certain. Of the Polish freighters, twenty-five were referred to as *Pan* (a term often reserved for noblemen). In 1716, out of fifty-seven non-Jewish freighters, eight were explicitly identified as *chłop* (peasant). If this year is typical, then the percentage of peasant freighters was approximately 10 percent.

[65] For complete lists of products see Rosman; cf. what the freighters carried with other lists of products carried by Jewish merchants: Hundert, "Security and Dependence," pp. 131, 178–79; Leszczyński, *Żydzi*, pp. 154–58, 170–87; Wyrobisz, "Materiały," pp. 703–12; Morgensztern, "O działalności gospodarczej," pp. 13–27. See also the 1703 customs schedule published in *Volumina Legum*, vol. 6, f. 134. The freight lists also demonstrate that Jews usually carried larger quantities of each product than the others did.

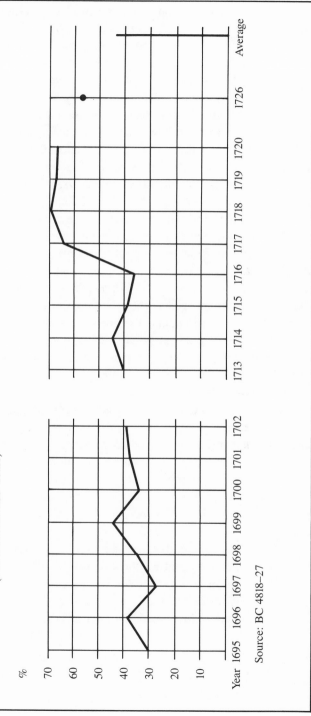

Figure 4.1: Percentage of Jews in the Total Number of Freighters Who Participated in the Sieniawski *Spław* Expeditions (For Documented Years)

Source: BC 4818–27

As a group, Jews carried about one-third more types of products to Gdańsk and about one and three quarters more to Sieniawa. The differential is even larger with regard to the number of types of products carried by each individual. By far the most common commodity carried by freighters to Gdańsk was linen (*płótno*). This was handled in small or large quantities by almost every freighter. Some supplemented it with small quantities of two or three other commodities, such as skins, wax, or tallow, but only occasionally would a freighter transport more than three or four products to Gdańsk.[66] Still, on the average, each Jew carried almost one and one-half times as many types of products to Gdańsk as non-Jews. On the return trip the disparity shot up to 400 percent (Figure 4.2).

Even more striking is the contrast between the Jewish contribution to *spław* revenue and that of the others. During the years for which data exist, Jewish freighters furnished approximately 50 to 90 percent of the freight fees collected each year (Figure 4.3). Of the average annual *spław* revenue of 24,383 *tynf*, the Jews contributed 18,335 *tynf*. Even in the ten years when they composed less than 40 percent of the number of freighters, the Jews paid—on the average—more than 60 percent of the fees. A hypothetical average Jewish merchant would have paid 607 *tynf* per round trip, or four times the amount spent by his Polish or Ukrainian colleague.

If we focus on the group of sixty-five wealthiest freighters who supplied over 40 percent (161,757 *tynf*) of the total money collected from the *spław* for the years shown in the figures, we find that the Jews among them contributed more than 75 percent of the money (121,231 *tynf*) paid by this group, even though they numbered less than 50 percent (29) of it. Over the course of his career in the *spław*, each of these Jewish freighters paid on the average almost three and three-quarters times (4,180 *tynf*) what one of the thirty-six Poles or Ukrainians paid (1,126 *tynf*).

Looking at all the freighters, however, it was not the case that a few rich Jewish merchants raised the average for the group. Figure 4.4 shows that a large majority of Jewish merchants were in the middle categories, paying between 100 and 1,000 *tynf* each trip. More than 75 percent of the Polish and Ukrainian freighters paid less than 100

---

[66] See Burszta, ''Handel,'' pp. 202–205, Tables IX–X.

Figure 4.2: Ratio (Jews/Others) of the Number of Products Carried per Freighter (For Documented Years)

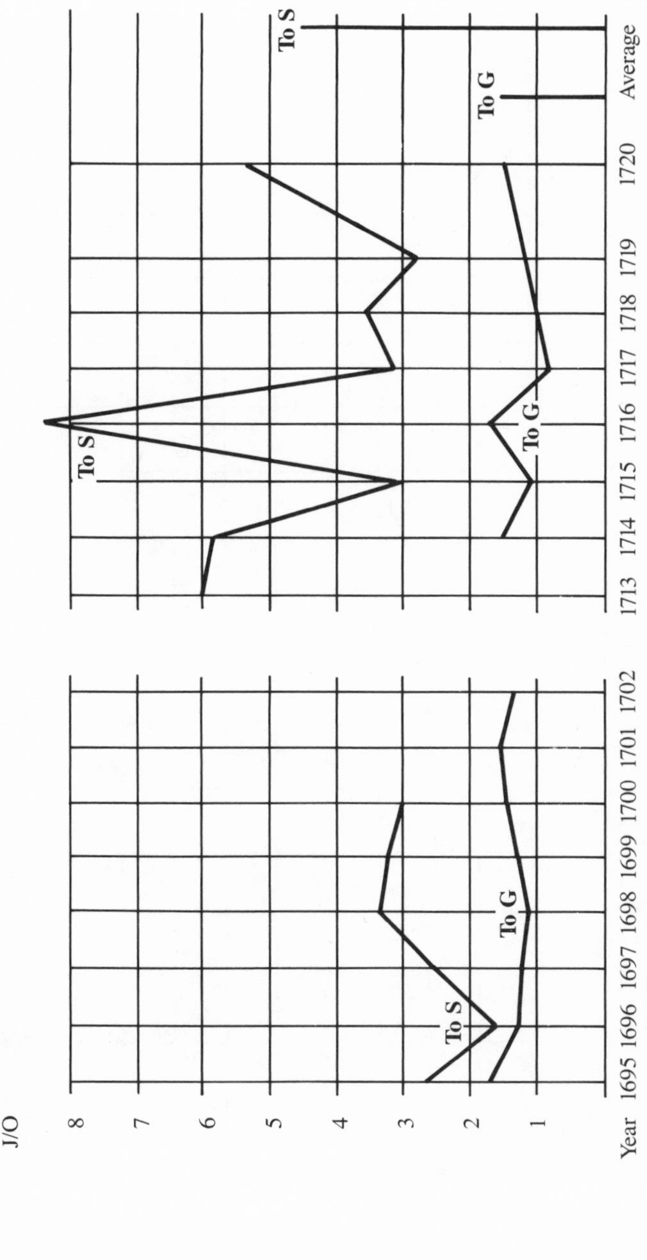

Source: BC 4818–27

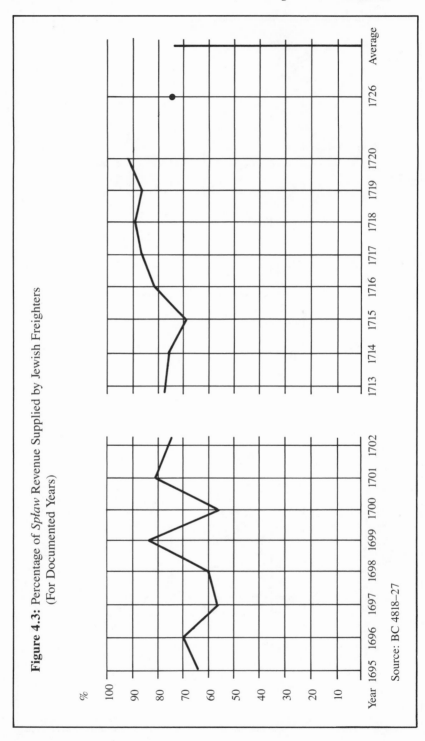

Figure 4.3: Percentage of *Splaw* Revenue Supplied by Jewish Freighters
(For Documented Years)

Source: BC 4818–27

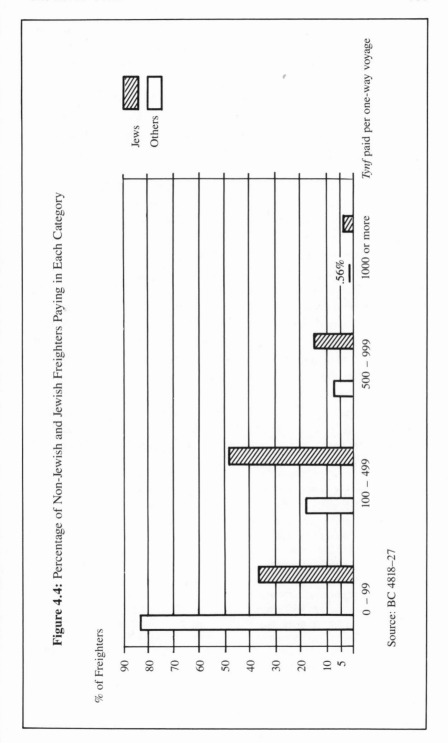

Figure 4.4: Percentage of Non-Jewish and Jewish Freighters Paying in Each Category

Source: BC 4818–27

tynf. While eight non-Jews paid between 1,500 and 6,000 *tynf*, twenty Jews were in this bracket. No Polish or Ukrainian freighter paid more than 6,000 *tynf* in freight fees for all the years he traveled; five Jews did so.

It is plain, then, that while Jews composed a majority of the freighters in only the last third of the period, they were consistently more likely to be repeating participants paying a much larger share of the freight fees than the Polish and Ukrainian freighters who accompanied them.

These statistics have two principal implications: First, Jewish participation was a key element in the conduct of the *spław*. Subtracting the Jews' 50 to 90 percent of the freight fees might have left the boats up to three-quarters filled with people but without enough merchandise and cash to make the trip worthwhile. Hence, the Jews were essential to this significant branch of latifundium income. The Sieniawskis were no doubt aware of this and tried to ensure that the Jewish merchants traveled on their boats and not those of other magnates.[67] To this end, Jewish religious sensibilities were respected during these voyages by not loading or embarking on the Sabbath or Jewish holidays, even though this prolonged the trip and cost money in provisions for the crew.[68] Perhaps more significantly, the post of *pisarz*, the man who had the most direct contact with the merchants, could be filled by a Jew.[69] Moreover, although Jews, as town residents, were frequently taxed at a higher rate than the Polish or Ukrainian residents of the same town, Jewish freighters did not pay

[67] There was competition between magnates to attract freighters; see above n. 60 and Burszta, "Handel," p. 201; EW 189 *Supl.* Fiszel Idzkowicz. Also, many of Sieniawski's freighters came from towns owned by others.

[68] BC 4818 *Inkwizycja* 9/13/1716 Testimony of Piotr Jabłoński, Stanisław Łańcucki, Haskiel Moszkowicz et al.

[69] I could find no *pisarz* named for the years before 1716. After that one non-Jew, *Pan* Orszulski, is mentioned once as participating in recruitment in 1726; see n. 60. Otherwise every *pisarz* and *szafarz* mentioned is named Hersz. Sometimes the surname is Moszkowicz and sometimes it is Tryplik, and sometimes it is missing. It is not clear whether two or more individuals are involved or one person with two different names, one his patronymic and one a nickname. See *Inkwizycje* at the end of BC 4818 and 4819; GOSP 478, p. 16; GOSP 991, 1724; GOSP 348, 1720, 1722; GOSP 1008, 1717; GOSP 1084, 1716; GOSP 773, 1729; GOSP 777, 1730; EW 144, 1734; BC 4819, pp. 135–36; BC 4820, before p. 93; BC 4822, pp. 14–15. Cf. Burszta, "Handel," pp. 190–91, 214.

any premium. If hostile testimony is to be believed, the Jews, by virtue of their importance, may have had more of a say than others in the skipper's decisions. In 1716 the Nemyriv freighter Wojciech Barszczowski charged that one of the reasons that the flotilla was delayed for weeks in Gdańsk was that the Jews had persuaded the skipper to wait for more boats bringing merchandise they could buy.[70]

The second implication of the Jewish predominance in terms of frequency, number of products, and amount of money paid is that, unlike most Polish and Ukrainian freighters, the Jews were usually professional merchants. The typical non-Jew was marketing his own produce or perhaps that of his immediate neighbors and buying enough goods to fulfill his own needs or theirs.[71] The Jewish freighters were marketing huge quantities of merchandise that could have been gathered only by buying up the produce of many peasants and petty noblemen either at markets or on buying trips into the countryside. By the same token, the variety and quantity of goods carried back from Gdańsk by the average Jewish merchant, as well as the frequency with which he traveled, indicate that he was bringing back stock either to sell wholesale to other merchants, or for his own store, or in fulfillment of specific orders. He had both the capital and the customers to enable him to invest in the trip to Gdańsk and in more expensive and exotic products. Thus, while the magnate purchased goods independently through the skipper, others, like the noblemen, clergy, townsmen, and even peasants, depended mainly on the Jewish merchants who went on the *spław* to supply them with sugar, spices, cloth, dyes, metal, and utensils.[72] Burszta has suggested that cash-starved noblemen may have struck deals with these Jewish merchants

---

[70] BC 4818 *Inkwizycja* 9/13/1716, pp. 249ff. The *Inkwizycje* also show that Jews played a leading role in negotiating with customs officials.

[71] Most non-Jewish freighters carried few types of merchandise in small quantities; see Burszta, "Handel," pp. 211–13, Table XI.

[72] BC 5934 R to ES 1.34657 2/8/1715 describing the murder of a Jew killed on a buying trip to a village; BC 3502 3/5/1720, p. 327 mentions peasants taking products to Sieniawa to be sold to Jews there; EW 402 notes peasants of Klevan' selling grain to Jews. See also: Burszta, "Handel," p. 206, 211–16; J. Goldberg, "Poles and Jews," pp. 262–63; Mahler, *Toldot*, pp. 261–62. On the question of peasant contact with markets, see: Rychlikowa, *Produkcja*, p. 126; Topolska, pp. 116, 122–24; Żytkowicz, "Okres gospodarki," pp. 250, 284–85. Cf. Wyrobisz, "Materiały," p. 713–14.

whereby the Jew took the nobleman's products to Gdańsk to be marketed in return for a set quantity of Gdańsk goods.[73]

By transporting commodities from the countryside to be exported
from Gdańsk and by purchasing imported goods in Gdańsk for distribution in the countryside, the Jewish freighters were continuing a traditional role of Polish Jews. They were the link between the big
import and export concerns on the one hand and the small-scale con-
sumers and suppliers on the other. Such merchants did not compete
with magnates in the main products of the Vistula trade—grain and
potash.[74]

Conclusion

What is true of the *spław* is largely true of Jewish-magnate commercial interaction in general. Economic powerhouses like the
Sieniawskis and Czartoryskis depended only secondarily on the Jews
as customers, suppliers, and marketers. While, at times, the Jews were
of service in these roles, the magnates' main interest was not in Jewish
commerce per se, but in its attendant financial gain. Most of the Jewish merchants did not earn their livelihood servicing the magnates'
commercial needs. Of more consequence than the transactions magnates conducted with a few Jews were the commercial opportunities
and support which, thanks to the magnates, were available to many
Jews.

If magnates and Jews were not each other's primary commercial
partners, neither were they competitors. The magnates specialized in
export and import via the Vistula, concentrating on a few large-
volume items and luxury goods. Jews dominated small local markets
and overland trade, dealing in a myriad of products and occupying
almost every rung of the commercial ladder. At points where their

---

[73] Burszta, "Handel," p. 215.

[74] Hundert, pp. 124–30, 142ff., 177; Schiper, *Dzieje handlu,* pp. 238–42;
Homecki, p. 117; Kremer, pp. 303, 307. There were, of course, Jews employed in the
magnate marketing network. They specialized in being warehouse supervisors and
factors who located customers and suppliers for the magnate. See Chapter 6 on Jews
in the administration.

activities intersected, such as in the grain trade or the *spław*, Jews took a subordinate, complementary role.[75]

The complementary nature of Jewish commercial activity, combined with its potential for indirectly enriching the magnates, created a powerful incentive for magnates to foster it. As a result, magnate towns became important commercial centers and the Jews' most congenial environment in Poland.

[75] Compare Bergerówna, pp. 316–17.

CHAPTER FIVE

The Jews as Latifundium Arrendators

While commercial collaboration between magnates and Jews was often subtle and indirect, their partnership in another important area of economic life, *arenda* (leasing), was self-evident. There was no other sphere in which magnate and Jewish interests were more obviously linked or their behavior more closely coordinated.

Arenda was one of the fundamental economic institutions in Poland. It began as early as the fourteenth century when the Polish kings leased out their salt mining, processing, and storage facilities. During the sixteenth, seventeenth, and eighteenth centuries, leasing took on major importance as the magnates sought an efficient, profitable method for exploiting their rapidly expanding holdings in the East. For reasons that will be discussed, they hit upon leasing, which always ranked, along with fixed payments and product sales, as one of the primary sources of latifundium income. In the Sieniawski-Czartoryski territories, for which quantifiable data are available, *arenda* constituted 20 to 65 percent of the revenue generated annually in each complex.

The owners appreciated this fact and gave their personal attention to the whole *arenda* process, from the recruiting of arrendators, to the negotiation of the contracts, to the enforcement of the contractual terms.[1]

For the Jews, too, *arenda* was a central institution. It provided a livelihood for a significant proportion of Polish Jewish families and

---

[1] The only monograph that exists on the central subject of *arenda* is A. I. Iaroshevych, "Kapitalistychna orenda na Ukraini za polskoi doby," *Zapysky Sotsialno-ekonomichnoho viddilu* 5–6 (1927), pp. 116–259. Many more recent works have touched on *arenda* in connection with other topics. One treatment that can serve as an introduction and includes bibliographical references is Baron, *History,* vol. 16, pp. 265–78, 443–48. On the proportion of Sieniawski-Czartoryski latifundium income represented by leases see Chapter 2, especially n. 46; cf. Iaroshevych, pp. 160–73.

was considered by non-Jews and Jews alike, particularly east of the Vistula, to be a traditionally Jewish occupation. In the Sieniawski-Czartoryski documents, as in other sources, the word "arrendator" is often used interchangeably with "Jew."[2]

The historian of Polish law, Dąbkowski, defined *arenda* as: "The leasing of immovable property or rights. The subject of the lease might be a whole territory, held either in ownership or in pledge . . . [or] the subject might be a tavern, mill, or the right to collect various payments such as a bridge toll or a payment connected with a jurisdiction."[3] In other words, in exchange for a pre-set rent the lessor agreed to transfer to the lessee control over property or rights to which the lessor was entitled. Such control meant that the lessee could pocket any income produced by the leased property or rights.

For a Polish magnate, who possessed many properties and a plethora of rights on them, leasing arrangements held several attractions. First, they provided him with the commodity that he thought he needed most and that was always in short supply—cash.[4] With the signing of the contract he was guaranteed a specific sum of money. This enabled him, or his representatives, to plan expenditures and to buy—or even borrow money in order to buy—consumer goods and services, in the knowledge that the money would certainly be available to pay the bills. It was also a means of raising quick cash to pay off pressing debts. Elżbieta Sieniawska wrote to Morzycki with regard to a debt she owed to a nobleman named Wilamowski that she had spent the money to be paid him on something else. She therefore ordered Morzycki to "lease out some village" in order to raise the needed cash.[5]

Second, this money was provided to the magnate with a minimum of effort on his part. The time consumed in negotiating and supervising a lease was a fraction of what would have been required had the

---

[2] Mahler, *Yidn*, pp. 100–102, 165 estimated that as many as 15 percent of urban and 80 percent of rural Jewish heads of households were occupied in some aspect of *arenda*; cf. H. H. Ben-Sasson, *Hagut Vehanhagah*, p. 58; M. Szczepaniak, *Karczma, wieś, dwór* (Warsaw, 1977), pp. 65–66.

[3] P. Dąbkowski, *Prawo prywatne polskie*, vol. 2 (Lviv, 1911), pp. 72–73.

[4] Burszta, *Wieś*, pp. 195–203; Czapliński and Długosz, pp. 70–89; Gierowski, *Między*, p. 76; Kula, *Economic Theory*, pp. 31–32, 36, 40.

[5] BC 5945 ES to Morzycki 1.37694 9/1/1720.

magnate attempted to perform the task of the lessee by himself, or through his subordinates. Compare, for example, the *arenda* of the tax and toll monopoly of the town of Jarosław, which in the early eighteenth century annually generated approximately 30,000 *zł.*, with the collection of taxes in Shkłoŭ, which ranged from 26,000 *zł.* to 36,000 *zł.*[6]

Once the contract was signed with the Jarosław arrendator the lord had very little to do. In case the arrendator's legitimate rights were challenged, the lord had to support him, with a detachment of soldiers if necessary. If he failed to provide cash on schedule, the owner threatened him with some punishment or confiscated his property. But the arrendator had to set up the tax and toll collecting apparatus, keep the books, and haggle with his subarrendators and the taxpayers.

In the Shkłoŭ complex each group of villages required a tax collector, each of whom had to be paid. They also were supervised to make sure that they were honest and efficient. Bookkeeping requirements were extensive, and any question with regard to tax exemption had to be brought to the owner's attention.[7]

In Jarosław, the arrendator held the responsibility for collection, with the lord entering the picture only in exceptional circumstances. In Shkłoŭ, the primary responsibility remained with the owner as the head of the administration. In this role he delegated the various tasks that had to be performed, kept track of their execution, and bore final responsibility for failure himself.

Whatever the charge might be, whether marketing latifundium liquor in a leased tavern, producing grain on a manor, mining salt, or developing a newly acquired property, by leasing, the magnate simplified his own role. The more properties a magnate owned, the more valuable the savings in time and effort.[8]

Third, leasing reduced risk. In theory, if not always in practice, if the property or right in question failed to produce more income than the rent that he paid, the lessee was expected to absorb the loss. This was one of the reasons that cash-endowed (*tanti*) lessees were sought after. If an individual had capital in addition to the lease income, he

---

[6] EW 133, 135 and Topolska, Table 40.

[7] BC 2940 Szkłów no. 16.

[8] Burszta, *Wieś*, pp. 195–98, 202–203; Wiatrowski, p. 128; Żytkowicz, "Okres gospodarki," pp. 263–64.

could be depended upon to fulfill the contract no matter what. In this way leasing insulated the owner, to some extent, against the exigencies of market and weather conditions, guaranteeing him a steady flow of cash regardless of what actually happened in his property. As one administrator put it in his financial report: income from the leases was "certain," while income from product sales depended on God.[9]

Leasing could be a convenient means of financing capital improvements on a property. Rather than having to raise the money and then supervise construction, the owner merely leased out the property and instructed the lessee to use the rent for building a new tavern or some other improvement. Sometimes the arrendator would even make essential improvements on his own initiative in order to assure efficiency and maximum profit.[10]

Of course, there were also disadvantages to leasing. *Arenda* may have reduced risk for the owner, but it also denied him the flexibility required to take advantage of market conditions. Lessees had to absorb losses, but it was they who enjoyed windfall profits. Moreover, risk was not lowered as much as might have been initially expected. Often either in the contract or in practice the arrendator was allowed a "discount" *(folga)* in case revenues were reduced drastically due to *force majeure*. In addition, a lessee could not be sure that his lease would be renewed. As a result, there was a tendency to overwork the land, peasants, and equipment in the short term without regard for long-term effects.[11]

Due to its advantages, *arenda* was one of the hallmarks of the period of latifundium expansion in the sixteenth and seventeenth centuries. But by the end of this period the disadvantages began to play more of a role. This was particularly true once a cadre of middle and petty noblemen administrators began to develop. Thus, during the

[9] Serczyk, p. 163; Żytkowicz, pp. 263–64. In 1704 when the Swedes occupied Jarosław, the drop in income from grain sales was 99 percent, while the drop in *arenda* income was only 65 percent, see EW 135. On the certainty of *arenda* income, see BC 3502 Toporów and Sokołówka 1711 Summary of Revenues, p. 235; Kula, *Economic Theory*, p. 56.

[10] Dąbkowski, p. 573; Rapoport, Orah Haim no. 4; cf. Maimon, *Autobiography*, pp. 17–19 where Maimon criticizes his arrendator grandfather for not taking such initiative.

[11] *Arenda* contracts BC 3499–3500; Serczyk, p. 163; Dąbkowski, pp. 574–75.

eighteenth century, leasing, particularly of property, decreased.[12] The percentage of income represented by leases was still relatively high, however, and leases remained a significant factor in latifundium economic life.

Arenda vs. Dzierżawa

In Polish there are two words that denote leasing. One is the Slavic *dzierżawa*, the other, the Latin loan word *arenda*. Semantically, the words are synonymous; in everyday usage, they were applied differentially. From the Sieniawski-Czartoryski material it is obvious that *dzierżawa* was employed in referring to leases of real estate—villages, manors, complexes—while *arenda* signified a lease of monopoly rights. This distinction is fixed in contracts, financial reports, and correspondence from the early eighteenth century on.[13] Sometimes when a property was let as a *dzierżawa* to one person, the rights to monopolies on that property—the *arenda*—were let to someone else. One lessee might be in charge of grain production, while someone else held the rights to the tavern income.[14]

This distinction takes on added significance when it is combined with the fact that the word "arrendator" (*arendarz*) was often used as a synonym for "Jew" (*Żyd*). The contracts and lists of arrendators and *dzierżawcy* reveal the basis of this usage. In the Sieniawski-Czartoryski holdings, arrendators were generally Jews, *dzierżawcy* were usually noblemen.[15] This apparently represents a change from

---

[12] Ber of Bolechow, pp. 31–32, 69; Burszta, *Wieś*, pp. 202–203. In light of the arguments adduced in favor of the abolition of the Council of Four Lands in 1764 this move can be seen as part of the antileasing trend; cf. *PVAA* pp. 440–41, LXXVI–LXXVII.

[13] For example, see contracts; BC 3499–3500; financial statements: BC 4101 Międzybóż, 1744; correspondence: e.g., BC 5897 Morzycki to ES 1.26556 1/21/1720. I. Halpern, "Gezeirot Voshchilo," *Zion* 22 (1958), p. 58 and n. 11, also documents this distinction. Cf. Iaroshevych, pp. 138–43.

[14] For example, BC 2702, pp. 147–58, 180.

[15] Contracts: BC 3499–3500; arrendator lists: EW 133 Jarosław 1711–18, EW 394 Jarosław 1724–28, EW 152 Sieniawa-Oleszyce 1727–29, EW 449 Sieniawa-Oleszyce 1695–1700, BC 4716 Zińków 1735, BC 4041 Międzybóż 1708–13, BC 4491 Szkłów 1724. These examples could be easily multiplied. There were exceptions to this general pattern; for example, BC 2581/2 Szkłów 1/24/1722: as a special

the pre-1648 period when Jewish lessees of newly established complexes were relatively commonplace.[16]

This shift is most likely due to the fact that in the post-1648 period many noblemen, who had lost their own lands due to destruction or dispossession, had no choice but to lease or administer the lands of the magnates. In the sixteenth and seventeenth centuries there had been little competition for an entrepreneurial-minded Jew who sought his fortune developing a new complex in the Southeast. By the eighteenth century, however, when these territories were well established and entrepreneurial skills were less necessary, there were, as a result of the post-1648 dislocations, many noblemen available who coveted the leases on the same territories.[17] It may also be that Jews, finding themselves exposed as *dzierżawcy* in the turbulent 1648–60 period, made a conscious decision to reduce their participation in a field that could have such dangerous consequences.

Somewhat more difficult to explain is why the competition from the noblemen after 1648 did not extend into the area of *arenda*. True, the 1633 constitution forbade noblemen to deal in commerce or liquor, under penalty of loss of nobility prerogatives.[18] But a prohibition in the law books was never sufficient reason to prevent someone from doing something financially advantageous in loosely governed Poland, and *arendy* were often lucrative. It is not true that only Jews had the capital to invest in leases, because the *dzierżawa* contracts clearly

---

reward Fajbisz Powzorowicz was granted a lease on a sizable piece of property; BC 5934 R to ES 1.34575 10/16/1709 *Pan* Stojnowski leased an *arenda* "like a Jew."

[16] Baron, *History,* vol. 16, pp. 28, 103–10, 123, 165, 270, 276; Ben-Sasson, "Takanot," pp. 190–91, 194; S. Ettinger, "Helkam Shel Hayehudim Bekolonizatzia Shel Ukraina," *Zion* 21 (1956), pp. 124–29, 132–37; Nadav, pp. 61–66, 149. In the rescension of the Sabbath regulations promulgated in 1700, published by Ben-Sasson, the laws regarding *dzierżawca* that had been included in the late sixteenth- and early seventeenth-century versions were omitted. This omission probably reflects the decline of Jewish participation in this field. See Nadav, pp. 127–28; E. Feldman, "Heikhan Ubishvil Mi Nitkanu Hatakanot Leissur Hamelakha Beshabbat Shel R. Meshullam Faibish," *Zion* 34 (1969), pp. 94–95.

[17] BC 5943 ES to Marysieńka 1.37133 8/7/1703; PHo no. 153; Baron, *History,* vol. 16, p. 448 (n. 77); Kula, *Economic Theory,* pp. 146–48; Kamiński, "Neo-Serfdom," pp. 262–63.

[18] *Volumina Legum,* vol. 3, f. 806; Kaczmarczyk and Leśnodorski, *Historia,* p. 208.

show noblemen and other non-Jews investing large sums of money in this type of lease.[19]

Perhaps the reason for continued Jewish domination of *arenda*, at a time when *dzierżawa* was losing much of the Jewish character it had, is to be found in the realm of sociology and tradition. While Jews may have been prominent as *dzierżawcy* during the sixteenth and seventeenth centuries, they never dominated the field, remaining a minority of land lessees.[20]

In contrast, the synonymity of "Jew" and "arrendator" bespeaks the numerical predominance of Jews in this sphere.[21] It was traditionally a Jewish field. For a dispossessed nobleman, seeking a livelihood after the catastrophes of the 1640s and 1650s, leasing land may have been less prestigious than owning it, but it entailed no essential change in life-style: he was still ordering around serfs; he was still heading an administration; and he was still concerned primarily with the "honorable" occupation of working the land to produce its bounty. A nobleman who accepted an *arenda* would not be suffering a mere decrease in prestige, he would be exchanging the noble occupation of agriculture for the gritty, petty, necessary evil of commerce. He would be taking up a livelihood that was the domain of not only non-noblemen, but of non-Poles—the Jews. Thus traditional Jewish domination of *arenda* and noblemen's reluctance to engage in an occupation that was considered undignified combined to discourage penetration by the nobility, keeping the field almost exclusively Jewish.[22]

Moreover, tradition was self-perpetuating inasmuch as it guaranteed training. Many noblemen were raised to be owners of manors and knew how to operate them, whether owned or leased. It is doubtful that any nobleman was ever trained by his father to be an

[19] Compare Ber of Bolechow, pp. 155–56, description of a non-Jew, (nobleman?) Abramowski, who lent money and received leases as security; Kula, *Economic Theory*, pp. 146–48.

[20] Ettinger, "Helkam," pp. 128, 135; Nadav, pp. 127–28; cf. Iaroshevych, pp. 219–20, 227–28.

[21] A. Leszczyński, "Karczmarze i szynkarze żydowscy ziemi bielskiej od drugiej połowy XVII w. do 1795 r.," *BŻIH* 102 (1977), pp. 77–78; by the 1770s, 94 percent of the tavernkeepers in the Bielsko region were Jews.

[22] At least east of the Vistula; cf. Baron, *History,* vol. 16, p. 366 (n. 33); Szczepaniak, pp. 65–66.

arrendator. Moreover, even when economics forced a nobleman to swallow his pride and take an *arenda*, it was "like a Jew"[23] and there was no guarantee of success. Elżbieta Sieniawska's opinion of noblemen arrendators was probably not unique. In 1703 she advised Queen Marysieńka against leasing an *arenda* to a nobleman because in the nobleman's hands, "There would be more arguments than money."[24]

Rights Available for Lease

Law and tradition bestowed on every Polish property owner the right to certain income-producing monopolies. The best known and most often exploited of these was the right to propination, meaning that a lord had the exclusive right to produce and sell alcoholic beverages within his domain. In the Middle Ages, the lord, in exchange for loyal services and low rent, usually favored a village official by voluntarily relinquishing the monopoly and granting to him a hereditary lease on very advantageous terms. But by the sixteenth century, when magnates were establishing their large latifundia based on grain monoculture, they realized that the liquor monopoly afforded an excellent opportunity for marketing grain—in the form of liquor. This was especially true in the Southeast where the grain-producing latifundia were often too far from transportation facilities to make conventional marketing profitable. They also saw it as an opportunity for siphoning off cash from their serfs—one way of cementing the latter's economic dependence on the latifundium.[25]

[23] BC 5943 R to ES 1.34575 10/16/1709.

[24] BC 5943 ES to Marysieńka 1.37133 8/7/1703. Similarly, in the same letter she informed Marysieńka that she was switching the *arenda* of the town of Jarosław from nobility to Jewish hands, "seeing that with the nobleman matters were bad"; cf. Ettinger, "Helkam," pp. 125–26.

[25] B. Baranowski, *Polska karczma-restauracja-kawiarnia* (Wrocław, 1979), pp. 9–10, 15–16; M. Bobrzyński, "Prawo propinacji w dawnej Polsce," *Szkice i studja historyczne*, vol. 2 (Cracow, 1922), pp. 238–52, 258–60, 290–91; Burszta, *Wieś*, pp. 20–30, 56–60, 65–68, 100–101; T. Czwojdrak and Z. Żak, "Przemysł propinacyjny i karczmarstwo w dobrach biskupa poznańskiego w XVII i XVIII wieku," *Studia i materiały do dziejów Wielkopolski i Pomorza* 2 (1956), p. 98; Kula, *Economic Theory*, pp. 134–44; J. Rafacz, "Przymus propinacyjny w dobrach królewskich koronnych w epoce nowożytnej," *Themis Polska* 8 (1933), pp. 35–102; Rychlikowa,

These considerations led the owners to harass and compete with the hereditary liquor producers. The widespread havoc of the late seventeenth and eighteenth centuries created a need for producing large sums with a minimum of investment, and this resulted in even greater pressure on the hereditary liquor producers. Consequently, by the mid-eighteenth century very few hereditary liquor producers were left. In their place, and in the newly developed territories in the Southeast, were arrendators who leased the liquor rights for usually no more than three years at a time, at a rather high rental.[26]

Terms varied from the arrendator who had the right to control all production and sales in all taverns in a particular area to the small arrendator who was still obligated to buy from the lord (or the large arrendator) and had the right to sell from one tavern (*karczma*) or bar (*szynk*) only.[27]

While the main motivation behind liquor production was profit, in actuality the arrendator of a tavern and the tavern itself served other functions for the owner and the latifundium. The *karczma* was not just a place where alcoholic beverages were served. It usually functioned as a restaurant, inn for travelers, and general store where food items, grain, cloth, and other consumer goods could be purchased. Beyond these money-making functions, the tavern was important in other ways. It was the setting for both formal and informal social occasions. People gathered on Sunday afternoons and in the evenings to drink, swap tales, sing folk songs and enjoy each other's company; weddings and other celebrations were catered there. The quickest way to take the measure of a town or village was to visit its tavern, and traveling merchants, beggars and thieves all made it their headquarters.[28]

Produkcja, pp. 45–46, 72–78, 138; cf. H. Levine, "Gentry, Jews, and Serfs: The Rise of Polish Vodka," *Review* 4 (1980), pp. 227–41.

[26] Baranowski, *Polska karczma*, pp. 12–13; Bobrzyński, pp. 260–71; Burszta, *Wieś*, pp. 37–39, 42–53, 194–95; Topolska, pp. 72–75; Żytkowicz, "Okres gospodarki," pp. 303–304.

[27] Compare Ben-Sasson, "Takanot," pp. 188–90 on "off-monopoly" liquor sales.

[28] Baranowski, *Polska karczma*, pp. 10, 16–22, 27; Burszta, *Wieś*, pp. 30–32, 119–30, 135, 162, 168–72; Leskiewiczowa, *Próba analizy gospodarki*, pp. 42–43; Szczepaniak, pp. 71–81. Not all of the social activity in the taverns was wholesome: Z. H. Kaidanover, *Kav Hayashar* (Frankfurt/Main, 1706), Chapter 24, p. 52d, criticized arrendators who "build a special building or room where non-Jews can drink

For the owner, the *karczma* and the arrendator who ran it also served a political function. Selling the peasants liquor and providing them with a social gathering place was not only a way of emptying their pockets, it was a means of defusing social unrest. Presumably, a peasant spending his leisure hours joking, singing and getting drunk with friends would be less likely to resist actively his master's demands. In case any nefarious plans were in the making, the owner relied upon the arrendator to inform him.[29]

In addition to their liquor monopoly, Polish landowners also enjoyed the exclusive right to operate grain, fulling, tanning, and saw mills on their property. They often leased these out as *arendy*. Besides the rent, the mill arrendator was usually responsible for pig fattening and carpentry work.[30]

There were other important types of *arenda* as well. The owner often leased out his right to collect tolls and liquor, market, or excise taxes in a given locality.[31] The Sieniawskis and Czartoryskis also commonly leased out their fish ponds.[32] Other kinds of leases mentioned in the sources include fairs, salt mines, grain warehouses, tobacco sales, and dairy production.[33]

In theory, the various types of *arenda* could be leased out separately, but a common form of *arenda* leasing involved lumping

---

and gamble and whore; a common failing in Poland and Lithuania.'' See also Burszta, *Wieś*, pp. 164–67.

[29] Baranowski, *Polska karczma*, pp. 15–16, 25–26; Burszta, *Wieś*, pp. 10, 18, 102–10, 151.

[30] BC 5882 Łukszyński to ES 1.23609 6/29/1718 makes it clear that the largest share of lease income in the Wysocki region came from the mill and tax leases; cf. Eliyahu ben Yehezkeil, no. 13. On the organization of the milling in general see: Rutkowski, *Badania*, pp. 155–96, 244–46; Opas, "Powinności," pp. 121–44; Rychlikowa, *Wodzicki*, pp. 136–42. On the issue of Jewish arrendators being involved with pig raising see Ben-Sasson, "Takanot," pp. 192–93.

[31] EW 189 *Supl.* Abram Irszowicz 1705, Sieniawa Targownicy (market tax lessees) 1720, 1733; BC 5806 Fejga to ES 1.10117 undated; cf. PHo nos. 108, 109, 227.

[32] BC 5881 Łukszyński to ES 1.23565 11/4/1716; BC 5934 R to ES 1.34674 11/14/1716; BC 5946 ES to Zabagłowicz 1.38022, 1.38025 9/24, 10/3/1726; BC 5972 Chaim Tywlowicz to ES 1.45319 undated.

[33] EW 255 *Punkta pospólstwa Jarosławia* undated; EW 394 *Punkta od Jakuba Oleszyckiego* ca. 1720; BC 5806 Fejga to ES 1.10153 1/15/1724; BC 5943 ES to Marysieńka 1.37133 8/7/1703; GOSP 1505 Sieniawa-Oleszyce 1703–1705 *Weryfikacja obór*; cf. PHo no. 230.

together most of the leases of a given area. This superlease, normally including the liquor production facilities, taverns, bars, mills, tolls, and taxes (and sometimes also the ponds and tobacco) of a town or group of villages, was referred to as the "general *arenda*," "town *arenda*," "village *arenda*," "principal *arenda*," or sometimes simply the "tavern *arenda*" or "brewery *arenda*." The general arrendator who held this lease usually leased out its components to subarrendators, keeping the most lucrative enterprises under his direct control.[34] Candidates for holding a general *arenda* were wealthy individuals or groups of individuals (sometimes it was the *kahal* itself) who could afford to invest a large sum. By leasing out the general *arenda* in piecemeal fashion, the arrendator hoped to realize a handsome profit on his capital. The subarrendators were people of modest means who viewed their lease—in the terminology of Jewish sources—as a "mihya," a means of making a living, not as a capital investment. They generally had no contact with the owner, who preferred to simplify matters by dealing with the general arrendator only. The latter negotiated the contracts and supervised the subarrendators, seeing to it that they made their payments. In exceptional circumstances, however, when the arrendator was too overbearing or when some catastrophe precluded their making their payments, subarrendators did address petitions directly to the owner.[35]

Local custom and the *arenda* contract determined the rights and obligations of the general arrendator. The lease was usually for one or three years. The following are common provisions.

---

[34] The considerations in favor of lumping leases together were substantially the same as those encouraging leasing in the first place. For examples of what was included in general *arendy* see: BC 4475 Szkłow 1693 *Arenda miejska punkta*; EW 185 *Punkta porządku arendy klewańskiej* 1719–20; BC 3499–3500 *Arenda* contracts. In PHo the people referred to throughout as *mahazikim* were general arrendators. Also S. Maimon's grandfather apparently was the arrendator of the village *arenda* for his area; see Maimon, *Autobiography*, p. 15. In Czartoryski's time, especially in the western parts of the latifundium, there was a tendency to eliminate the institution of the general *arenda* and to lease directly to small arrendators. This was part of the general decline in the utilization of *arenda* referred to above.

[35] EW 189 *Supl.* Sieniawa *Targownicy* 1720 who note that they are the subarrendators of the general arrendator Lejba Sukiennik; cf. Dąbkowski, p. 577.

Rights

- The right to do business in all taverns, bars, mills, etc. included in the *arenda*.
- The use of the lord's brewing and distilling facilities and/or the right to maintain separate ones.[36]
- Housing for the arrendator and his family.
- Tax exemption.
- The right to use fields, gardens, meadows, and any other land that traditionally "belonged" to the *arenda*, or to be given hay, vegetables, and other produce from the owner's lands.
- Protection from monopoly-busting by serfs, neighboring arrendators, or anyone else.
- A discount in case of *force majeure*.
- The rights to excise and market taxes.
- The rights to operate and collect fees from the town scales.
- The rights to bridge and highway tolls.
- The cooperation of local members of the lord's administration.
- The right to contract with subarrendators and to see to the profitability of their efforts.
- The right to expect equipment in good repair or to repair it at no cost to himself.

Obligations

- Serve good quality liquor.
- Keep honest measures.
- Allow the residents to distill their own liquor tax-free for special occasions such as holidays, during fairs, and for weddings.
- Collect the central government's excise tax on liquor (*czopowy*).
- Supply mutton legs to the owner's hunting dogs.
- Pay the rent in four installments and on time.
- Supply the lord's court with liquor.[37]

[36] Sometimes the arrendator was obligated to buy liquor produced by the lord; see Rapoport, Hoshen Mishpat no. 19; cf. Ben-Sasson, "Takanot," pp. 188 – 90.

[37] These lists are based on the following sources: BC 2581/2 Międzybóż no. 63 9/1/1717; BC 2702 *Arenda* contracts of MZSC 1730 – 31, pp. 1 – 18, 37 – 39, 41 – 57, 69 – 71; BC 2902 Cieplice 1728, pp. 359 – 60; BC 3499 – 3500 Sieniawa-Oleszyce contracts 1628 – 1829; BC 4180 *Inwentarz Zińków* 1740, p. 3; BC 4474 – 75 Szkłów, 1688, p. 126 – 27, 1693, pp. 68 – 70; BC 5881 Łukszyński to ES 1.23565 11/4/1714;

Exactly whose liquor was sold in the tavern varied. If the owner
retained control over part of his distilling and brewing facilities, he
was likely to require the arrendators to purchase at least some of what
they sold from him.[38] Frequently, however, all production facilities
were included in the lease and the arrendator and/or subarrendators
produced what was sold in the bars in their areas. Usually the arrendator had to buy his own raw materials—primarily grain and wood—
either from the lord or on the open market.[39] Sometimes, however, the
contract or dire circumstances required that the owner supply these
commodities free.[40]

Labor and equipment were largely the responsibility of the owner.
As mentioned by the contracts and specified in the inventories and
accounts, some of the serfs in each village "belonged" to the *arenda*.
This meant that the arrendator had the right to their labor dues. He
used them to haul wood and grain, to help with the brewing and distilling, to serve as bartenders, to work in the mill, and to work on the
lands granted to him as part of the lease. He normally did not have

GOSP 1468 *Rachunek Sieniawa-Oleszyce i Lubaczów* 1717–25; EW 172 contracts
between AAC and various arrendators; EW 179 *Supl. Szaja Arendarz*; EW 185
Klewań contracts 1673–1793; EW 394 *Punkta od Jakuba Oleszyckiego* ca. 1720. It
is not clear from the contracts whether the arrendators were obligated to keep their
taverns open on Saturday. In Peretz b. Moshe, *Beit Peretz*, (Zhovkva, 1759), p. 26a,
Jewish tavernkeepers are blamed for keeping their taverns open in violation of the
Sabbath with the excuse that "our livelihood and lives depend on it and the law of the
land is the law"; cf. *PML* 1639 no. 358 p. 74, 1676 no. 713 p. 175; Ben-Sasson,
"Takanot," pp. 187–88.

[38] GOSP 232 Międzybóż 1734, pp. 24–30; Topolska, p. 73; Rapoport, Hoshen
Mishpat no. 19; cf. Czwojdrak and Żak, pp. 92–93.

[39] BC 5897 Morzycki to ES 1.26690 6/24/1724; BC 5946 ES to Morzycki 1.37899
10/27/1723; BC 5997 A. Zelmanowicz (?) to ES 1.50300 8/29/1723; GOSP 597
Sieniawa-Oleszyce *Intrata* 1731–42, p. 58; EW 185 *Punkta porządku arendy
klewańskiej* 1719–20, pt. 9; Klewań *Arenda* contract, 1722; Krzesz. 141 Tenczyn
1708; Krzesz. 142 Tenczyn 1713.

[40] BC 5935 S. Rubinowicz to ES 1.34962 6/4/1720; BC 5945 ES to Morzycki
1.37645 9/24/1719; BC 5963 H. Szmuyłowicz to ES 1.42441 undated, Szmuyło *Arendarz* to Lubiszewski 1.42437 12/22/1716; cf. *SB*, p. 171. Grain was also given to
serfs in trouble; see Chapter 3.

the right to money and kind rent from them. These remained obliged to the owner.[41]

As to equipment, again it was the owner's basic responsibility to see to it that the tavern and brewing facilities were in good repair. When a tavern burned down, he had to rebuild it; if vats wore out or were not returned by the previous arrendator, the owner had to replace them. In practice, the owner was not always quick to honor such costly obligations, and sometimes, so as to be able to stay in business, the arrendator would prefer to make repairs at his own cost first and try to collect from the owner later.[42]

The benefits of a general *arenda* included much more than the income from liquor sales or milling. The fringe benefits of tax exemption, housing, and use of land, labor, and equipment were of considerable value and enhanced the attractiveness of an *arenda*. It is no wonder that competition for lucrative leases was often cutthroat in nature.[43]

The *arenda* was a business opportunity, and the arrendator was primarily an entrepreneur and business administrator. This was especially true of a general arrendator. For while the subarrendator of one tavern might be, with the aid of his family, brewmaster, distiller, bartender, and business manager all in one, an arrendator of several taverns, mills, and so on could not hope to conduct personally all of

[41] Krzesz. 6 *Inwentarz* Tenczyn 1733, p. 22; Krzesz. 4 *Inwentarz* Tenczyn 1722, pp. 4, 9, 11; EW 86 *Supl.: Gromada* Stawnica undated pt. 16, *Gromada* Parchomowiec, *Gromada* Złotarynek pt. 4; EW 449c *Rachunki* Sieniawa-Oleszyce 1727 *Regestr poddanych do arend nalażących*; GOSP 537 *Inwentarz* Międzybóż 1727, e.g., Przedmieście Perehonka: Two out of twenty-eight peasant households belonged to the *arenda*; BC 4035 *Inwentarz* Międzybóż 1717, note Christian householders nos. 52, 56, 57, and 1 (in Słoboda) who are bartenders living in the homes of Jewish arrendators; BC 5881 Łukszyński to ES 1.23516 1715; cf. Rychlikowa, *Wodzicki*, pp. 131–36; Goldberg, "Poles and Jews," p. 260.

[42] EW 179 Moszko *Arendarz* to the *Komisarz* of the Sataniv region; EW 185 Klewań *Arenda* contract 1722; BC 5806 Fejga to ES 1.10121 undated, 1.10123 undated; BC 5881 Łukszyński to ES 1.23436, undated; arrendators have three brewing kettles of their own and two belonging to the owner; BC 5934 R to ES 1.34574 2/14/1709, 1.34756 11/25/1722; BC 5945 ES to Morzycki 1.37755 9/15/1721. Cf. n. 10; Maimon, *Autobiography*, pp. 17–19.

[43] See below, the case of Fejga against Majer Jakubowicz; cf. *SB* pp. 128, 200–201; C. Szmeruk, "Hahasidut Veiskei Hahakhirot," *Zion* 35 (1970), pp. 182–85.

the enterprises under his control. He devoted his attentions to negotiating contracts, collecting payments, enforcing serf labor dues, keeping accounts, and serving as the owner's local bank branch. The
actual brewing, distilling, milling, and bartending were done either by
professional artisans taken in as partners or hired, by subarrendators,
or by serf labor.[44]

Choosing an Arrendator

The chief considerations of the owner in choosing an arrendator
were his ability to pay and his capabilities as an administrator.[45] If one
were to take at face value the statutes and declarations laid down by
the various Jewish communal bodies in the seventeenth and eighteenth
centuries, however, it would appear that the owner of a latifundium
could never choose an arrendator. Rather, the arrendator was to be
chosen for him by the local *kahal*. Over and over again the communal
record books emphasize that no one may accept an *arenda* of any type
without being granted permission to do so by his *kahal*. The *kahal*
was to grant a license (*hazaka*) to potential arrendators allowing them
to bid on given *arendy*. The two main determinants of who received
this license were how long a particular license for an *arenda* had been
held by an individual or members of his family, and whether the successful candidate was prepared to pay the *kahal* the required license
fee or commission. Once members of a family had established themselves as lessees of some *arenda*, they would normally not be replaced
so long as they paid the *kahal* for the continual right to retain their
license.[46]

[44] BC 5997 A. Zelmanowicz to ES 1.50302, 1.50303 3/23/1724; Opas,
"Powinności," pp. 138–41; Szczepaniak, pp. 51–67, cf. *SB* pp. 37, 194–95;
Topolska, pp. 71–72. Cf. *PVAA* pp. 483–87.

[45] EW 525 Szkłów 1725 *Informacja*, pt. 23; BC 5943 ES to Marysieńka 1.37133
8/7/1703.

[46] EW 185 Klewań Arrendators vs. *Kahal* 3/19/1719; *PVAA*, no. 352 pp. 148–50;
PML, nos. 64–66 p. 13, nos. 73, 75, 77 pp. 14–15, nos. 83, 85 p. 16, nos. 104, 106,
107 pp. 24–25, no. 404 p. 83; PHo, nos. 83, 286; S. Buber, *Kirya Nisgava* (Cracow,
1903), pp. 86–87, 95; S. Ettinger, "Hayishuv Hayehudi Beukraina min Haihud Halublini ad Legezeirot Takh," doctoral dissertation, Hebrew University, (Jerusalem,

Such an arrangement worked in real life if economic conditions kept competition at a relatively low level. But when a shortage of *arendy* increased competitive pressures, there was little to prevent a potential arrendator from circumventing the *kahal* and approaching the lord on his own. The lord, of course, would normally grant the lease to the highest bidder. Hence, in reality, the license worked only when there were no incentives to the owners and potential arrendators not to honor it. That this was rarely the case is evident from the number of times that communities reiterated prohibitions against competitive bidding for *arendy*; from the large number of rabbinic responsa dealing with cases of *arenda* competition; from *ex post facto* settlements between successful bidders and the *kahal*; from mentions of this problem in homiletical literature; and from Polish sources showing that the lord did not feel bound to honor the *kahal* license.[47]

As early as the sixteenth century, in the responsa of R. Shlomo Luria, the statement is found that the practice of direct tendering of competitive bids was "a custom that bedevils the entire country."[48] Even the Lithuanian Council, in 1637, noted that there were many fewer *arendy* than potential arrendators and gave any fifteen householders in a town the right to sue in rabbinic court to have the *arenda* license rescinded from its current holder and opened up to competitive bidding.[49]

Thus, while communities tried to maintain the licensing system,[50] it

---

1957), pp. 135–40; Maimon, *Autobiography*, p. 23; M. Schorr, *Organizacja Żydów,* p. 40.

[47] The following Sieniawski-Czartoryski documents indicate that *arenda* leases were granted on the basis of competitive bidding or favoritism, apparently without regard for *kahal* licensing procedures: BC 5944 ES to Gowarczowski 1.37513 7/9/1713; BC 5886 Szawel Markiewicz to ES 1.24370 undated; BC 5935 R to ES 1.34805 2/18/1724; BC 5756 Michał Abramowicz to MZSC 1.9 3/24/1731; EW 176 *Supl.* Jews from Zińków 1737; EW 179 *Supl.* Jews from Satanów 1737; EW 525 Szkłów 1725 *Informacja* pt. 23; see also the correspondence recording the struggle between Fejga and Majer Jakubowicz for the Końskowoła *arenda* below. Cf. PHo no. 84; Buber, p. 140; *ABK* no. 219; Dinur, pp. 118–20; Schorr, *Organizacja Żydow*, p. 42; Szmeruk, pp. 182–87; *SB* pp. 128, 200–201.

[48] R. Shlomo Luria, *Responsa* (Jerusalem, 1969), no. 35.

[49] *PML*, no. 308, pp. 67–68.

[50] BC 5881 Łukszyński to ES 1.23458, undated, does mention the family of Sender the *balchazaka* (holder of the license) and there were cases of arrendators holding their lease for several terms, even passing it on to their sons; e.g., BC 5844 Szymon

could not be effective against the competitive pressure between potential arrendators and the lord's desire to maximize profit. The Sieniawskis were aware of this and tried to encourage competition. In 1725, Adam Mikołaj Sieniawski observed that the likelihood of getting an increment (*aukcja*) in an *arenda* price was greater if competition was intensified. He therefore ordered that contracts be let for one year instead of three.[51] In 1713, Elżbieta Sieniawska instructed her administrator, Gowarzowski, to lease the Laszków *arenda* to Marek Lwowski because he "is offering an increase of 1,000 *złoty* which the previous arrendators don't want to match."[52]

Of more significance than the license in determining who would be the arrendator—at least for leases not negotiated personally by the owner—were the local administrators. In outlying complexes the *komisarz* or *ekonom* was entrusted with the task of finding and negotiating with arrendators. His mandate was to find someone responsible and willing to pay an increment over the previous contract,[53] but much depended on his discretion. This opened the way to corruption. For instance, Berko Jakubowicz offered in writing to pay Czartoryski's administrator, Aleksander Walicki, a bribe if he would not include an increment in the new contract.[54] In other localities the practice of administrators granting leases to their favorites was protested in petitions from potential arrendators whose higher bids were not considered.[55]

Despite the general trend in the eighteenth century toward increased competition for *arendy*, sometimes an *arenda* was simply not prof-

---

Józefowicz to ES 1.16866 5/25/1723. In view of the evidence cited in note 47, however, the fact that such families possessed the *kahal* licenses was probably not the determining element in their longevity as arrendators. Cf. Ettinger, "Hayishuv," pp. 135–40, however, who maintains that, at least in the pre-1648 period, communities were fairly successful in protecting the *Hazaka* system in the face of competitive pressures.

[51] EW 525 Szklów 1725 *Informacja* pt. 23.

[52] BC 5944 ES to Gowarzowski 1.37513 7/9/1713.

[53] BC 5944 ES to Morzycki 1.37591 8/9/1718; BC 5946 ES to Morzycki 1.37899 10/27/1723; EW 525 Szklów 1725 *Informacja* pt. 23.

[54] BC 5840 Berko Jakubowicz to A. Walicki 1.16065 7/7/1744.

[55] EW 176 *Supl.* Jews from Zińków 1739; EW 179 *Supl.* Jews from Satanów 1737; BC 5806 Fejga to ES 1.10159 10/7/1724; BC 5963 L. Szmujłowicz to ES 1.42442 7/22/1716.

itable, and the owner's problem was not finding the highest bidder, but finding anyone willing to accept the lease. In such circumstances, either the outgoing arrendator was prevailed upon to stay on, or a new person was forced to accept the lease, or the *kahal* was given the responsibility. In one case, Szejna, the widow of Abramko of Sawnica, recalled how her husband died as a result of being imprisoned and beaten in order to force him to accept the *arenda*. In 1733, Jewna Lejbowicz went into hiding in order to avoid being coerced into continuing as arrendator of Nowa Sieniawa. Moszko Ankielowicz asserted that since he held the lease of Ivankiv only as a service to Czartoryski, seeing that no one else would take it, it was unconscionable to demand an increase from him.[56]

Once an arrendator had been chosen and held the contract for one term, he had the presumptive right to have the contract renewed. This was subject, however, to the owner's desire to obtain an increment. The arrendator, of course, wanted to keep the price as low as possible and so a negotiation process ensued. Geography and commitments permitting, the lord or lady negotiated contract renewals in person. If the *arenda* was in one of the outlying complexes, Sieniawska would typically write to the administrator in charge, instructing him how much of an increment to obtain. The administrator then presented a contract to the arrendator. If he refused to sign, then either the administrator or the arrendator or both might write to the owner explaining their view of the situation and asking for a proposed settlement. The Sieniawski correspondence has preserved at least some of the letters exchanged during one negotiation of this type.

Most *arenda* contracts started from April 24 or June 24 and ended one year later. In 1723, June 24 came and went, and the arrendator of Tenczyn still had not signed his contract. Sieniawska was demanding 6,000 *tynf* per year; the arrendator, Lewek Lejzorowicz wanted to pay

---

[56] Ew 86 *Supl.* Szejna undated, *Supl.* Jewna Leybowicz ca. 1733; EW 179 *Supl.* Moszko Ankielowicz; 1744; EW 189 *Supl. Pospólstwo Żydowskie* to Szumanczowski, ca. 1730. See also BC 5844 Szymon Józefowicz to ES 1.16738–39 5/1/1723; BC 5881 Łukszyński to ES 1.23502 7/3/1714; cf. Ber of Bolechow, pp. 157–64; *SB* p. 171.

only 4,000. On August 2, 1723, Sieniawska wrote to the administrator in charge, Morzycki:[57]

> From the Tenczyn *arenda* you must finally do your best to get the arrendator to pay 6,000 *tynf* per year, seeing that he has so many villages under him and now a newly constructed tavern for guests; besides being allowed in the woods as much as he wants contrary to the prescriptions of the contract . . .

She repeated this order in letters of August 15 and October 13, apparently to no avail.[58] On October 24, Morzycki informed her of the arrendator's persistent refusal to come to terms,[59] and Lewek himself wrote, at about the same time, that her demand for an increase was unreasonable because: he controlled only fifteen taverns and not twenty as she had claimed in the letter of August 15; the peasants had decreased the amount of drinks they were purchasing, reducing the volume of his sales; the price of grain had risen, hiking his costs; the amount of wood he was taking from her forest was inconsequential; no one had complained about him; he was running an honest and efficient operation that caused Sieniawska no inconvenience.[60]

Sieniawska did not accept these arguments nor others that must have been presented in a letter which has not been preserved, for on October 27 she wrote to Morzycki:[61]

> If he does not want to sign the contract for the specified sum [6,000 *tynf*] . . . I will most assuredly send my representative there who will immediately and deliberately note down all of the misdeeds he has committed as well as the damage he has done to the forest and all of the profit he has made thereby. Without doubt he will have to answer for everything in irons. Neither will I take the slightest notice of the fact that he is a royal Jew. There was once an arrendator of my father's in Willanów who also belonged to the king. He just alternated between the king's irons and my father's.

[57] BC 5946 ES to Morzycki 1.37887 8/1/1723.
[58] BC 5946 ES to Morzycki 1.37890, 1.37898, 8/15 – 10/13/1723.
· [59] BC 5897 Morzycki to ES 1.26664, 10/24/1723.
[60] BC 5870 Lewek Lejzorowicz to ES 1.21189 undated.
[61] BC 5946 ES to Morzycki 1.37899, 10/27/1723.

After she had expressed similar sentiments on November 3 and November 10,[62] Morzycki, exasperated, wrote on November 20, "I cannot continue haggling with the Tenczyn arrendator. On the one hand, he says that he cannot pay more than 4,000 *tynf*; on the other he desires to keep his lease...."[63]

At least three more letters were exchanged on this subject.[64] In the final one (December 11, 1723), Morzycki informed Sieniawska that, "I have not given the contract to the arrendator because he has not yet returned from visiting the rabbi in Staszów; but as soon as he comes back I will immediately give it to him."[65] Six months after the customary signing date the contract for the Tenczyn *arenda* was still not settled.

This case is instructive in several ways. It shows how important it was to the owner that the *arenda* be settled and an increment obtained. Sieniawska's persistence in demanding that the contract be signed, her refusal to compromise on the price, and her readiness to send a special envoy to handle the matter all indicate that she felt this was an affair of some import.

Just as impressive is the arrendator's power to resist. Having stalled past the period when arrendators were customarily recruited,[66] he was in no hurry to sign the contract on unfavorable terms. He obviously was not afraid of Morzycki and probably put little stock in Sieniawska's threat. He may have eventually capitulated, but only after causing much annoyance to both Morzycki and Sieniawska.

Another interesting point is the rationality displayed by Sieniawska. In contrast to the stories about capricious noblemen like Prince Marcin Radziwiłł, who beat or used his Jews for sport at the slightest

[62] BC 5946 ES to Morzycki 1.37901, 1.37903, 11/3 – 11/10/1723.

[63] BC 5897 Morzycki to ES 1.26666 11/20/1723.

[64] BC 5946 ES to Morzycki 1.37906 11/24/1723 1.37908 12/1/1723; BC 5897 Morzycki to ES 1.26667 12/11/1723.

[65] BC 5897 Morzycki to ES 1.26667 12/11/1723.

[66] Normally, the arrendators informed the administrators of their intentions in advance of the lease expiration date; e.g., BC 5881 Łukszyński to ES 1.23438 undated. It was evidently more difficult to find a good arrendator after the usual negotiating season; see BC 5934 R to ES 1.34674 11/14/1716; BC 5935 R to ES 1.34890 7/3/1726.

pretence,[67] here Elżbieta Sieniawska demonstrated that she was much more interested in accumulating money than in beating the Jew. Furthermore, she did not demand the money arbitrarily, but presented a reasoned argument justifying the increase. On another occasion she even ordered Morzycki not to demand an increment because the arrendator had convinced her that the *arenda* revenues didn't justify it.[68]

Data on *arenda* prices for the Sieniawa-Oleszyce complex, which Sieniawska dealt with personally, are available. These also support the idea that the magnate was rational and knew that every lease had a market value, which could go up or down.

In the first quarter of the eighteenth century the prices of the seven general *arendy* in the Sieniawa-Oleszyce complex offer an interesting pattern of *arenda* payments. The range is from 750 *zł.*/yr for Dakhnivs'ka and 11,500 *zł.*/yr for Sieniawa (the smallest and largest *arendy*) in 1708 to 1,300 and 20,500 for these same leases in 1726. The trend is upward, but it took nineteen years before even one lease, Oleszyce, doubled in price. As Table 5.1 shows, price hikes were not a matter of course. In each case the probability that the price would remain the same or decrease was close to or higher than the probability that it would increase. When increases—and decreases—did occur, they were not standardized. Increments fluctuated between 1.5 and 66.6 percent, while decrements ranged from 3.4 to 30 percent. All of this is an indication that the price of the *arenda* was not merely a function of the magnates' whims. Negotiations were meaningful, and variables affecting the profitability of the *arenda* in any given year were taken into account. The owners, in the inflationary atmosphere of the early eighteenth century, kept pressing for increments, but the resistance of the arrendators seems to have tempered their lords' demands, forcing them to adjust their desires to reality.

[67] See M. Bałaban, *Letoldot Hatenuah Hafrankit*, vol. 1 (Tel Aviv, 1934), pp. 83–87; Dubnov, *Toldot Hahasidut*, Introduction; Maimon, *Autobiography*, pp. 63–67.

[68] BC 5944 ES to Morzycki 1.37591 8/9/1718; she also commanded him to do everything in his power to aid the arrendator so that an increment could be obtained the following year. Note that even in her threat to punish Lewek, ES admitted to the necessity of her honoring the letter of the contract; cf. EW 255 *Supl.* Jarosław arrendators 1721–22.

TABLE 5.1
SUMMARY OF ARENDA PRICES FOR SIENIAWA-OLESZYCE COMPLEX 1708–26

TOWN:	Dachnów	Dzików	Majdan	Mykolaiv	Oleszyce	Sieniawa	Ułazów
Number of years	18	19	19	13	19	19	19
Price in First year (zł)	750	3,640	2,000	2,500	5,200	11,500	1,300
Number of Increments	8	7	8	6	11	10	6
Average %	18.75	20.1	15.7	6.25	14	6.4	26.6
Number of Decrements	3	8	3	3	4	1	4
Average %	21.6	10.1	16.9	4.4	19	3.4	18
Number of times the price did not change	6	3	7	4	3	7	8
Price in last year	1,300	5,100	3,500	2,600	10,500	20,500	2,300
% Increase 1708–26	73.3	39.7	75	4	101	82	76.9

Points of the *arenda* contract other than price were also negotiable. In return for an increment, the lord was sometimes obliged to grant concessions such as canceling privileges entitling certain individuals not to honor the *arenda* monopoly, providing wood, allowing price increases, constructing a new building, enlarging the geographic area of the monopoly, or promising better enforcement of the monopoly. Also, the owner preferred one-year leases, but the lessee sometimes could hold out for a longer term.[69]

The Payment Order System

While the heart of every *arenda* contract was the amount of rent to be paid, the manner in which the money was remitted was highly significant. Typically, the contract specified that the rent was to be paid in four equal quarterly installments (*rate*), less any down payment. Commonly, however, the money was not forwarded to the owner in a lump sum every three months. Rather, the sum due every quarter represented the limit on how much money the owner could require the arrendator to spend on his behalf in that quarter. The money was actually paid out throughout the quarter in small amounts according to the instructions of the owner or his representatives as expressed in payment orders (*asygnacje*).

The system built around the payment orders was similar to a modern checking account. For instance, if the owner had 1,000 zł. due from an arrendator on April 23, rather than waiting for that date, whenever the owner wanted to purchase something or had to pay an obligation, he would give the provider of the goods or services a payment order which the latter would present to the arrendator in exchange for cash. A characteristic payment order reads: "*Pan* Lewko, arrendator of Jarosław, is to pay in exchange for this, my pay-

---

[69] EW 179 *Supl.* Lejzor Lejbowicz and Moszko Wolfowicz 1737; EW 185 Klewań *Arenda* contracts 1722, 1729; EW 394 *Punkta od Jakuba Oleszyckiego*; EW 525 Szkłów 1725 *Informacja* pt. 23; BC 3499 Sieniawa 1706 contract; BC 5840 Berko Jakubowicz to A. Walicki 1.16065 7/7/1744; BC 5944 ES to Gowarczowski 1.37513 7/9/1716; ES to Morzycki 1.37591 8/9/1718; BC 5963 Szmuyło Arendarz to Lubiszewski 1.42437 12/29/1716.

ment order, to Franciszek 300 *taler bity* which should be entered into the account. As confirmation I am signing.''[70]

The payment order was then presented to the arrendator, who paid the bill, countersigned the payment order, and sent it back to the owner, to verify that it was paid. He also entered the amount into his account book and subtracted it from what he owed in rent. By the end of the quarter it was usually not money that the arrendator handed over to the owner, but his account book specifying exactly how the *arenda* money had been spent, with any surplus or shortfall being counted against the next quarter's payment.[71]

This system saved time and trouble for the magnate. Rather than have all the money sent under guard to a central or regional treasury where it would have to be counted and stored and then kept track of as it was spent, the lord simplified matters by having the arrendator maintain the responsibility for the actual handling of the money. This required careful and honest bookkeeping on the part of the arrendators, and the owners strived to ensure this.[72] But the gains in efficiency, security, and flexibility evidently outweighed the possibility of malfeasance, and this decentralization of the latifundium banking and treasury functions, largely in the hands of the arrendators, persisted.[73]

[70] For examples of payment orders (*asygnajca*) see BC 2647 *Kwity i asygnacje*; 1668–1731; BC 3507 *Asygnacje i dyspozycje Sieniawskich* 1721–1809. Contracts sometimes specify the duty of arrendators to pay payment orders; for example, BC 3499 Sieniawa *Arenda* contract 1707. Financial accounts also mention that bills were paid by arrendators; for example, BC 2904 where Mowsza Szkolnik and Żyd Aleksandryjski pay most of the bills. Arrendators had to be on the lookout for counterfeit payment orders, and when suspicious they would refuse to pay until the owner sent them written confirmation; see BC 5806 Fejga to ES 1.10116, 1.10118 undated; BC 5934 R to ES 1.34677 4/30/1717.

[71] For examples of such account books see EW 449c *Sieniawa-Oleszyce rachunki arendowe* 1699–1737; BC 4041 *Arendy Klucza Sieniawy-Oleszyckiego* 1695–98; cf. BC 5882 Łukszyński to ES 1.23629 7/26/1719. In BC 5943 ES to Lejmin 1.37126 4/26/1700 ES specified that she did not want *arenda* money paid in drips and drabs that quarter, but collected and forwarded as a lump sum. Thus sometimes sacks of money were sent to the magnate's residence.

[72] EW 525 Szkłów 1716 *Informacja*; BC 5946 ES to Zabagłowicz 1.37968 8/5/1725.

[73] Compare Leszczyński, *Żydzi,* pp. 214–15; Prochaska, *Historja,* p. 46. Arrendators were not the only people who handled money. Administrators who collected tax money also paid payment orders; e.g., GOSP 1576.

In addition to running latifundium enterprises and paying the magnate's checks, arrendators fulfilled several ancillary functions. They were an excellent source of information as to what was happening in their section of the latifundium, whether it was troop movements, peasant restlessness, or administrator corruption. They heard about business and investment opportunities and could provide the owner with reliable tips. Arrendators could also serve as factors, procuring necessities, especially comestibles for the local latifundium staff, marching troops, or the owner's entourage whenever it passed through.[74]

The Arrendator's Position

Many descriptions of arrendators emphasize their helplessness in the face of the lord and other powers. The classic description by Shlomo Maimon of how his grandfather, a general arrendator, and his family cringed before every passing nobleman has been taken as normative, and arrendators have been characterized as having the same status as serfs.[75] The anecdotes behind this characterization are no doubt true, and they attest to the employment of force as one means of dealing with arrendators. The Sieniawski-Czartoryski documents also show signs of arrendators suffering rough treatment at the hands of administrators, usually in the form of imprisonment or drubbing intended to force the arrendator to accept a lease or make a payment.[76] This conception of the arrendator, however, fails to recognize the fact that the utility of the arrendator, especially the general arrendator,

---

[74] BC 5806 Fejga to ES 1.10121 undated, 1.10122 undated, 1.10123 undated, 1.10131 5/3/1721, 1.10134 2/1/1724, 1.10137 6/7/1722, 1.10154 2/16/1724, 1.10157 undated (bound with letter from 8/12/1724); BC 5997 A. Zelmanowicz to ES 1.50297 undated.

[75] Maimon, *Autobiography*, pp. 16–17; Burszta, *Wieś*, pp. 126–30; Bałaban, *Letoldot Hatenuah Hafrankit*, pp. 86–87; Dubnov, *Toldot Hahasidut*, pp. 9–12; Szmeruk, p. 190; cf. I. Halpern, ed., *Beit Yisrael Bepolin*, vol. 2 (Jerusalem, 1953), no. 49; *SB*, pp. 102, 115, 128–29, 145–46, 171–72.

[76] EW 86 *Supl.* Irsz; EW 179 *Supl.* Szejna; cf. Goldberg, "Poles and Jews," p. 261; Weinryb, *Jews*, pp. 10–11, 352 (n. 1).

as a rule gained for him the support, not the ire, of his lord.[77] This support endowed the arrendator with a measure of real power. To judge from the petitions submitted to the Sieniawskis and Czartoryskis, the typical general arrendator was by no means a cowering sycophant, but a man who was as much aware of his rights as of his obligations and who was not afraid to demand the support and consideration to which he was entitled.

This judgment is based on three categories of incidents. In the first group are:

- Lewek Lejzorowicz's refusal, mentioned above, either to sign a disadvantageous *arenda* contract or to give up his *arenda* even in the face of threats from Elżbieta Sieniawska herself;
- attempts by arrendators to renegotiate their contracts in the middle of the term;[78]
- numerous petitions asking for discounts;
- many letters and petitions demanding more protection of the monopoly and enforcement of the arrendator's rights so that he could turn a decent profit.

These actions reflect self-confidence and the belief that the arrendator-owner relationship was a contractual one, not a modified version of slave and master. The second group of incidents shows this even more clearly.

On August 24, 1715, the Christian town council of Jarosław sent a petition to Sieniawska claiming, among other things, that the Jewish general arrendator was refusing to pay 600 *zł.* of the 1,200 *zł.* he was obliged to contribute toward certain municipal projects.[79] In a different, undated petition, one Wojciech Pomolecki asserted that Sieniawska's court, headed by her commissioner, had rendered a judgment in his favor against the arrendators Zelman Jakubowicz and

---

[77] Cordial relations between lord and arrendator were common enough for the Dubno Magid to compare God's relationship with Israel to a lord's relationship with his arrendator; see Y. Krantz, *Kol Yaakov*, Shir Hashirim Kol Yeshorer (Lemberg, 1804), p. 14b; cf. Weinryb, *Jews*, pp. 10–11, 352 (n. 1).

[78] EW 185 Klewań 1721–22; EW 179 *Supl.* Arrendator of Satanów.

[79] EW 255.

Jakub Kiwowicz for 583 *zł*. The arrendators were refusing to pay.[80] A petition from the millers of Sataniv requested that the arrendator, Śprynca, be enjoined from building a mill that would pose unwarranted competition to them.[81]

These cases all indicate that an arrendator—at least if he leased a large enough *arenda*—had the power to resist other authorities, be they council, court, or custom. Apparently none of the accused arrendators feared being beaten, placed in irons, or baptized forcefully. They understood their value to the lord and assumed that this would keep them from harm.

The third category shows arrendators not merely confidently negotiating with their lord, or defiantly resisting other authorities, but forcibly imposing their will upon others.

Matjasz Rogola of Ivankovych complained that Moszko, the Sataniv arrendator, commandeered Matjasz's farm hands to bale his own hay.[82]

The Jewish community of Nowa Sieniawa complained that the new arrendator had arbitrarily decided that each Jew must pay taxes on two brewing kettles whether he actually possessed them or not. He also imposed other new, illegal taxes and raised the quota of wood due to him.[83]

In 1740 and 1743 the Christian council of Sataniv, together with the *kahal*, complained that the arrendator was overzealous in collecting customs and tolls, collecting illegally high rates, and collecting from exempt people and on duty-free items.[84]

In 1712, Jacenty Ordyński of Sataniv wrote, "God is on high and My Lord is far away, but Berko the arrendator is near." He claimed that Berko sent sixteen soldiers to wreck his house and left him impoverished.[85]

These cases, and others like them,[86] demonstrate the power enjoyed

---

[80] Ibid.
[81] EW 179.
[82] Ibid.
[83] EW 86.
[84] EW 179.
[85] Ibid.
[86] For example, BC 5881 Łukszyński to ES 1.23429 undated; EW 86 *Supliki* of peasants vs. Liber *Arendarz*; EW 176 *Supl.* Satanów 1737; Zińków 1739; EW 179 *Supl.* Semian Piasecki, Herszko Tysmienicki; EW 525 Szkłów 1716 *Informacja* pt. 1;

by at least some arrendators. They did not have to answer to anyone but the owner and were able to call upon troops to enforce their will. In this way, a general arrendator could approach the power of a high latifundium official. His subarrendators were analogous to minor officials under an *ekonom* or *podstarosta*. Thus, while it is true that arrendators were often victims of highhandedness, there were those among their number who could call others to account.

In the absence of information on *arenda* profit margins, the financial rewards gained from leasing are difficult to gauge. The impression left by such phenomena as the generally high level of competition, the steady, though not continuous, rise in *arenda* prices, the high tax rates for arrendators, and by anecdotes like those told by Solomon Maimon is that *arenda* could be a good way to earn a living.[87] It is also obvious that, however profitable it may have been, the *arenda* did open up other opportunities to enterprising arrendators. Mention has already been made of the fields, meadows, gardens, animals, and serfs placed at the disposal of most general arrendators. Agricultural accoutrements of this nature meant that an arrendator who knew how to employ these resources could enter the agricultural produce market.[88] Being located advantageously to gain information, arrendators not only passed on to the owner intelligence concerning promising business deals, but put such knowledge to use in their own ventures.

When an arrendator informed the owner of an opportunity, he could expect to be the instrument by which the deal was consummated, thereby gaining a commission for himself.[89] Arrendators also could attract business for themselves. Lejba Sukiennik, the arrendator of Sieniawa, was, in addition, an important supplier of cloth for uniforms

---

cf. Prochaska, *Historja*, pp. 113 – 15; *SB*, pp. 43 – 44, 183 – 84, 215 – 17.

[87] Maimon, *Autobiography*, pp. 15, 20, 23; cf. Prochaska, *Historja*, p. 109; Weinryb, *Jews*, p. 11; idem, *Mehkarim*, p. 84. A complete assessment of *arenda* profitability would have to deal with issues such as the likelihood that general arrendators reaped huge profits while subarrendators just got by, the representativeness of the many petitions asking for discounts due to natural or man-made calamities, and the percentage of *arendy* that had to be forced upon arrendators as a result of unprofitability.

[88] See above and Mahler, *Toldot,* pp. 285 – 88.

[89] BC 5806 Fejga to ES 1.10117 undated, 1.10120 undated, 1.10148 2/22/1723; BC 5840 Majer Jakubowicz to ES 1.16068 6/8/1714; cf. Rychlikowa, *Produkcja*, p. 116.

to the Sieniawskis.[90] The extraordinary privileges that Sieniawska granted in 1712 to Zelman Jakubowicz, the arrendator of Jarosław, brought down the wrath of the Jewish community.[91]

Perhaps the best advantage offered by a lucrative *arenda* was the opportunity it afforded to build up a cash reserve. If the magnate did not write too many payment orders, an arrendator could accumulate cash waiting to be collected. Astute arrendators invested this reserve in agricultural produce or merchandise, which they marketed, either locally or long-distance.[92] They also often engaged in petty moneylending to noblemen and peasants.[93]

Arrendator-Magnate Relations

As we have seen, there were many elements that a magnate had to coordinate and balance in order to operate the latifundium. Among these the Jewish arrendators, who provided so much of the latifundium cash as well as banking, administrative, and other services, were essential to successful operation.

The arrendators, however, faced certain difficulties in carrying out their task. Chief among these was the conflict of interest between them and other latifundium constituencies: peasants, townsmen, other arrendators, administrators, and rivals for the *arenda* leases.

Relations between the arrendator and the villagers who lived in the region of his monopoly were normally peaceful.[94] Still, the potential for conflict was present in the tendency of the arrendator to try to maximize the profit of his *arenda* combined with the fact that the

[90] BC 2527, pp. 26, 27, 40; BC 2904, no. 51; cf. Leszczyński, *Żydzi,* p. 191.

[91] M. Steinberg, *Żydzi w Jarosławiu* (Jarosław, 1933), pp. 34–35.

[92] BC 4819, pp. 21–22, 31; BC 4820, pp. 110–11; BC 5806 Fejga to ES 1.10132, 1722; 1.10145 1/2/1723; BC 5963 Herszko Szmujłowicz to ES 1.42441, undated, notes that he did not invest his money in other types of commerce, implying that other arrendators did, cf. Maimon, *Autobiography*, p. 17; H. H. Ben-Sasson, "Poland," *EJE* 13, pp. 728–29; Leszczyński, *Żydzi*, pp. 215–16, 221–22.

[93] BC 4495 Szkłów 1765, p. 6; BC 5806 Fejga to ES 1.10140 8/18/1722, 1.10145 1/2/1723, 1.10146 1/10/1723 BC 5829 Hajzyk wnuk Chaimow to ES 1.14238–40 undated; BC 5897 Morzycki to ES 1.26531 5/6/1719; cf. Burszta, *Wieś*, p. 148; Prochaska, *Historja*, p. 111. See Chapter 3 on multiple occupations.

[94] Compare Baron, *History*, vol. 16, pp. 274–75; Czwojdrak and Żak, p. 105.

peasants were prevented by their feudal obligations from shopping around. The arrendator could charge as high a price as practicable for drinks, insist that all duties to him be paid scrupulously, and strictly enforce his monopoly rights. Some arrendators apparently went even further by demanding payments and services not due to them according to custom or contract, by watering down liquor, and by using dishonest measures.[95]

For their part, the peasants tried to minimize the amount of cash they placed in the arrendator's pocket. Their means of doing this was "to mutiny" (*buntować się*) by producing their own liquor, by buying it from sources outside the monopoly, or by simply refusing to render labor dues to which the arrendator was entitled. In some cases, peasants violently attacked the arrendators.[96]

For the same reasons and in the same ways in which arrendators came into conflict with peasants, they could find themselves at loggerheads with townsmen.[97] In towns there was the added dimension of commerce, leading to the complaint that high tolls, tariffs, and excise taxes and stringent attempts to collect them made it difficult for marginally profitable enterprises to survive.[98]

Peasants and townsmen who—in the phrase of the time— "harmed the *arenda*" (that is, broke the monopoly) often did so by buying liquor or by using stills not controlled by their region's arrendator, and thereby patronized a different arrendator. Fejga the arrendator wrote,

[95] EW 86 *Supliki* of peasant councils; EW 179 *Supl.* Semian Piasecki; EW 189 *Supl.* Cieplice, Majdan millers, Dobropol; EW 282 *Supl. Gromada* Podmanostyrka; BC 3503 Międzybóż ca. 1738 three Jews fined for beating a serf; BC 3814, no. 73; EW 525 Szkłów 1716 *Informacja Suplika* pt. 1; BC 3499 Majdan *Arenda* contract 4/23/1707; cf. *SB*, pp. 115, 242; Goldberg, "Poles and Jews," pp. 264–68.

[96] BC 5806 Fejga to ES *passim*; BC 5935 Szmojło Rubinowicz to ES 1.34963 8/5/1722; BC 5997 A. Zelmanowicz to ES 1.50301 12/28/1723 1.50302 undated; EW 176 reply to *Punkta gromady gluszkowskiej*; EW 1509 *Supl.* of Iwan, Parzyło et al.; cf. Bursztâ, *Wieś*, pp. 71–77, 79–84.

[97] BC 3499 Sieniawa *arenda* contract 1704; BC 5897 Morzycki to ES 1.26556 1/21/1720; BC 5963 Szmuyło *Arendarz* to ES 1.42439 6/14/1724. Among those who harmed the *arenda* could be the subarrendators; e.g., EW 188 *Supl.* Moszko of Klewań, Lewko Zysklewicz of Jarosław; cf. *PML*, no. 809 p. 211.

[98] EW 255 *Punkta pospólstwa Jarosławia*; EW 282 *Supl.* Berezhany shoemakers; BC 5767 Borgolt to ES 1.2742 5/28/1721; BC 5860 A. Kowalski to MZSC 1.19708–709, 1.19711 July–August, 1730; cf. Goldberg, "Poles and Jews," pp. 274–75.

in 1721, that two people she sent to investigate in a village near Końskowola discovered liquor belonging to the arrendator of Zosin instead of Fejga.[99] Evidently neighboring arrendators were not always careful in verifying the feudal obligations of their customers. The 1689 contract for the *arenda* of Dobropol specified a fifteen *grzywny* fine for any outside arrendator who sold to people who lived within the Dobropol *arenda* region.[100]

While there may have been an inherent conflict of interest between an arrendator on the one hand, and peasants, townsmen, and other arrendators on the other, the relationship between arrendators and members of the administration was, in theory, one of mutual dependence. They served complementary functions: the administrator was responsible for the order and general profitability of the complex under his control; the arrendator was responsible for producing a large part of the income on that complex. Each needed the cooperation of the other to accomplish his job. An administrator saddled with an incompetent arrendator could expect a hail of letters from the owner demanding to know why there wasn't more income. The arrendator normally depended upon the local administrator to render "justice" (*sprawiedliwość*); that is, to enforce the monopoly against those who sought to spend their money elsewhere. A hostile administrator could make it very difficult for an arrendator to earn a profit.

In 1720, Berko Szmulowicz of Jarosław wrote directly to Elżbieta Sieniawska, "because there are so many officials, but one does not know who will listen."[101] He charged that the new arrendator of the village of Nowotny was being ruined because the administrator, Łukszyński, was friendly with the previous arrendator, Szajka. Łukszyński, Szajka, and other Sieniawski officials "often drink and play music together."[102] Łukszyński failed to give the new arrendator possession of the millstones, brewery, and brewing kettles and

[99] BC 5806 Fejga to ES 1.10131 5/3/1721. See also: 1.10123 undated, 1.10134 4/22/1721, 1.10160 2/3/1725; BC 2702, p. 572; BC 3814, no. 73; Ew 179 *Supl.* Lejzor Lejbowicz and Moszko Wolfowicz 1738.

[100] BC 3499 Dobropol *arenda* contract; cf. Burszta, *Wieś*, pp. 71–77, 79–85.

[101] BC 5963 Berko Szmulowicz to ES 1.42440 8/26/1720.

[102] Ibid.

allowed the peasants to buy wherever they wished.[103] The Sieni-awski-Czartoryski sources contain many similar complaints by arren-dators that administrators, either through incompetence or by design, failed to execute "justice," with the consequence that the monopoly was violated and little income was forthcoming.[104] In some cases, the administrators themselves competed with or actively oppressed the arrendators.[105]

With the common exceptions of cases of bribery and personal predilection, the probable explanation for the lack of cooperation on the part of administrators is the fact that the administrator was respon-sible for maximizing agricultural production on his complex. To do this he needed the cooperation of the peasants. If an administrator felt that enforcing the monopoly somehow made his job of compelling the peasants to work—and to work efficiently—more difficult, he prob-ably would not have been too conscientious about it. It is easier to deal with one disgruntled arrendator than to try to control the illegal activities of hundreds of peasants. Faced with this kind of conflict between arrendator and administrator, the owner had to proceed with caution. If he significantly damaged the ability of either man to do his job, the results for the complex could be disastrous.

Conflict of interest was most blatant when a lucrative *arenda* was coveted by more than one bidder. The arrendator who held such a lease had to work very hard to keep it. The example of Końskowola

[103] Ibid.; cf. EW 139 Satanów 1727 abstract of petition vs. Šprynca, who with the aid of the administrator Siedlicki harassed the new arrendator.

[104] BC 5806 Fejga's correspondence with ES contains many complaints about the administrators Karetta and Narkiewicz; BC 5756 Lewek Abramowicz to AMS(?) and ES 1.5 undated; BC 5829 Michał Abuszewicz to Lubiszewski 1.14152 3/12/1716; BC 5881 Łukszyński to ES 1.23522 undated (?); BC 5935 S. Rubinowicz to ES 1.34965 10/8/1721; BC 5997 A. Zelmanowicz to ES 1.50300–303 Dec.–Jan. 1723–24; EW 86 *Supl.* Chaim arrendator of Nowa Sieniawa 1719, Jewna Lejbowicz 1733; cf. Maimon, *Autobiography*, pp. 15–17; Shlomo of Helma, *Mirkevet Mishna* (Jerusalem, 1975), Haftarat Vayera, p. 16: "... for in general the King or the magnate himself does justice ... but the officials and army officers, whose hands are stretched out to receive bribes so as to influence cases, sometimes prevent justice."

[105] BC 5782 M. Czaplic to ES 1.5892 1/30/1715, 1.5900 9/7/1712 1.5901 10/11/1712, 1.5902 6/14/1715, 1.5909 8/27/1715; BC 5997 A. Zelmanowicz to ES 1.50302 ca. Jan. 1713.

illustrates the tactics that could be utilized to fend off competition and shows how bitter the struggle could become.[106]

The antagonists in this case were Majer Jakubowicz and Fejga, wife of Józef Lejbowicz. From the dates on the correspondence between Sieniawska and these two individuals, it appears that Majer assumed the Końskowoła *arenda* sometime early in the second decade of the eighteenth century and held it until 1721. If Fejga is to be believed, Majer lost the lease to her because of debts he owed to Sieniawska and the Polish royal treasury, and because Fejga tendered a higher bid.[107]

Majer did not accept his ouster with equanimity. According to Fejga, he engaged in a full-scale campaign to dislodge her and regain the *arenda*. His first tactic was harassment. He registered complaints about Fejga, claiming that she did not observe the terms of the contract. Second, Fejga stated, "[The Jews] have mutinied against me due to the incitement of Majer; because he hired them and pays them to ruin me."[108]

Fejga claimed that through bribery Majer enjoyed the support of Sieniawska's local administrators, for neither Narkiewicz nor Karetta, his successor as *ekonom*, would lift a finger to help Fejga enforce the monopoly and stop the "mutiny." Karetta even issued, at Majer's behest, an open invitation to anyone with a claim against Fejga to sue her in his court. Majer also collected briefs (*instancje*) from several Polish notables attempting to convince Sieniawska to cancel his debts and grant him the lease. Of course he promised that eventually she would realize handsome monetary rewards.

On her own behalf, Fejga reminded Sieniawska of how she had

---

[106] The sources for this case are: BC 5806 Fejga to ES 1.10126 undated, 1.10127 undated, 1.10128 undated, 1.10132 1722, 1.10133 1/3/1722, 1.10138 6/12/1722, 1.10139 7/24/1722, 1.10141 9/7/1722, 1.10142 11/2/1722, 1.10143 11/9/1722, 1.10144 11/16/1722, 1.10158 9/16/1724, 1.10159 10/7/1724; BC 5840 Majer Jakubowicz to ES 1.16068 6/8/1714, 1.16069 8/22/1714, 1.16079 5/30/1715, Majer to Lubiszewski 1.16071 2/28/1713, Majer to AMS(?) 1.16088 7/24/1719. Unfortunately all of the correspondence preserved from Majer relates to the period before the dispute with Fejga, ca. 1722–25. Thus we are dependent upon Fejga's letters alone for information on what transpired. For a case similar to this one see EW 179 Satanów 1737 Nine Jews vs. Śprynca.

[107] L.10158 may imply that Fejga held the *arenda* once before, ca. 1715–18, and that Majer won it back, ca. 1718–21.

[108] L.10128.

paid rent in advance and had discharged her other obligations, such as providing oats, before the deadline. This was in contrast to Majer, who owed money from as far back as 1713. As to Majer's promises of huge future profits, Fejga matched them and noted how Majer had lied in the past. Majer, Fejga claimed, was harming the *arenda* with the cooperation of the administrators. This would hurt Sieniawska's interests and had to be stopped.

While the sources do not elucidate the outcome, it is clear that the struggle between Majer and Fejga even took on a violent aspect. Fejga charged that in the synagogue during Sabbath prayers, Majer threatened to beat her husband and that Majer's son did beat up Fejga's messenger, who had gone to market to buy oats for "My Lady's needs."[109]

Besides being called upon to take the part of his arrendator in conflicts with others, there was another type of problem that the magnate was expected to help the arrendator solve. Every arrendator assumed a risk when he signed his contract. He gambled that revenues would exceed the rental fee. There were many factors that could make this gamble a bad one. Even if peasants, townsmen, rival arrendators, administrators, and competing bidders did not harm the *arenda*, many other agents could. The Sieniawski-Czartoryski sources are replete with requests from arrendators asking for abatements due to objective difficulties: flood or drought made mills unworkable; an epidemic prevented peasants from patronizing the tavern and merchants from traveling and paying tolls; local battling forced temporary abandonment of a town or resulted in the destruction of the *arenda* equipment; personal misfortune prevented the arrendator from tending to his business. Sometimes arrendators complained that they were being sent payment orders faster than they could take in revenues.[110]

---

[109] L.10158; cf. Ew 179 Satanów 1737 *Supl.* vs. Ŝprynca and *Pan* Siedlicki.

[110] For examples of requests for abatements due to problems, see: BC 5756 Aron Abramowicz to (?) 1.3 undated: epidemic; BC 5806 Fejga to ES 1.10145 1/2/1723: fire; BC 5840 Irsz Jakubowicz to ES 1.16066 10/20/1722: drought; BC 5882 Łukszyński to ES 1.23609 6/29/1718: drought; BC 5897 Morzycki to ES 1.26564 5/4/1720: fire; EW 179 *Supl.* Moszko Łysowodzki and Jona Abramowicz: war; *Supl.* Satanów Mill arrendators: flood; *Supl.* Lejba Mędlowicz: death in the family. For complaints about the number of payment orders, see: BC 5806 Fejga to ES 1.10149 4/10/1723, 1.10152 10/24/1723; BC 5844 Szymon Józefowicz to ES 1.16738, 16739,

The magnate's decision on whether to respond positively to arrendators' pleas for support in conflicts with others or in the face of natural or man-made calamities was not always an easy one to make. At first glance it might seem that an owner would have every reason to support his arrendators in any way necessary, since the more successful they were, the higher the rent the owner could charge. In reality, however, the magnate had to balance his interests in supporting the arrendator against his interests in supporting other constituencies important to the latifundium's functioning.

For example, in conflicts between peasants and arrendators the owner could be placed in the following uncomfortable position. When negotiating a new contract, the arrendator would refuse an increment on the grounds that the peasants were mutinying and that he was not gaining any profit. Meanwhile the peasants might petition for relief from high prices and highhanded collection practices. If the owner acceded to the petition, he was apt to undermine the *arenda*. If he supplied the arrendator with better means of enforcement, he was liable to drive the peasants to more active resistance or to abandonment of his territory.[111] Similar dilemmas arose with regard to the conflicts between the arrendators and the other groups.[112] The delicate balance that had to be struck in such situations is reflected in a letter written by the Staszów administrator, Kowalski, to Czartoryska. He said: "In the matter between the salt miners and the arrendators of Staszów, I achieved a compromise so that people would not be hurt by the arrendators while revenues owed to the treasury will not be diminished."[113]

Even concerning the simpler problem of whether or not to grant a discount, there was always the question of how necessary the relief was. Perhaps imprisonment of the defaulting arrendator might be more effective.

It is impossible to determine how the owners responded to most

---

16866, May 1723; BC 5886 Szawel Markiewicz to ES 1.24369 undated; BC 5932 Rubcio to Lubiszewski 1.34338 6/26/1714; BC 5997 A. Zelmanowicz to ES 1.50298 7/16/1723.

[111] Gierowski, *Rzeczpospolita,* pp. xxii – xxiv, 44, 52; J. Burszta, "Zbiegostwo chłopów znad Sanu w I ćwierci XVIII wieku," *RDSG* 17 (1955), pp. 55 – 80.

[112] Compare Baron, *History,* vol. 16, p. 402 (n. 21).

[113] BC 5860 A. Kowalski to MZSC 1.19709 7/23/1730.

arrendator requests for aid. Even in cases where their responses are preserved, one cannot always discern the immediate circumstances that prompted them to act as they did. On the basis of the existing responses, however, it is possible to isolate the magnates' apparent guiding principle: maximize profit but preserve capital.

Actions such as making a loan to rebuild brewing facilities after a fire, prohibiting peasants from using their cattle as payment on debts to arrendators, fining those who harmed the *arenda*, or ordering an arrendator to lower prices, all show that the lord was willing to absorb a short-term loss in order to guarantee the long-term ability of his capital to generate income.[114]

Conclusion

For the magnate, Jewish arrendators were an important source of both money and services. Without arrendators, administration, revenue collection, and bill paying would have been much more cumbersome, and cash would have been in much shorter supply. Because of their importance, they were usually treated rationally and were generally lent support. Their demands were, at times, given precedence over those of competing constituencies on the latifundium.

For the arrendator, the contract with the magnate often yielded high financial returns as well as a measure of power to wield over inhabitants of the latifundium. While fundamentally economic in nature, the relationship between the magnate and the arrendator had other aspects that went beyond the mutual economic benefits. The wealth accumulated by a successful arrendator could buy for him not only material objects, but social and political prestige as well. Because of the competitiveness generated by the *arenda* system, the arrendator might find himself at odds with other Jews or with the Jewish community. The contractual nature of the *arenda* put the arrendator, unlike most Jews, in a direct individual relationship with the magnate. Arrendators'

---

[114] EW 179 *Supl.* Helka córka Fajbina of Sieniawa; EW 189 *Supl.* Hercyk Dawidowicz of Sieniawa; EW 525 Szkłow 1716 *Informacja*; BC 4201 Zińków 1745 *Inwentarz* p. 36; BC 5806 Fejga to ES 1.10142 11/2/1722; BC 5946 ES to Zabagłowicz 1.37972 9/1/1725.

power could be employed to do more than enforce the terms of the *arenda* contract. All of this meant that the arrendators in each town enjoyed a special status that potentially enabled them to oppose or dominate their communities. This phenomenon was of crucial importance to the Jewish institutional structure and to the magnate's ability to realize his goals *vis-à-vis* the Jewish community.[115]

[115] See Chapter 7.

CHAPTER SIX

The Jews in the Latifundium Administration

By the eighteenth century, the trend was for the magnates to depend less on leases and more on direct administration as the best means of operating their feudal complexes. By exercising direct control, the magnate might have to exert more effort, but he would gain direct access to the huge profits that his lessees had purportedly been concealing and enjoying. The establishment of a sophisticated administration was facilitated by the existence of a large pool of noblemen who had been dispossessed by the wars and devastation of the mid-seventeenth to early eighteenth centuries.[1] Much of their land was acquired by the magnates, and a natural move for these property-less noblemen was into leasing or administering, on behalf of the magnates, the lands they formerly owned themselves.[2] In this manner noblemen came to dominate the *dzierżawa* leases that still existed.[3] They also formed the main corps of latifundium administrators, entrusted with the task of organizing and increasing agricultural production. They were employed as general managers (*ekonom*) of

---

[1] Kamiński, "Neo-Serfdom," pp. 262–63; W. Kula, "L'histoire économique de la Pologne du XVIII siècle," *APH* 4 (1961), pp. 138–39. On the growing monopoly of magnates over royal leaseholdings (*królewszczyzna*), see Zielińska, *Magnateria polska,* Chapter 2. For statistical analyses of the tendency for nobles with less land to lose it and those who were large landholders to augment their holdings see: T. Sobczak, "Zmiany w stanie posiadania dóbr ziemskich w województwie łęczyckim od XVI do XVIII wieku," *RDSG* 18 (1955), pp. 163–93; W. Szczygielski, "Zmiany w stanie posiadania i w strukturze własnościowej szlachty powiatu wieluńskiego od połowy XVI do końca XVIII wieku," *Rocznik Łódzki* 1 (1958), pp. 295–81; Zytkowicz, "Okres gospodarki," pp. 253–56.

[2] Gierowski and Kamiński, "Eclipse," p. 706; Kula, *Economic Theory,* pp. 146–48.

[3] See Chapter 5, nn. 15–17.

complexes, administrators (*podstarosta*) and assistant administrators (*dwornik*) of manors, and stewards (*marszałek*) of palaces.[4] The lower members of the administration, the employees in charge of sheep, forests, dairy and poultry production, gardening, cooking, and the like were recruited from the peasantry. For them a job in the manorial service (*służba folwarczna*) was one of the few paths leading to a modicum of economic security and social mobility.[5]

Noblemen and peasants possessed the skills and traditions appropriate to managing agricultural production, and considerations of economics and prestige prompted them to place their skills at the service of the magnates. It is therefore not surprising to find that Jews appear infrequently as agricultural managers in the Sieniawski-Czartoryski sources.[6] In my examination of the material, I found no Jewish *podstarosta* or *dwornik*. The one Jew who appears in a position that dealt with agriculture, the *ekonom* Rubinowicz, was a general manager whose responsibilities included many things in addition to agricultural production.[7] Jews who aspired to positions of agricultural management had to compete directly with noblemen,[8] and face the resistance of both nobility and peasantry to the Jews serving in administrative positions.[9] Jews, then, did not typically make their careers in

[4] Szkurłatowski, p. 156; Pośpiech and Tygielski, pp. 227–31; cf. A. Makowska, "Pracownicy najemni wielkiej własności na przykładzie dóbr sandomierskich Czartoryskich w XVIII wieku," *Społeczeństwo Staropolskie*, vol. 2, A. Wyczański, ed. (Warsaw, 1979), pp. 315–36; Bergerówna, pp. 176–229.

[5] Szkurłatowski, p. 156.

[6] Sieniawska's *ekonomi* in Tenczyn were, successively, Stanisław Lublicki, Piotr Morzycki, and Andrzej Zabagłowicz. Similarly, the list of *ekonomi* and *podstarości* for the Sieniawa-Oleszyce complex (BC 4824, pp. 326–34) does not include any Jews. Analogously, in the *spław* trade Jews were neither skippers nor sailors, but were *szafarze* and *pisarze*; see Chapter 4.

[7] On the responsibilities of an *ekonom* see n. 51; as to Rubinowicz's variegated activities, see below.

[8] Goldberg, "Poles and Jews," p. 262; B. D. Weinryb, *Neueste Wirtschaftsgeschichte der Juden in Russland und Polen* (Hildesheim–New York, 1972), pp. VIII*–XI*.

[9] *AGZ*, vol. 23, no. 5.21; vol. 25, nos. 16.13, 174.34, 307.40; EW 1509 *Supl.* Iwan Parzyło et al., undated; EW 394 *Reflexje nad przyrzeczonym kontraktem*. Of course resistance to Jews in these positions is virtually incontrovertible proof that they occupied them. In the Sieniawski territories, however, the resentment seems to have had an effect and only a few Jews, such as R, could attain the coveted positions. Even this small number was enough to induce rivals for their posts to keep up the pressure. Cf.

manorial management. When they were able to overcome these obstacles and rise to such positions, their circumstances were less secure than those of other administrators.[10]

Jews were virtually absent from the other main branch of the latifundium staff, the court (*dwór*). The Sieniawski-Czartoryski payrolls and lists of court retainers and servants outfitted with uniforms include hundreds of people, but only one Jew.[11] Here, in addition to factors of economic tradition and competition, the lack of Jews can be attributed to social-cultural factors. The magnate court was a hub of Polish cultural life and rich camaraderie based on common values and cultural traditions.[12] The court staff had to be immersed in Polish culture in order to facilitate or participate in court life. Jews, who were unversed in Polish culture and who were bound by Jewish laws governing diet and social behavior, would have had great difficulties participating either as principals or servants in the Polish-style court life, with its un-Jewish food, dress, and modes of behavior.

On the basis of the available Sieniawski-Czartoryski sources, it is apparent that on the latifundia Jews performed control and distribution functions. Jews were concentrated in the positions of overseer (*dozorca*), stackyard supervisor (*gummienny*), steward (*szafarz*), clerk (*pisarz*), and factor (*faktor*).[13] All but the last of these were respon-

---

Bałaban, *Historja Żydów,* vol. 2, pp. 154–56; Bergerówna, pp. 184, 193; Halpern, "Gezerot Voshchilo," pp. 64–75; M. Lech, "Powstanie chłopów białoruskich w starostwie krzyczewskim (1740 r.)," *PH* 51 (1960), p. 316.

[10] See the difficulties faced by Rubinowicz described below.

[11] BC 2527 Accounts of all the Expenses for Staff . . . 1713–20; BC 2626 Army Accounts of AMS, pp. 11–15 is a register of AMS's entourage for 1703. Pages 37 and 42–44 are court payrolls for Berezhany in 1706; BC 2677 Budget for AMS's Kitchen . . . 1711, the only Jew identified among the members of the kitchen and household staff is: "*Żyd Szafarz* (The Jewish Steward)"; BC 2904 no. 51 Miscellaneous Accounts for the Court of AMS 1717–26; included are lists of all the *dwór* staff outfitted with uniforms during this period. In all of these lists the only identifiable Jew is "*Żyd Szafarz.*" It is noteworthy that this one Jew on the household staff served in a typically Jewish capacity, i.e., as a control official.

[12] Pośpiech and Tygielski, pp. 224–336.

[13] This statement is based on information culled from the following files: BC: 2165, 2581/1, 2626, 2677, 2904, 3507, 4065, 4075, 4818–22, 5782 1.5897 7/18/1712, 1.5903–904 6/27/1713, 7/5/1713, 1.5906 3/25/1714, 5806 1.10086–0087, 1/25/1723, 6/3/1727, 5881 1.23468–72 ca. 1712, 5886 1.24374 7/11?/1717, 5897 1.26494 8/7/1717, 5943 1.37133 8/7/1703, 5972 1.45326 11/20/1714. EW: 133, 135, 171,

sible for keeping track of what was produced or purchased and how it was distributed.[14] The need for a sophisticated control and distribution administration was the result of the development of the latifundia on a large scale. The items produced on the latifundia or collected as taxes had to be shipped to a central location, stored, distributed internally, or marketed. This required organizational capabilities, literacy and accurate record keeping, arithmetic and bookkeeping skills, and the ability to handle money. Moreover, allocation of latifundium resources and marketing of surplus inventory required a degree of entrepreneurial experience enabling the administrator to judge the most opportune time to buy or sell.[15]

In other words, the requirements of control and distribution called for skills of a commercial nature. As we have seen, Jews were the preeminent commercial group on the latifundia. They were also probably the most highly literate group in Poland—albeit in Hebrew or Yiddish.[16] Centuries of commercial experience conditioned them to manage money,[17] warehouses, granaries, and larders. Jewish entrepreneurial traditions, passed down through the generations, trained them to make informed marketing decisions. All of these factors favored the concentration of Jews in the control and distribution sector of the administration.

Probably the latifundium position most commonly identified with Jews was that of factor. This term was used broadly in Poland and connoted different responsibilities in different contexts.[18] According to the Sieniawski-Czartoryski sources, factors were utilized as a means of:

176, 189, 282, 394; GOSP: 340, 407, 428, 478, 574, 597, 602, 853, 1014, 1015, 1104, 1472, 1505.

[14] Arrendators, though not salaried members of the administration, also fall into this category, since they marketed grain in the form of liquor and paid many of the magnate's bills. In some cases the town arrendator continued to serve as *de facto ekonom* of the private city as had been the case before 1648; cf. S. Ettinger, "Helkam," pp. 136–38.

[15] Baron, *History*, vol. 16, p. 234; C. Biernat, *Statystyka obrotu towarowego Gdańska w latach 1651–1815* (Warsaw, 1962), p. 23.

[16] W. Urban, "Umiejętność pisania w Małopolsce," *PH* 68 (1977), pp. 236–53.

[17] Ettinger, "Helkam," p. 126 (n. 70); Czapliński and Długosz, p. 89.

[18] Cf. Nadav, p. 128.

- procuring supplementary food or other needs for the local complex, commonly when the owner was coming to visit and extra grain and food were required to feed his entourage.
- procuring specialty items for the magnate or supplementing the major purchases made in Gdańsk during the *spław* expeditions; buying diamonds or locating vinegar, for example.
- marketing surplus latifundium produce not shipped to Gdańsk, such as dairy products and, in some years, grain.
- serving as the owner's agent in locations outside of the latifundium and for special missions such as negotiating land sales with another magnate or a foreigner.

Remuneration for factor services usually consisted of a commission based on the value of the goods procured or marketed or the value of the deal negotiated.

While factors can be described as middlemen, they did not all serve identical functions or enjoy equal status. There were petty factors who engaged in sporadic procurement or marketing on a small scale at the order of a latifundium official. There were also factors who regularly handled large quantities of expensive items and dealt directly with the owners. What does seem to be true is that despite the application of the title "factor" to certain individuals, factoring was not a full-time occupation. Rather, individuals who engaged in pursuits that put them in a good position to render factor services—merchants or arrendators—were called upon more or less frequently to perform the factor functions. Being a factor was but one source of an individual's livelihood, although the title probably conferred a degree of prestige that aided his other endeavors.

Dr. Mojżesz Fortis

At least some of the aspects of factoring, including its part-time nature, are illustrated by the career of the most prestigious of the Sieniawski factors, Dr. Mojżesz Fortis.

The Jewish doctor who, through his medical skill, becomes the confidant and agent of powerful non-Jews, thereby attaining wealth and power, is a common phenomenon in Jewish history. Mojżesz Fortis, as physician and factor to Elżbieta Sieniawska, held true to this pattern. Since he knew Latin[19] and was almost certainly part of the famous Fortis family,[20] it is probable that Fortis, like many other Polish Jews, received his medical training at either the University of Padua or at one of the German universities that opened their doors to Jews in the second half of the seventeenth century.[21]

[19] BC 5809 F to ES 1.10736 – 53 9/22/1714 – 9/24/1726, passim.

[20] This was a family of Italian and Polish doctors and rabbis. The most distinguished member of the Polish branch was Abraham Isaac Fortis, d. ca. 1731, who served as court physician to the Potocki and Lubomirski magnate families. He was a central figure on the Council of Four Lands and played a pivotal role in the communal controversies of his time. On his activities and biography see *PVAA* Index s.v. Fortis; *EJG*, vol. 6, p. 1055 (M. Bałaban); *EJE*, vol. 6, p. 1443 (I. Halpern); and bibliography in all three places. Bałaban in the *EJG* article claimed that Mojżesz was probably one of Isaac's sons. If this is so then he was probably the eldest because he was already established as a factor and doctor in 1710, while Isaac's son Solomon only began medical school in Padua in 1716, and his daughter Haya married Jacob Haim Halpern in the 1720s, at the earliest. It may be that Mojżesz was a nephew or cousin or even brother of Isaac. Given their distinctive last name and the fact that it is traceable to a specific family line in Italy (see: I. Levi, "Famiglie Distinte e Benemerite della com. Isr. di Mantova," *Il Vessilo Israelitico* 54 [1906], pp. 19,76 – 77), it is almost certain that they were related.

[21] On Jews in these universities, see: A. Freimann, "Briefwechsel eines Studenten der Medizin in Frankfurt a.d. Oder mit dem in Halle Medizin studierenden Isak Wallach im Jahre 1702," *Zeitschrift für Hebräische Bibliographie* 14 (1910), pp. 117 – 23; H. Friedenwald, *The Jews and Medicine*, vol. 1 (Baltimore, 1944), pp. 221 – 40; L. Lewin, "Die Jüdischen Studenten an der Universität Frankfurt a.d. Oder," *JJLG* 14 (1921), pp. 216 – 38, 15 (1923), pp. 59 – 96, 16 (1924), pp. 43 – 86; idem, "Jüdische Aerzte in Gross-Polen," *JJLG* 9 (1911), pp. 367 – 420, see especially p. 378; A. Modena and E. Morpugo, *Medici e Chirughi Ebrei Dottorati e Licenziati nell' Universita di Padova dal 1617 al 1816*, (Bologna, 1967); M. Richarz, *Der Eintritt der Juden in die Akademischen Berufe* (Tübingen, 1974), pp. 28 – 82; P. Rieger, "Deutsche Juden als Heidelberger Studenten im 18. Jahrhundert," *M. Philippson Festschrift* (Leipzig, 1916), pp. 178 – 83; J. Warchal, "Żydzi polscy na uniwersytecie padewskim," *Kwartalnik poświęcony badaniu przeszłości Żydów w Polsce* 1 (1912), pp. 37 – 72; Solomon Fortis is listed as entering the University of Frankfurt/Oder in 1716 (Lewin, "Jüdische Studenten, " vol. 16, pp. 60 – 61). Bałaban stated, *Die Judenstadt von Lublin* (Berlin, 1919), p. 70, without references, that Isaac Fortis attended the same institution, but Lewin did not list him. Lieberman Levi Ostilla, who was Isaac Fortis's partner in Lublin and who was, perhaps, his brother as well (Bałaban assumed so, probably based on the etymological connection between Ostilla and Fortis and the fact that both had fathers named Samuel), was listed by Modena and Morpugo, under no. 89, and by Warchal, pp. 62, 65. Halpern assumed that Isaac Fortis completed his medical training in Italy and Modena and Morpugo, no. 145

Fortis must have faced the problems common to all Jewish medical students of his era. Such men had to acquire the necessary preparation in languages and science, overcome conflicts between religious and academic obligations, and deal with discrimination against Jews in the forms of higher fees, harder examinations, hostile faculty attitudes, and reluctance to grant formal degrees.[22] Once they completed their training, they were confronted by Christian doctors, who resented competition, as well as by Church doctrine—repeatedly reaffirmed in Poland—which prohibited Jewish doctors from treating Christian patients.[23] Nevertheless, the shortage of doctors, the low standard of medical training in Poland, and superstitions about the Jews and medicine created a demand for university-trained Jewish doctors. Polish kings, magnates, and even highly placed members of the clergy employed Jewish physicians, so that it was no novelty for Elżbieta Sieniawska to choose to take advantage of Fortis's services.[24]

The sources do not mention when Fortis began treating Sieniawska, but he was already established as one of her factors—and presumably as her doctor—in Jarosław as early as 1710 and was still practicing medicine in 1731. In 1720 Fortis moved to Wrocław where he was

---

listed "Forti Isacco, ebreo . . ." who graduated from the Padua school on June 18, 1700. It may be that this was the Isaac Fortis of later Polish fame. Other members of the Fortis family listed are nos. 111, 134, 144, 145. Mojżesz Fortis may be signified by Warchal, p. 62, Modena and Morpugo, no. 110, "Polacco Mose qm. Isacco, ebreo di Lublino . . ." graduated Oct. 14, 1687.

[22] On the problems of Jewish medical students in this period, see: A. Berliner, "Aus den Memoiren eines Römischen Ghetto-Jünglings," *Jahrbuch für Jüdische Geschichte und Literatur* 7 (1904), pp. 110–32; T. Cohen, *Maaseh Tuvia* (Venice, 1707), Introduction of the author, pp. 5b–c; Friedenwald; Lewin, "Jüdische Studenten."

[23] Isaac Fortis and Lieberman Levi Ostigla (Ostilla) were sued in the Crown Tribunal in Lublin in 1710 for treating Christians, see Bałaban, *Judenstadt von Lublin*, p. 70. See also: Lewin, "Jüdische Studenten," vol. 14, pp. 218–21; N. M. Gelber, "Letoldot Harofim Hayehudim Bepolin Bameah Ha-18," *Shai Leyeshayahu* (Tel Aviv, 1957), p. 347.

[24] Gelber, "Letoldot Harofim Hayehudim Bepolin," pp. 347, 352–53. It may not be coincidental that Mojżesz Fortis was in ES's employ. She was a Lubomirski, and Isaac Fortis was physician to the Lubomirski court in Rzeszów.

attached for a period of several years to the court of Prince Konstantyn Sobieski, brother of Sieniawska's lover.[25]

It is evident from the correspondence that Fortis's medical services were in demand. He treated Sieniawska and members of her family and was at the disposal of her officials. The letters record how Sieniawska sent Fortis to treat her husband and had him take care of her daughter. She also asked him to prescribe medicine for sick administrators, and the administrators sometimes summoned Fortis on their own. In addition, he was apparently free to receive patients not directly connected to the magnate court.[26]

One striking feature of Fortis's medical practice was its geographic range. The letters specifically record his being called to Jarosław, Rzeszów, and Sanok, a radius of thirty-five miles, to treat patients. In addition, he probably made occasional trips to Sieniawa and elsewhere. The *ekonom* Rubinowicz once went all the way from Rytwiany to Jarosław, about one hundred miles, to be treated by Fortis.[27]

Besides practicing medicine, Fortis dealt in pharmacology. As was characteristic for the era, he derived part of his income from the concoction of proprietary medicines for specific patients. Sometimes he forwarded them from his laboratory by post after having made the diagnosis in person.[28]

One of the crucial elements in Fortis's success was his ability to gain the trust of his powerful patients. Their confidence paved the way for him to broaden the scope of his services to include political and economic activity. He appears in the Jarosław accounts with the

[25] GOSP 602, p. 151; BC 5767 Borgolt to MZSC 1.2901 6/27/1631; Lewin, "Jüdische Studenten," vol. 16, pp. 84–85. On ES and Prince Aleksander Sobieski see Brablec, pp. 29–30. By 1730 F was apparently back living in Jarosław; see: BC 5767 Borgolt to MZSC 1.2873 9/27/1730, 1.2901 6/27/1731.

[26] BC 5767 Borgolt to MZSC 1.2873 9/27/1730, 1.2901 6/27/1731; BC 5809 F to ES 1.10742 3/21/1721, 1.10743 4/9/1721, 1.10747 3/5/1724; BC 5881 Łukszyński to ES 1.23494 4/29/1714; 1.34684 3/16/1719; BC 5943 ES to AMS 1.37125 11/30/17(??).

[27] BC 5809 F to ES 1.10742 3/21/1721; BC 5881 Łukszyński to ES 1.23494 4/29/1714; BC 5934 R to ES 1.34684 3/16/1719.

[28] BC 5809 F to ES 1.10743 4/9/1721, F to R 1.10754 8/3/1721.

title of factor,[29] and the correspondence confirms the fact of his nonmedical activity on behalf of Sieniawska.

In his role as factor, the Sieniawski-Czartoryski correspondence records Fortis's activities in procuring goods, especially luxury items, for the use of the magnates, as well as his serving as Sieniawska's business representative in locations removed from the latifundium. The story of how, on two occasions, Fortis served these functions sheds much light on the institution of the factor.

By 1720, Fortis had moved from Jarosław to Wrocław, where he lived for several years. One of his first acts there was to fill Sieniawska's order for some diamond brooches.[30] In June 1720 he negotiated the purchase with a Jewish diamond merchant, settling on the price of 235 *czerwony złoty*. Fortis advanced the merchant a down payment of 35 *cz. zł.*[31] out of his own funds and promised to pay the rest by August 22. In the meantime, he sent the brooches to Sieniawska, requesting that she remit the full amount immediately. After some delay she sent the money but said nothing about the brooches. After several of his letters asking her if she was pleased with them went unanswered, Fortis began to fear that she did not like the brooches and that he had fallen from favor. As a result, he offered to return the brooches, absorbing any consequent loss himself.[32]

This episode demonstrates the requirements as well as some of the risks of factoring. Fortis was valuable to Sieniawska because she could trust him, because he had the contacts that enabled him to purchase diamonds easily and at a reasonable price, and because he had enough of his own cash to be able to advance the down payment. He risked Sieniawska's failure to send him the balance of the money on time or her displeasure with the merchandise. Yet the potential benefits from his relationship to Sieniawska must have outweighed the

[29] GOSP 602, p. 151.

[30] The first letter posted from Wrocław is BC 5809 F to ES 1.10740 7/16/1720. F received official permission to settle in the city 9/9/1721; see Lewin, "Jüdische Studenten," vol. 16, pp. 84–85. The datelines on the letters show that F did a lot of traveling back East. On the diamond brooch incident, see BC 5809 F to ES 1.10740 7/16/1720.

[31] By way of comparison, in 1731 the license for the Sieniawa rabbinate for three years cost 80 *czerwony złoty*; see BC 2905, no. 119.

[32] BC 5809 F to ES 1.10739 10/22/1720 (where he refers to other, nonextant letters on this topic, 1.10740 7/16/1720, 1.10741 11/26/1720.

risks, for Fortis seems to have been much more disturbed by the prospect of losing Sieniawska as a client than by the loss of 35 *cz. zł.* As he wrote,[33]

> I told the servant who picked up the brooches that in case they were not pleasing they should be returned here immediately and I would collect 200 *cz. zł.* for them; because the Jew who sold them assured me that if they were not pleasing that only the 35 *cz. zł.* down payment would be lost, but that he would refund the 200 *cz. zł.* If, then, this is the reason for the lack of My Lady's favor let My Lady quickly send the brooches here and I will collect the 200 *cz. zł.*, adding my own 35 *cz. zł.* so that My Lady will not incur any loss. I will remit the money to whomever My Lady designates because I esteem My Lady's favor more than money. However poor I may be, even if I lose everything, I will remember to preserve my honor. . . . Such is my sorrow over My Lady's disfavor that I do not know how I can live. . . .

Fortis evidently reached some accommodation with Sieniawska, for two years later, in 1722, he was involved as her business agent in a most sensitive negotiation. The German-Jewish banker, Behrend Lehmann, had assumed the debts of Stanisław Leszczyński, the sometime king of Poland.[34] In return he acquired the rights to the city of Leszno, worth more than 20,000 *zł.* annually, and offered to sell them to Elżbieta Sieniawska. Sieniawska sent Fortis to Germany to enter into negotiations with Lehmann, and he successfully concluded a preliminary agreement. Fortis wrote to Sieniawska, urging her to finalize the deal in Warsaw, stressing the need for haste so as not to keep Lehmann waiting. Lehmann's influence was needed to expedite Sieniawska's affairs that Fortis was conducting in Berlin and it was important to show him every courtesy.[35]

This incident also serves to illustrate the factor at work. It demon-

---

[33] BC 5809 F to ES 1.10741 11/26/1720. Cf. Gierowski, "Wrocławskie interesy," pp. 232–33.

[34] On Behrend Lehmann, see E. Lehmann, *Der Polnische Resident Behrend Lehmann* (Dresden, 1885); J. Meisl, "Behrend Lehmann und der Sächsische Hof," *JJLG* 16 (1924), pp. 227–52; S. Stern, *The Court Jew* (Philadelphia, 1950), see Index. On Lehmann's financial dealings with Leszczyński and his acquisition of the rights to Leszno and environs, see L. Lewin, *Geschichte der Juden in Lissa* (Pinne, 1904), pp. 127–29.

[35] BC 5809 F to ES 1.10744–46, 8/18/1722, 9/15/1722, 5/9/1723.

strates that Fortis was no mere order-filler, but rather a trusted pleni-potentiary who was expected to use his discretion and judgment. He both conducted sensitive negotiations and offered his assessment of the matter. His imparting of advice implies that his word carried weight, and his reminding Sieniawska of the interconnection between the business at hand and her interests in Berlin suggests that he was more conversant with this facet of her operations than she was.

As busy as Fortis may have been as physician and factor, his liveli-hood was not limited to these pursuits. Sometimes he represented other people's business interests, such as those of his brother-in-law and the Wrocław merchant firm of Tarone and Bordalo.[36] He also mentioned two other enterprises in the correspondence.

Fortis wrote to Sieniawska from Wrocław several times to request that she protect property he left behind in a building in Jarosław owned by one Boruchowicz, since deceased. He emphasized that in addition to his personal property, the cache included chattels of noblemen—pledges taken from his noblemen debtors. Moreover, Fortis insisted that he had the right to seize Boruchowicz's building as payment for a debt. Thus it is obvious that Fortis derived part of his income from moneylending.[37]

Fortis was also one of the few Jewish *dzierżawcy*. In a series of letters he asked Sieniawska's intervention in his struggle against the *starosta* of Stara Krupica and his peasant administrator. They were trying to dislodge Fortis from his *dzierżawa* there, resorting to force and accusations of blasphemy in order to do so.[38]

There is a clear connection between Fortis being a Jew and his occupations. As physician, factor, and moneylender, he was engaged in traditionally Jewish endeavors. His common language—literally and figuratively—with other Jews such as the diamond merchant and Behrend Lehmann enhanced his efforts. As *dzierżawca* he was con-fronted with the usual resistance that nobles and peasants displayed toward Jews in this post.

---

[36] Gierowski, "Wrocławskie interesy," p. 232. F also advised ES about other land deals; e.g., BC 5809 F to R 1.10754 8/3/1721.

[37] BC 5809 F to ES 1.10738 10/6/1718, 1.10739 10/22/1720, 1.10741 11/26/1720, 1.10746 5/9/1723.

[38] BC 5809 F to ES 1.10747–53 3/5/1724, 1/18/1724, 8/26/1724, 9/17/1724, 11/24/1724, 12/3/1724, 9/24/1726.

Yisrael Rubinowicz—General Manager

Fortis was not the only Jew to reach the upper echelons of the Sieniawski-Czartoryski administration. One of the key positions in the latifundium, that of general manager (*ekonom*)[39] of the Rytwiany-Lubnice complex, including the town of Staszów, was occupied for many years by Yisrael Rubinowicz. His example illustrates the upper limits to which a Jew could rise in the administration, and his experiences exemplify some of the problems faced by Jewish administrators.

More than four hundred letters were exchanged between Rubinowicz and Elżbieta Sieniawska and the Czartoryskis, and mention of Rubinowicz is found in Sieniawska's correspondence with her husband and her officials in Tenczyn. It is obvious from these references that Rubinowicz was a central figure in the Sieniawski-Czartoryski administration.[40] Elżbieta Sieniawska personally conducted the affairs of her territories around Lublin and in Red Russia, where she spent most of her time. She rarely crossed the Vistula to visit her property around Cracow and Sandomierz, however. The administration of this westernmost part of the latifundium was the responsibility of Rubinowicz and the successive managers of Tenczyn.[41]

The correspondence confirms the description of Rubinowicz written by R. Jacob Emden in his autobiography, *Megilat Sefer*.[42] Emden, recounting the tribulations of his father, the Hakham Zvi Ashkenazi, told how finally the unfortunate rabbi came under the patronage of

the famous and praiseworthy R. Yisrael of Rytwiany,[43] an official,

[39] See Chapter 1; cf. Makowska, pp. 317–20.

[40] BC 5934–35 R to ES, AAC, MZSC and others, 1.34553–1.34961, 1705–42; BC 5943 ES to R 1.37211 6/1/1708. ES to AMS 1.37260 6/8/1709; BC 5944–45 ES to Morzycki 1.37500 2/19/1716, 1.37597 9/11/1718, 1.37689 7/21/1720, 1.37691 8/4/1720, 1.37704 10/19/1720, 1.37747 8/11/1721, 1.37762 10/12/1721, 1.37786 2/3/1722; BC 5946 ES to Zabagłowicz 1.37965 7/16/1725.

[41] Gierowski, "Wrocławskie interesy," pp. 222–23. For a description of this administration in the second half of the eighteenth century, see Makowska.

[42] Y. Y. Emden, *Megilat Sefer* (New York, 1956), p. 44.

[43] I am certain that Emden's R. Yisrael is the Rubinowicz of the Polish sources on the following counts:

a) R. Yisrael was Sieniawski's *ekonom* in Rytwiany for a period that included the years ca. 1714–18 when the Hakham Zvi took shelter with him.

called *ekonom*, of the great magnate Sieniawska who owned vast territory and many towns in Poland, and many serfs. This R. Yisrael was appointed over her property as head official. He controlled all of the income and disbursements of the magnate. Everything was done by him. He was the chief. Thus he was very powerful. . . .

The sources do not yield very much biographical information about Rubinowicz, nor do they recount how he rose to his post. It is known, however, that in April 1724 his first wife died after thirty years of marriage,[44] and that in April 1736 he requested the appointment of his grandson, Simha, as rabbi of Kalush. (This was the young man's second rabbinical post.)[45] In July of that year Rubinowicz referred to himself as "old and weak; I can't work."[46] Thus it is reasonable to assume that Rubinowicz was born before 1675.

His earliest existing letter to Sieniawska is dated January 8, 1705.[47] In a letter to August Aleksander Czartoryski on July 7, 1736, Rubinowicz noted, "I have been *ekonom* here for several decades."[48] The

---

b) Rubinowicz was Sieniawska's *ekonom* in Rytwiany ca. 1705–42, including the years 1714–18.

c) In this period there is no other *ekonom* on record in Rytwiany nor any other Jewish *ekonom* on record in any of the Sieniawski territories.

d) It was very common in Poland for Jews to refer to each other by first name as "Reb so-and-so," while in Polish documents the first name and patronymic or patronymic alone was employed (Rubinowicz = son of Rubin).

e) In AKP D.S. 2 Inventory for Staszów, the main town of the Rytwiany *Klucz*, April 22, 1733, p. 32, the largest house belonged to Israel (= Yisrael) Rubinowicz.

f) A letter from Fortis to Rubinowicz (BC 5809 1.10754 8/3/1721) is addressed in Polish to "*Pan* Rubinowicz" and in Hebrew to "the Katzin Mar Yisrael" (see below p. 172 and n. 113).

[44] BC 5935 R to ES 1.34808 4/19/1724.

[45] BC 5935 R to AAC 1.34931 4/28/1736.

[46] BC 5935 R to AAC 1.34934 7/7/1736.

[47] BC 5934 R to ES 1.34568 1/8/1705, the subject is marketing latifundium salt. The first actual reference to him as "*Pisarz i Rachmistrz Generalny*" occurs in BC 5943 1.37211 6/1/1708 in the address of a letter ES sent to R. Since this is also the earliest extant letter from ES to R, it is probable that he assumed his title earlier but not too much so because ES inherited this territory from her uncle, Stanisław Opaliński, only in 1704 and could not have appointed R to his post before then. See Brablec, pp. 57–58, 125–26.

[48] BC 5935 R to AAC 1.34934 7/7/1736.

last dated letter he wrote to Czartoryski was on June 29, 1742.[49] From these dates and my assumption about his age, it appears that Rubinowicz assumed his responsibilities while in his thirties and served for almost forty years. He served longer than any other administrator whose correspondence is collected in the archives.[50]

The day-to-day conduct of business catalogued in the correspondence casts Rubinowicz's professional responsibilities into sharp relief. As manager of a large complex, Rubinowicz answered directly to Elżbieta Sieniawska (and later to her daughter and son-in-law), a very demanding boss who issued precise instructions and knew what results she wanted. His job required an ability to deal with the peasants, nobility, and townsmen connected with the latifundium and an absolute commitment to increasing the income of the owners.[51]

Rubinowicz's Jewishness did create obstacles to his performance. To begin with, it was illegal for a Jew to be an *ekonom*, and so Rubinowicz had to be content with a lower-grade title. As he noted in 1736, "A Catholic manager would be called *ekonom*, but I with the title of *pisarz* (clerk) oversee everything."[52] Second, many Poles were

---

[49] BC 5935 R to AAC 1.34961 6/29/1742.

[50] See Indeks Archiwum Książąt Czartoryskich I. Oddział listów. The fact that Rubinowicz was always addressed by his patronymic may hint that his father preceded him in serving the Sieniawskis and that his position as administrator was inherited. Other biographic details on R that can be gleaned from the sources are: He had at least two daughters and one son. One daughter married a certain Judka who was a rabbi and served in Sieniawa and Kalush. (In Hebrew his name was R. Yehuda Leib ben Simha Zunz.) See Z. H. Horwitz, *Letoldot Hakehillot Bepolin* (Jerusalem, 1978), p. 523; note that, contrary to Horwitz's statement, R. Zunz did not sign the pro-Eybeshutz Proclamation of 1753 (see Y. Eybeshutz, *Luhot Eidut*, Altona, 1755, pp. 50–51). The fact is that, according to Rubinowicz, he died in 1736 (see BC 5935 R to AAC 1.34931 4/28/1736). See also: N. Z. Friedman, *Otzar Harabanim*, (Bnei Brak, n.d.), no. 6829. In 1710 R built a house in Koniemłota, but ES requested that he live in one of her castles in either Rytwiany or Lubnice and he apparently complied. In 1713 R was seriously ill, and after the death of his first wife he remarried.

[51] On the responsibilities of an *ekonom*, see Bergerówna, pp. 183–91; Rychlikowa, *Wodzicki,* pp. 73–86; Serczyk, pp. 33–34; Szkurłatowski, p. 154. On ES's style as manager of the entire latifundium see: Brablec, pp. 30–32, 134–37; Gierowski, "Wrocławskie interesy," pp. 222–26.

[52] In BC 5934 R to ES 1.34581 4/24/1710 and BC 5935 R to AAC 1.34934 7/7/1736 R described himself as an *ekonom*. In BC 5943 1.37211 6/1/1708, ES addressed him as "Pan Rubinowicz, *Pisarz i Rachmistrz Generalny* Dóbr Moich." Emden, p. 44, called Rubinowicz "*ekonom*." The reason for this discrepancy is

unwilling to cooperate with a Jew wielding authority. Despite this, Rubinowicz insisted that he did his job well. As he once remarked to Sieniawska, "It is said that in this country where it is sometimes necessary to be harsh and to threaten that authority should not be granted to a Jew . . . I request that My Lady withdraw the authority if I have served you poorly."[53] Later, he wrote to Czartoryski,[54]

> I have been *ekonom* here for several decades. There were at different times Swedes, Moscow [*sic*], Saxons, and Cossacks as well as several floods; but the people, revenue and property remained. Only construction was a perennial problem. But in the worst of years, when there was a flood or some ruinous calamities, the property generated up to 60,000 *złoty*. . . .

Rubinowicz's responsibilities included supervising all branches of latifundium industry, serving as the owner's representative, and managing finances.

Supervision of latifundium industries. The primary industry, from the perspective of effort invested, was grain and vegetable production. Rubinowicz, through his subordinates, ensured that peasants had enough seed to sow, enforced feudal dues, kept track of how much was harvested, and saw that it was stored and distributed properly. This involved much paperwork, inspection trips to the manors, and, when necessary, forcing the peasants to live up to their obligations.[55]

---

explained by R in the citation given here, BC 5935 1.34934 7/7/1736. Sometimes, however, even ES's official documents recognized reality and gave R's title as "*ekonom*"; see AKP D.S. 80, 84. Makowska, p. 317 pointed out that the title "*pisarz generalny*," denoting the highest official on the Rytwiany-Lubnice complex, was applied to Rubinowicz's successors. It is noteworthy that Polish sources give Radziwiłł's famous administrator, Szmul Ickowicz, the title "*Kasjer Generalny*" which is equivalent to "*Rachmistrz*," i.e., cashier, treasurer; see Lech, pp. 315–16; Halpern, "Gezeirot Voshchilo," p. 60. His power, however, like R's, went far beyond financial record keeping; cf. Bergerówna, pp. 184–93.

[53] BC 5934 R to ES 1.34633 4/16/1714. For similar expressions by R on the difficulties of being a Jewish administrator and his success nonetheless, see BC 5934 R to ES 1.34583 5/14/1710, 1.34588 12/19/1710.

[54] BC 5935 R to ES 1.34934 7/7/1736.

[55] See, for examples, BC 5934–35 R to ES 1.34554 undated, 1.34569 1/16/1705, 1.34575 10/16/1709, 1.34583 5/14/1710, 1.34606 11/11/1712, 1.34625 8/15/1713, 1.34633 4/16/1714, 1.34870 5/3/1724, 1.34872 12/5/1725; BC 5943 ES to R 1.37211 6/1/1708; AKP D.S. 84.

Similarly, Rubinowicz had to account for the livestock (cattle, swine, poultry, and sheep) in addition to the wool, tallow, skins, meat, and dairy products they produced. He also supervised the management of the fish yield, the mineral and forest industries, the saber factory, and the hay-cutting in the meadows.[56]

In addition, Rubinowicz found arrendators, negotiated contracts, collected payments, and protected arrendators from elements that threatened their capacity to earn a profit. He also oversaw compliance with the contracts and punished those who were delinquent.[57] When, for instance, the distillery of Lubnice burned down due to the carelessness of the arrendator, Rubinowicz ordered him to rebuild the enterprise at his own expense or be put in irons.[58] Sometimes, however, he had to compromise, as in the case of the ''short Jewess'' who was 750 zł. in arrears. Rubinowicz said, ''I was forced to settle for 150 zł. and I don't know if she will pay that.''[59]

Essential to the functioning of the complex were the hundreds of buildings and pieces of equipment it contained. Rubinowicz also was in charge of these. He had to be apprised as to the state of barns, taverns, and breweries, and it was his responsibility to be sure that he had the budget, materials, and workmen to maintain and repair them.[60] Besides this routine care of buildings and equipment, special construction projects also came under the manager's aegis. At one point he complained that for two years construction projects had required most

[56] BC 5934–35 R to ES and AAC 1.34564 undated, 1.34569 1/16/1705, 1.34574 2/14/1709, 1.34575 10/16/1709, 1.34640 7/18/1714, 1.34872 12/5/1725, 1.34873, 1.34875, 1.34879, ca. 1726, 1.34887 5/15/1726, 1.34894 7/24/1726, 1.34941 9/25/1738, 1.34942 11/18/1738; BC 5946 ES to Zabagłowicz 1.38022 9/24/1726, R to Zabagłowicz 1.38025 10/3/1726; AKP D.S. 84.

[57] BC 5934–35 R to ES and AAC 1.34574 2/14/1709, 1.34575 10/16/1709, 1.34584 7/8/1710, 1.34615 4/11/1713, 1.34632 (?) 4/6/1714, 1.34686 7/30/1719, 1.34724 10/30/1721, 1.34733 6/10/1722, 1.34737 7/10/1722, 1.34805 2/18/1724, 1.34888 5/29/1726, 1.34890 7/3/1726, 1.34934 7/7/1736; AKP D.S. 84.

[58] BC 5935 R to ES 1.34839 1/3/1725; cf. 1.34890 7/3/1726 where R refuses to allow an arrendator in financial straits to abrogate his contract but does ask ES to grant him some relief from further *asygnacja* payments.

[59] BC 5934 R to ES 1.34614 ca. 1713.

[60] BC 5934–35 R to ES 1.34555 12/31/17(??), 1.34557 undated, 1.34573 2/16/1704, 1.34574 2/14/1709, 1.34583 5/14/1710, 1.34633 4/16/1714, 1.34638 6/20/1714, 1.34643 9/7/1714, 1.34698 ca. 1720, 1.34756 11/25/1722, 1.34871 11/14/1725.

of his attention, and that from 1719 to 1724 a major portion of his time was devoted to building the palace in Lubnice.[61]

The owner's representative. As *ekonom*, Rubinowicz frequently fulfilled roles and made decisions that were the owner's prerogative. For example, when subjects were faced with some sort of problem they often turned to Rubinowicz for help. It was Rubinowicz who had to deal with attempts by noblemen, who had leased royal revenues, to force the Sieniawski arrendators to pay inordinate sums. Such attempts, if successful, would exert a deleterious effect on the ability of arrendators to meet their obligations to the Sieniawskis. Rubinowicz, in the name of the owner, strongly resisted them. In one case he noted that a certain nobleman leased the liquor excise tax (*czopowe*) for the Sandomierz county and behaved cruelly toward the arrendator of Staszów by demanding that he pay an extraordinary and unjustifiable sum. The arrendator turned to Rubinowicz who "ordered the arrendator not to pay one *taler bity* more than the old contracts specify must be paid."[62]

Rubinowicz also recommended action to the owner or himself acted upon problems of peasants and others. The records show how he dealt with cases of peasants whose water supply was ruined by a passing Swedish army, a cavalry mercenary whose horse had been stolen by a nobleman, and the cossack Janoszowski—"an honest and upright person"—who had given good service to the Sieniawskis and whose house had burned down.[63]

In addition, Rubinowicz was called upon to manage emergency situations. In September 1720, when plague was spreading

[61] BC 5934–35 R to ES 1.34564 undated, 1.34690, 1.34692, 1.34695, 1.34697 ca. 1719, 1.34761, 1.34765, 1.34768, 1.34771, 1.34773, 1.34776, 1.34779, 1.34780, 1.34785, 1.34794, 1.34795 ca. 1723, 1.34819, 1.34830, 1.34833, 1.34834, 1.34835, 1.34838, 1.34844 ca. 1724–25; Bohdziewicz, *Korespondencja artystyczna Elżbiety Sieniawskiej,* pp. 19–57, 187–216.

[62] BC 5934 R to ES 1.34868 10/8/1725. See similarly: 1.34661 7/6/1715, 1.34677 4/30/1717, 1.34686 7/30/1719, 1.34694 11/28/1719. Non-Jewish administrators also defended the rights of "their" arrendators; see BC 5881 Łukszyński to ES 1.23561 10/7/1716 where Łukszyński requests a reduction for the arrendator of Jarosław. On the question of *protekcja*, see Chapter 3.

[63] BC 5934 R to ES 1.34576 1/27/1710, 1.34580 4/13/1710; BC 5943 ES to R 1.37211 6/1/1708. Later, in 1.34610 1/1/1713, R recommended favoring a petitioner whose interests clashed with Janoszowski's.

throughout the area, he informed Elżbieta Sieniawska that "thanks to God" the people of her town, Staszów, were healthy. To keep them that way, he forbade the Jews—who normally traveled on business—to leave the town for four weeks. He directed the town elders to deny reentry to any Jew who left the town in defiance of the order.[64]

Besides acting as the Sieniawskis' representative to the inhabitants of their territories, Rubinowicz was also their agent in dealings with outside elements. Frequently he was confronted by different army units in the area demanding food and supplies.[65] Another common situation is typified by the following: In September 1722 two canons of Chodzika came to Rytwiany, "with a retinue,"[66] in order to collect a debt Sieniawska owed them. At first Rubinowicz tried to talk them out of collecting the debt but succeeded only in obtaining a four-day postponement. Consequently, he wrote to Sieniawska that he had decided to pay them as much as possible out of what remained from the peasant taxes and to obtain the rest by borrowing "from the Jews or from somebody."[67]

Sometimes Rubinowicz conducted business with other magnates on the owner's behalf. When approached by a magnate with an offer to sell some property, Rubinowicz would begin the negotiations and proceed according to Sieniawska's instructions.[68] He was also called upon to defuse potential conflicts with neighboring magnates.

An example of this occurred in February 1715. A peasant belonging to the castellan of Radom came to Staszów and proposed to one of the Jewish merchants there that he come back to the village to purchase honey and wax waiting to be marketed. The Jew went along, taking with him enough cash to make the purchase. About a quarter of a mile outside Staszów, the peasant killed the Jew and took the money. After investigating the matter, Rubinowicz sent one of his subordinates to the castellan to demand that the culprit be caught. The

---

[64] BC 5934 R to ES 1.34702 9/7/1720; cf. Rychlikowa, *Wodzicki,* pp. 75–76.

[65] BC 5934 R to ES 1.34554 undated, 1.34564 undated, 1.34570 1/17/1705, 1.34580 4/13/1710, 1.34664 11/29/1715.

[66] BC 5934 R to ES 1.34752 9/30/1722.

[67] On money owed to other monasteries see BC 5934 R to ES 1.34575 10/16/1709 and AKP D.S. 84.

[68] BC 5934–35 R to ES and AAC 1.34553 undated, 1.34563 undated. 1.34927 2/4/1735 (the p.s.).

peasant was arrested; he confessed, returned the money, and showed where the Jew's body was hidden. This was not enough for Rubinowicz. He elicited a promise from the castellan that there would be a formal trial and appropriate punishment. It was important that the peasants realize that the castellan's protection over them did not extend to murdering the subjects of other magnates. The castellan procrastinated, however, and after three weeks Rubinowicz asked Elżbieta Sieniawska to intervene personally.[69]

The owner's financial manager. Emden, in his description of Rubinowicz, observed that "he controlled all of the income and the disbursements of the magnate." The "Summary of the Account of Rubinowicz; Both Income of All Types of Revenues as Well as Disbursements for Payment Orders (*asygnacja*) of the Lord and Oral Orders . . ."[70] for 1708–19, and the more detailed "Notation of Cash Income and Disbursements for the Year 1708 made by *Pan Ekonom* Rubinowicz,"[71] show just how true Emden's statement was.

During the period 1708–19 Rubinowicz's complex generated total revenue of 423,000 zł. with which to pay obligations and purchase goods and services required for the successful maintenance of the complex and the Sieniawskis' personal needs. This annual average of more than 35,000 zł. may appear modest compared to the 60,000 zł. Rubinowicz bragged about it in 1736, but in reality is remarkable in the years and territory in question. This was the period of the Northern War. Battles, roaming troops, natural disasters, and peasant revolts combined to wreak havoc on the Polish economy and devastate many manors. Despite these difficulties Rubinowicz's complex still was profitable, which must have been due to a combination of luck and managerial skill.

In managing a large budget of this nature Rubinowicz faced two basic problems: the need for accurate recordkeeping and, more difficult, the challenge of managing the cash flow. All of the non-*arenda* income was seasonal. Taxes were due on specified dates, and

[69] BC 5934 R to ES 1.34657 2/8/1715.

[70] AKP D.S. 84.

[71] AKP D.S. 80. See also: BC 5934–35 R to ES 1.34555 12/31/17(??), 1.34561 4/11/17(??), 1.34575 10/16/1709, 1.34579 4/10/1710, 1.34580 4/13/1710, 1.34587 11/26/1710, 1.34614 ca. 1713, 1.34640 7/18/1714, 1.34643 9/7/1714, 1.34693 10/25/1719, 1.34694 10/28/1719, 1.34887 5/15/1726.

agricultural products could only be sold when available. The maximum that could be collected from arrendators was at least theoretically limited by their contracts. On the other hand, payments were hard to anticipate or to limit. Payment orders were liable to be presented at any time, and goods and services had to be paid for as needed. One never knew when an army unit might appear demanding food, and the owner would frequently send urgent requests for cash, which was always in short supply.[72]

Rubinowicz had to be ingenious enough to find the cash when it was needed. This meant that he had to be well-informed as to the status of his different revenue resources: How much of their contractual obligations had the arrendators already paid out in payment orders? How soon would he be able to market agricultural products and at what prices? How large a harvest could he expect? Would the peasants be able to meet all their obligations to the lord this year or would they need aid?

Based on these reckonings, Rubinowicz had to plan for the regular expenses: debt payments, salaries, religious contributions, preplanned visits by army units. The irregular expenses he had to estimate. He then had to apportion the different financial obligations among his revenue items. Thus, to the arrendators he assigned part of the expenses for building maintenance and construction, food, salaries, debts and other obligations to the clergy, as well as general payment orders. The remainder of the expenses he paid out of the general fund.[73] Sometimes, however, planning was to no avail, as in April 1710, when he informed Sieniawska that, despite her pressing need for cash, poor market conditions prevented his selling wool.[74] In November 1710 an arrendator died, necessitating the postponement of two financial obligations.[75] Occasionally the usual sources of cash

[72] BC 5934–35 R to ES 1.34554 undated, 1.34614 ca. 1713, 1.34618 6/28/1713, 1.34888 5/29/1726 demonstrate how carefully ES examined the accounting books and how important accuracy was. On the magnate need for and shortage of cash see Chapter 2.

[73] AKP D.S. 84; BC 5934–35 R to ES 1.34575 10/16/1709, 1.34614 ca. 1713, 1.34887 5/15/1726.

[74] BC 5934 R to ES 1.34579 4/10/1710.

[75] BC 5934 R to ES 1.34587 11/26/1710; similarly, see: 1.34615 4/11/1713 and 1.34890 7/3/1726 (inability of arrendators to pay), 1.34702 9/7/1720 (R's cashbox is empty).

dried up and Rubinowicz had to resort to borrowing funds or to payment in kind.[76]

Managing finances was such a central part of Rubinowicz's job that he used images borrowed from this realm of experience in his everyday speech. In one letter he apologized to Sieniawska for a delay in submitting an accounting report by explaining that he had been very sick. His wife, he said, had already given him up for dead. But his time had not come; as he phrased it, "The account was not toted up, the books were not balanced."[77]

Marketing manorial products. Some of the agricultural, animal, forest, and mineral products produced on the manors were not required for seed, salary, or other internal needs. This surplus was either sent to be consumed on other parts of the latifundium or marketed for profit.[78] In Chapter 4 I emphasized that the task of transporting and marketing these products was not usually delegated to private merchants. The Sieniawskis' own administrators were in charge of finding the wagons or boats, hiring the personnel, safely loading and unloading the cargo, and taking it to its final destination. In the Rytwiany-Lubnice area these responsibilities fell squarely on Rubinowicz. As he wrote on September 1, 1714, "I must complain to My Lady that when *Pan* Zabłocki or anyone else sends anything to My Lady from the Cracow area it always goes through Lubnice and I must forward it to My Lady."[79] The correspondence confirms that, under Rubinowicz, Lubnice was the main depot for products sent to Sieniawska or to market from this region. Purchases made from the Wrocław merchants and supplies from Cracow were usually sent to Tenczyn and then to Rubinowicz, who shipped them on to Sieniawska. Rubinowicz also forwarded salt and grain as well as

[76] BC 5934–35 R to ES 1.34752 9/30/1722, R to MZSC: 1.34915 10/19/1730.

[77] BC 5934 R to ES 1.34618 6/28/1713.

[78] BC 5934 R to ES 1.34558 4/25/17(??), 1.34560 undated, 1.34561 4/11/17(??), 1.34605 10/6/1712, 1.34606 11/11/1712; BC 5943 R to ES 1.37211 6/1/1708; BC 5945 ES to Morzycki 1.37751 8/24/1721; see also: Gierowski, "Wrocławskie interesy," p. 244. Accounts of disbursements of products show that products were used routinely for paying part of the salaries; e.g., BC 4046 "Account of Grain and Other Products for Międzybóż *Włość*, 1724–27," BC 4081 similarly for Międzybóż *Klucz*, 1740. The best example of marketing is represented by the records of products shipped from the Sieniawski holdings in Red Ruthenia to Gdańsk, BC 4818–4835.

[79] BC 5934 R to ES 1.34643 9/7/1714.

various supplies needed in other parts of the latifundium and supervised the marketing of the cattle, grain, wood, calamine, lime, and gypsum produced in this section. Except for the cattle, the products were normally shipped by boat to either Warsaw or Gdańsk or sold locally. Cattle were usually driven overland to Silesian markets.[80]

It was also Rubinowicz's responsibility to organize the *spław* expeditions from this part of the latifundium. He found freighters to fill up the extra space on the boats and secured passports from Sieniawska to guarantee that the materials could pass to Gdańsk duty-free.[81] All of these tasks as well as the ones described in the preceding paragraph were administrative. At this point, however, Rubinowicz's entrepreneurial skills came into play, because in addition to arranging for the boats and crews, Rubinowicz had to decide on the most advantageous and profitable way to market the products: to sell locally or to ship to a large market, to sell immediately or to postpone. In 1709, for example, he recommended driving the cattle to Cracow and selling them there rather than in faraway Silesia.[82] The differential in price was not great, there were plenty of butchers in Cracow who would buy them, and the Sieniawski arrendators in the area could provide feed while the cattle were awaiting sale. In 1731, he recommended to Maria Zofia Denhoffowa (soon to be Czartoryska) that more money was to be made by selling grain locally to Jewish merchants than by sending it all the way to Gdańsk.[83]

---

[80] BC 5934–35 R to ES and AAC 1.34558 4/25/17(??), 1.34560 undated, 1.34558 4/25/17(??), 1.34568 1/8/1705, 1.34574 2/14/1709, 1.34575 10/16/1709, 1.34605 10/6/1712, 1.34606 11/11/1712, 1.34640 7/18/1714, 1.34848 4/3/1725, 1.34954–61 ca. 1740–42; BC 5945 ES to Morzycki: 1.37597 9/11/1718, 1.37674 ca. 1720, 1.37677, ca. 1720, 1.37689, 7/21/1720, 1.37691 8/4/1720, 1.37704 10/19/1720, 1.37747 8/11/1721, 1.37751 8/24/1721, 1.37762 10/12/1721, 1.37786 2/3/1722; BC 2744, pp. 477–78 Rybczyński to ES 7/5/1714; see also Gierowski, "Wrocławskie interesy," p. 225; Prochaska, *Historja,* p. 110; see n. 78.

[81] BC 5934–35 R to ES and AAC 1.34579 4/10/1710, 1.34583 5/14/1710, 1.34585 8/19/1710, 1.34627 9/10/1713, 1.34640 7/18/1714, 1.34642 9/21/1714, 1.34848 4/3/1725, 1.34870 5/3/1724, 1.34871 11/14/1725, 1.34887 5/15/1726, 1.34924 9/12/1735; BC 5946 ES to Zabagłowicz 1.37965 7/16/1725; Gierowski, "Wrocławskie interesy," p. 235.

[82] BC 5934 R to ES 1.34575 10/16/1709.

[83] BC 5935 R to MZSC 1.34918–20 Jan.–Feb., 1731; see Chapter 4. GOSP 51 shows the figures for grain sold locally 1731–35. On the sale of salt locally see:

To be able to make decisions such as these, one had to be acquainted with market conditions and aware of alternative marketing possibilities. Undoubtedly, an aid to Rubinowicz's success in his job was his contacts with other Jews, which provided him with both the information and the marketing options necessary to maximize the Sieniawskis' profits.

The commercial services provided by Rubinowicz to the Sieniawskis were not limited to marketing latifundium products to the outside. Rubinowicz also procured various goods both for the personal use of Elżbieta Sieniawska and for the latifundium. In particular the letters mention building materials, pet dogs, copper for brewing kettles, rapiers, oats, charm water to induce pregnancy, and, as was characteristic for Polish Jews, horses and Hungarian wine.[84]

Of course Rubinowicz did not fulfill his responsibilities singlehandedly. He had many subordinates who contributed to his efforts; comptrollers who handled the bookkeeping and helped in managing the finances, *podstarości* who managed the agriculture, arrendators who provided cash, skippers who operated the *spław*, overseers of granaries and stackyards, and factors who procured goods, to name the most important. But even in the unlikely event that all of these were totally honest and optimally efficient, supervising and coordinating their activities required skill and a huge investment of time and effort.

Rubinowicz's Wealth, Status, and Power

Jewish homiletical writers of the late seventeenth and eighteenth centuries frequently attacked individuals—most of them "intimates of the regime," that is, tied to the Polish king or nobility—who amassed tremendous fortunes and acquired thereby undeserved honor and

---

BC 5935 R to MZSC 1.34912 6/25/1730. On finding markets for gypsum see 1.34954–61 ca. 1740–42.

[84] BC 5934–35 R to ES 1.34553 undated, 1.34602 9/8/1712, 1.34614 ca. 1713, 1.34894 7/24/1726; BC 2905 no. 146 3/24/1736 R to AAC; BC 2531 3/3/1709 after p. 83, R to ES; BC 5809 F to R 1.10754 8/3/1721; BC 5943 ES to R 1.37211 6/1/1708; BC 2903, no. 13 1716.

power in the community.[85] The following passage from R. Shmuel Kaidanover's *Kav Hayashar* is typical:[86]

> For all of the false honor which exists now in these times is based on wealth. Fools bring proof from Rabbi [Judah the Patriarch d. ca. 225 C.E.] who honored the rich, but they do not know that our Holy Rabbi also honored the poor who studied Torah, for they are the possessors of deeds. In the world-to-come honor will be given according to the amount of good deeds and not according to the amount of wealth.

Rubinowicz, well compensated for his services to the Sieniawskis, was a wealthy man. If Emden's description is indicative, however, he used his wealth to do good deeds. As Emden related,[87]

> He gave my father a large house to live in rent-free and provided for him a servant on duty day and night prepared to deal with all of the household chores. He also gave him cows which provided ample milk, butter and cheese for the needs of his entire household. He sent him as much wood and fire as he needed for heating as well as fowl and abundant fresh fish from the ponds under his control. Everything was absolutely free. He supplied almost all of his needs Only non-essential items and clothing would my father buy out of his own money. This wealthy man would sometimes even give my father many gifts of all sorts of treats, spices, sugar and delicacies which he could procure, in order to give my father pleasure and find favor in his eyes. R. Yisrael gave everything generously and with great delight. For several years he bore all of my father's needs with love, goodwill and much kindness, until 5478 A.M. [1718] when my father of blessed memory was accepted as rabbi of Lwów and the surrounding region. Then the notable R. Yisrael was sorry that this great *mitzva* was lost from his home which had served as a hospice of Torah for several [years].

---

[85] For examples of this type of criticism see: Dinur, pp. 121–23; see also, Kaidanover, pt. 1, pp. 7b, 10c, 89c, pt. 2, pp. 19c, 51b; Yosef ben Yehuda Yidel, *Yesod Yosef* (Shkłoǔ, 1785), pp. 51, 71b, 29c–d. For examples of this type of criticism in earlier centuries, see H. H. Ben-Sasson, *Hagut Vehanhagah*, Index, s.v. "Ashirim" (wealthy people).

[86] Kaidanover, pt. 1, p. 19c.

[87] Emden, pp. 44–45.

It is not surprising that Rubinowicz possessed such wealth. In addition to his high salary,[88] he received income from his own private enterprises. In the letters he specifically mentioned land that he bought and on which he built huts and settled serfs.[89] Sieniawska allowed him to market the grain grown on this land via her *spław* boats, duty-free.[90] He was also allowed to build his own brick factory.[91] Under Czartoryski he leased a mill *arenda*.[92] Moreover, through his horse- and grain-trading activity, contract letting, and *spław* organizing on behalf of the owners, Rubinowicz must have established contacts and gained knowledge of market conditions that enabled him to make shrewd investments and to take advantage of commercial opportunities when they presented themselves.[93] Finally, his wealth was augmented by fringe benefits that the Sieniawskis granted to *ekonomi* in general. Among these were a weekly fish allotment, horses at his disposal, personal use of meadowlands, gifts of building material, and free housing.[94] All of this income combined to

[88] See Makowska, pp. 319–24.

[89] BC 3826, no. 81; cf. BC 2581/2, p. 215 1/24/1722, which records that as a special reward AMS leased out twelve *włoki* of the Shkłoŭ complex to Fajbisz Powzorowicz. It was illegal for Jews to control real estate as owners or lessees. (See *AGZ*, vol. 22, 120.62, 125.63; vol. 25, 174.37). It was, however, common for magnates, when it suited their purposes, to allow Jews to break laws regarding settlement, occupation, or land ownership; cf. Hundert, "Security and Dependence," p. 120; Goldberg, "Poles and Jews," p. 260.

[90] BC 5935 R to ES 1.34870 5/3/1724 (cf. BC 4825, p. 11, a list of administrators exempted from freight payments), 1.34640 7/18/1714.

[91] BC 5935 R to MZSC 1.34912 6/25/1730; BC 3826, no. 81.

[92] BC 2905, no. 167 Hubiński to AAC 8/20/1738.

[93] Other Jews in the Sieniawskis' employ certainly did; see BC 5943 ES to Queen Marysieńka Sobieska 1.37133 8/7/1703, where she noted that she had granted the *arenda* of the Jarosław Fair to her Jewish *pisarz prowentowy* there (probably Lewko); also BC 4180 *Inwentarz Klucz Zińków*, 1740, p. 4, which records how AAC's Jewish factor Srewel bought a mill. It should be recalled, too, that the Ickowicz brothers, connected to Radziwiłł, were both members of the administration (Szmul as *Kasjer Generalny*, Gdal as factor) and were allowed to possess *dzierżawy*; see Halpern, pp. 60, 62 and Lech, pp. 315–17. Non-Jewish administrators also had their own enterprises, e.g., Morzycki who owned his own cattle, BC 5945 ES to Morzycki 1.37699 9/21/1720.

[94] BC 3826, no. 81; in 1.34579 4/10/1710 R requested from ES that he be allowed to live in the home he built for himself in Koniemłota, but from BC 3826, no. 81 it appears that he eventually settled in one of the castles in either Rytwiany or Lubnice.

make Rubinowicz a very rich man, whose wealth was at least equivalent to that of a prosperous nobleman owner of several villages. He could easily afford to support the Hakham Zvi in the manner Emden described.

There were other parallels between Rubinowicz and well-to-do owners of several villages. In the correspondence most Jews were addressed or referred to as "Żyd X" or simply "X" without benefit of title. Rubinowicz was often addressed or referred to as *"Pan."*[95] As a landowner and administrator he had serfs under his control, and his problems and interests were like those of noblemen in a similar position. He even had "his" Jew who served him as errand-runner and factor.[96]

Evidently, Rubinowicz was also capable of wielding authority among noblemen—both his subordinates on the latifundium staff and others who were not formally bound to obey him. For instance, in October 1725, Vice Regent Gawroński was sent to the village of Strzyżowice to confiscate part of the estate of a deceased nobleman named Dembicki. Gawroński's superior, Demboli, wrote to Rubinowicz informing him of the mission and requesting his help. In response, Rubinowicz said, "I immediately gathered several noblemen who went with me."[97] He then led his group to rendezvous with Gawroński in Opatów and they proceeded together.

Like noblemen administrators,[98] Rubinowicz was frequently required to reply to complaints about his performance. The correspondence includes Rubinowicz's reactions to many such charges. Peasants complained of being overworked or overtaxed.

---

[95] AKP D. S. 80; BC 5943 ES to R 1.37211 6/1/1708; BC 2905, no. 106 Mickiewicz to ES 6/25/1725; BC 2647, pp. 327–42. For examples of Jewish *dzierżawcy* being called *"Pan"* see *ABK*, no. 12.

[96] BC 5934 R to ES 1.34620 7/13/1713 R spoke of his *"żydek."*

[97] BC 5935 R to ES 1.34864 10/25/1725.

[98] BC 5881 Łukszyński to ES 1.23456 undated, 1.23458 undated, Łukszyński, administrator of holdings around Jarosław, defended himself against charges of corruption; BC 5884 Chaim Mairowicz to ES 1.23930 2/26/1725, Chaim accused Łukszyński of arbitrary behavior and misappropriation of funds; BC 5945 ES to Morzycki 1.37699 9/21/1720, ES accused him of grazing his own cattle while inventing an excuse not to take care of hers. The *ekonom* Stanisław Lublicki was dismissed for malfeasance; Gierowski, "Wrocławskie interesy," p. 224.

Townsmen claimed that he tax-gouged, was corrupt, and drove settlers away. Nobles accused him of disobedience or disloyalty to the owners. Jews, for reasons of revenge, jealousy, or profit, tried to have him removed or aided in the efforts of others to do so.[99]

As a Jew, Rubinowicz was more vulnerable to all these attacks.[100] There was a predisposition in Polish society to believe the worst about a Jew. Terms such as "Jewish tricks" and "sly Jew" were evidently common expressions. At times, Elżbieta Sieniawska even applied them to Rubinowicz.[101]

Rubinowicz, while suffering numerous accusations, tried to turn this suspicious inclination to his advantage. He countered his accusers, in part, by ascribing their motives to Jew-hatred, thereby casting doubt *a priori* on the merits of the charges. He continually stressed the necessity for him, a Jew, to avoid the slightest hint of corruption or disloyalty. Once in replying to a charge of misappropriating tax money, he observed that "Because I am a Jew there will be more than one unkind charge."[102] On another occasion, he ended his defense against an accusation that he diverted grain to his own use by saying, "I most fear the Lord's anger because whatever may befall someone else the briefs multiply on his behalf, but as for me, a Jew, anything might be a pretext for accusations."[103] Hence, Rubinowicz maintained, his dedication to his work and loyalty to his employers were absolute. As he remarked in the dramatic style of the age,

---

[99] BC 5934 R to ES 1.34588 12/19/1710, 1.34625 8/15/1713, 1.34633 4/16/1714, 1.34737 7/10/1722, 1.34817 6/30/1724; BC 3826, no. 81 8/24/1729; in BC 5935 R to ES 1.348176 6/30/1724 R remarks, "Were it a Jew who concocted this I would know to what to attribute it."

[100] According to BC 5935 R to AAC 1.34934 7/7/1736 R was granted a privilege by ES protecting him from claims made by other officials. The necessity of such a privilege implies that his position was not usual.

[101] In BC 5935 R to ES 1.34888 5/29/1726, R replied to ES's charge that the account he presented was the product of either "Jewish tricks or stupidity." BC 5782, M. Czaplic to ES (?) 1.5892 1/30/1715 speaks of the "Sly Jews." In BC 5809 F to ES 1.10736 undated, F found it necessary to say: "I am a Jew but honorable." BC 5881, Łukszyński to ES 1.23557 3/18/1716: "The Jews played tricks. . . ."

[102] BC 5934 R to ES 1.34588 12/19/1710.

[103] BC 5934 R to ES 1.34583 5/14/1710. See similar expressions in: 1.34633 4/16/1714, 1.34817 6/30/1724.

"Anything which you say to me is as a command of the Jewish God."[104]

Rubinowicz's defenses and protestations of loyalty and honesty were apparently believed,[105] for he served the Sieniawskis until their deaths and, despite an attempted overthrow,[106] successfully weathered the transition to rule by Maria Zofia and her second husband, August Aleksander Czartoryski.

The confidence the owners displayed in him not only gained him wealth and status, but also opened the path to power in dealing with both Poles and Jews in areas not directly related to his professional responsibilities. Rubinowicz's connection to the magnates gave him three principal tools to use to gain power in society:

- the right to employ force;
- discretionary power to allocate contracts, jobs, money, and minor appointments; and
- direct access to and influence on the magnate.

The right to employ force. In Poland, when a person broke a law, failed to honor an order issued by a court or lord, or did not pay his taxes or other obligations, he could be subjected to an *egzekucja*, a posse of soldiers or noblemen who came to his home, arrested him, seized property, or burned the house. While in theory *egzekucje* were authorized by a court, in reality whoever controlled or held influence over a court—such as a high administrator or an important arrendator—could obtain authorization to assemble a posse to carry out an *egzekucja*.[107]

As observed in the last chapter, powerful arrendators, by way of collecting their due, sometimes seized people or their property. Acts like these were done by means of *egzekucje*. Presumably, Rubinowicz

---

[104] BC 5934 R to ES 1.34614 ca. 1713; cf. 1.34588 12/19/1710: "I neither serve nor accommodate anyone save The One and Only Lady whose bread I eat"; 1.34633 4/16/1714: "I am the serf of My Lady to the end of my life. Whatever order of My Lady comes down to me I will fulfill."

[105] For example, BC 2514, pp. 385–90, in a letter to AMS, ES stated "Everything about Rubinowicz is untrue."

[106] By *Pan* Dunin; see BC 3826, no. 81.

[107] Kaczmarczyk and Leśnodorski, *Historia*, vol. 2, Index, s.v. *Egzekucja*.

employed *egzekucje* in collecting taxes from recalcitrant peasants, whose resultant complaints were alluded to above. He may also have been tempted to use force or the threat of force to collect personal debts or to settle personal scores. Anyone lacking a detail of soldiers at his disposal would have been at a disadvantage when dealing with Rubinowicz.

Allocation of contracts, jobs, money, and minor appointments. In September 1726 Elżbieta Sieniawska had Rubinowicz send a townsman to check the ponds at Tenczyn to see which would be worth leasing out.[108] This was no doubt one of hundreds of opportunities Rubinowicz had to appoint someone to do an errand, carry a message, or fulfill some task. Such patronage power could be used to build a cadre of loyal suporters who could then be counted on to support Rubinowicz in the event of a dispute with a member of the Jewish community or an investigation by a commission sent by the owners. Rubinowicz's power to arrange contracts and make purchases was even more important. Even in lean years Rubinowicz controlled a large budget and lucrative contracts. Moreover, he marketed products shipped from other areas. Those people hired as workmen and artisans for the construction projects he supervised were assured employment. The Jewish merchants to whom he chose to sell the grain in 1731, in place of shipping it to Gdańsk, received a windfall that assured them a very successful year. The people awarded *arenda* contracts were thereby granted promising economic opportunities. The cloth merchants from whom Rubinowicz bought the crepe for the elegant funeral he planned in 1722 must have been the envy of their competitors.[109] In short, Rubinowicz's power to allocate economic opportunity meant that he could profoundly affect the economic fate of individuals and even communities.

Direct access to and influence on the magnates. Rubinowicz was in constant written communication with his employers. He also made occasional trips to meet with them personally, and on rare occasions was visited by them.[110] A frequent feature of the letters Rubinowicz sent is the brief (*instancja*).

---

[108] BC 5946 ES to Zabagłowicz 1.38022 9/24/1726.
[109] BC 5934 R to ES 1.34555 undated.
[110] AKP D.S. 84 includes a food budget for such visits.

From time to time Rubinowicz would ask Elżbieta Sieniawska or August Aleksander Czartoryski to grant a favor to someone under their control. The request may have been to be lenient with an arrendator who could not meet his payments, or to loan or give money to rebuild after a fire, or to intervene with ecclesiastical authorities to get permission to build a synagogue.[111] Rubinowicz's right to approach the magnate with such requests meant, in effect, that he shared the power to grant them, for if he refused to submit a petition it was dealt a severe blow. Any request that was granted would mean that the petitioner was in Rubinowicz's debt as well as that of the magnate.

While Rubinowicz's right to use force, his power to allocate resources, and his access to the magnate enhanced his standing with the Poles he encountered,[112] these prerogatives had an even greater impact on the Jewish community to which he naturally belonged. Poles may have granted him the simple honorific *"Pan"*; but Dr. Mojżesz Fortis, in a letter written in 1721, [113] addressed him as "The Noble Sir Rubinowicz." Indeed, Fortis went beyond this, signing himself "the fortunate brother and servant of the *"WMMMM Pan* . . .*"*, where the multiplying of *"M"*'s denoted a very high degree of power possessed by the "Great Sir" Rubinowicz. This honorific was often applied to magnates. In the Hebrew address Fortis called Rubinowicz "The notable (*katzin*) Sir (*Mar*) Yisrael." Emden also emphasized Rubinowicz's high standing, describing him as "an important notable (*katzin*), one of the dignitaries of the land of Poland, the famed and praiseworthy, R. Yisrael of Rytwiany."[114]

These forms of address bespeak a high degree of respect shown to a powerful man within the Jewish community. What is not clear is in what ways Rubinowicz wielded the power he possessed. Even though Fortis and Emden regarded Rubinowicz's high status and magnate

---

[111] BC 5934 R to ES 1.34576 1/27/1710, 1.34657 2/8/1715, 1.34749 9/9/1722.

[112] These prerogatives also made him the target of attempts by Poles to unseat him; see BC 5934–35 R to ES and AAC 1.34583 5/14/1710, 1.34588 12/19/1710, 1.34633 4/16/1714, 1.34934 7/7/1736; BC 3826, no. 81 8/24/1729.

[113] BC 5809 F to R 1.10754 8/3/1721: the Polish address on the envelope reads: "Imci Panu Rubinowiczowi oddać należy w Rytwianach" (To the Noble Sir Rubinowicz, to be delivered at Rytwiany). The salutation reads: "Mój Kochany Mci Panie Bracie" (My Dear Powerful Sir [and] Brother); the signature is: "WMMMM Pana życzliwym bratem i sługą. . . ."

[114] Emden, p. 44.

affiliation positively, in Jewish homiletical and legal literature of the late seventeenth and eighteenth centuries, Jews who maintained close relations with Poles and derived power thereby were regarded ambivalently, if not negatively. This was so because Jews with connections in high places often used the power they obtained in ways that were undesirable from the community's perspective.[115]

The dearth of Jewish sources makes it impossible to determine whether Rubinowicz used his power to become a despot over the Jewish community. There is no way of knowing whether he wielded influence with the Council of Four Lands or conducted personal vendettas. Some of the correspondence, however, shows that, within the Jewish community, Rubinowicz knew how to use his power to further his own interests and those of his family.

He secured the position of Rabbi of Sieniawa (and later Kalush) for his son-in-law Judka and, by appeal to Maria Zofia Czartoryska, helped Judka keep the job despite opposition within the community. When Judka died, Rubinowicz used his magnate connections to insure that Judka's son, Simha, would succeed to the Kalush rabbinate, even though a rival faction supported a different candidate.[116]

Another time, Rubinowicz obtained a three-year exemption from all Jewish and Polish taxes for his son Marek.[117] On the other hand, Emden's description—albeit written more than thirty years after the fact by the son of a beneficiary of Rubinowicz's kindness—inclines one to believe that if Rubinowicz was a despot, he was a benevolent one who was "famed and praiseworthy." Rubinowicz apparently regarded it as an honor to support a genuine scholar of the Hakham Zvi's stature, and he performed communal-minded acts such as

[115] Dinur, pp. 121–23; see Chapter 7.
[116] BC 5934–35 R to ES 1.34767 2/21/1723, R to Królikiewicz 1.34908 2/23/1727, R to MZSC 1.34909 3/31/1730, 1.34912 6/25/1730, R to AAC 1.34921 11/25/1732, 1.34931 4/28/1736, 1.34932 5/19/1736, 1.34938 11/26/1736; cf. M. Bałaban, "Z zagadnień ustrojowych żydostwa polskiego," *Studja Lwowskie* (Lviv, 1932), pp. 52–54; and Dinur, pp. 106–10. Both of these discuss how magnates' Jews used their influence to persuade the magnate to appoint their relatives and friends to rabbinic posts.
[117] BC 5935 R to ES 1.34786 9/1/1723.

interceding with Sieniawska to have the synagogue built in Staszów.[118]

Fortis, Rubinowicz, and Polish Culture

As traditional Polish Jews, Rubinowicz and Fortis and the other Jewish members of the Sieniawski-Czartoryski administration were deeply rooted in Jewish society and Jewish culture. Common characteristics of Polish Jews, such as commercial acumen and facility with languages, enhanced their value to the magnate. But what uncharacteristic behavior—for Jews—was necessary to their success? Did service in the magnate administration require some degree of acculturation?

I have already observed that one barrier to Jewish occupation of high administrative posts and participation in the court entourage was the Jews' lack of assimilation into society and culture. It does seem possible, however, that, while the Jews were not polonized, the closer to the Poles they became the more elements of Polish culture they had to master. The Sieniawski-Czartoryski sources allow consideration of this question from the perspective of language. The speed with which an immigrant minority masters the majority's language and the degree to which it uses that language are excellent indicators of the degree to which the minority has adapted itself to and become a part of the host society.[119]

How much Polish did Jews in the magnate's administration know? Common sense dictates that Jews living in the southeastern part of the Commonwealth and dealing with non-Jews in business must have had at least a rudimentary command of spoken Polish or Ruthenian and that the more extensive their non-Jewish contacts, the more extensive

[118] BC 5934 R to ES 1.34749 9/9/1722. After the departure of the Hakham Zvi, Rubinowicz became the patron of another rabbi, Moszko of Leżajsk, ca. 1721–29, see BC 3826, no. 82.

[119] On this question, see: E. Haugen, *Bilingualism in the Americas* (Alabama, 1956), pp. 99–106. Note especially his statement on p. 99: "In most cases, however, linguistic and social acculturation go hand in hand."

their knowledge of the non-Jewish language would have been.[120] The following passage from an eighteenth-century homiletical text illustrates this rule of thumb:[121]

> We have seen in our days that the great merchants consider themselves accomplished sages while they consider those who continuously sit and learn in school to be cattle; saying about them that they do not know how to talk to the people of the world, *not being able to speak the vernacular like them.*

This reflects a *sitz im leben* where the ivory-tower yeshiva students and rabbis knew little, if any, Polish or Ruthenian, while the merchants, out in the non-Jewish world, were able to deal fluently in the language of the land. The *Memoirs* of the wine merchant Ber of Bolechow contain an historical example of this reality. In 1753, the Rabbi of Lviv, the distinguished R. Haim Rapoport, was charged before August Aleksander Czartoryski with accepting bribes in connection with his arbitration of a disputed inheritance. Czartoryski's commissioner, Cieszkowski, set about prosecuting the rabbi for this offense, and R. Rapoport realized that the seriousness of the accusation merited a sophisticated defense. He was stymied by his lack of facility with Polish. As Ber tells it, R. Rapport said: "If I could only find someone who writes Polish well I could explain to the commissioner the whole affair of this lawsuit ... I myself know the Polish language a little, but not perfectly; and when a gentile writes for me he never expresses my meaning properly." So Ber was recommended to the rabbi as someone fluent and literate in Polish. He was engaged and composed an affidavit that convinced Cieszkowski of the rabbi's innocençe. Later, in 1759, Ber served as R. Rapoport's interpreter during the famous debate with the Frankists in Lviv.[122]

---

[120] This is buttressed by scholarly opinion; M. Altbauer, *Achievements and Tasks in the Field of Jewish-Slavic Language Contact Studies* (Los Angeles, 1972), p. 2; Baron, *History,* vol. 16, pp. 74–79; Weinryb, *Jews,* pp. 93–94. Urban, p. 236, found Jews signing in Latin letters as early as 1576 and four Jews who signed their names in polonized form in the 1630s; cf. *SB*, p. 37.

[121] Mordekhai ben Naftali Hertz, *Pithei Yah* (Lviv, 1799), p. 25a (emphasis mine).

[122] Ber of Bolechow, pp. 60–67; A. Brawer, "Makor Ivri Hadash Letoldot Frank Vesiyato," *Hashiloah* 38 (1917), p. 17. See also R. Rapoport, "Even Haezer,"

Among the magnate-connected Jews, the degree of their knowledge of Polish seems to have been directly related to their closeness to the magnate court. Evidently, a lower-ranking official like a *dozorca* or *pisarz* did not necessarily have to be able to write Polish himself, although he did have to read or at least speak it. For example, Hersz Moszkowicz, *pisarz* and *szafarz*, kept his registers in Yiddish and was assisted by a non-Jewish clerk, Dębicki, who wrote out Polish documents.[123] Most documents submitted to Jewish *pisarze* or arrendators have on the back in Yiddish or Hebrew a one-line *précis* of the contents of the Polish text—implying that the Jew read the document in Polish but for filing purposes wrote on it in the language in which he was more comfortable and fully literate.[124]

There were Jews associated with the administration who may have written in Polish, however. Most correspondence in the Sieniawski-Czartoryski archive, whether authored by the magnates, Jews, or others, is written in the characteristically broad pen strokes and grammatically correct language of the professional scribes of the time. But judging from the sloppy penmanship, poor spelling, grammatical errors, and incorrect usage in some documents it appears that at least a few Jews—and others — could write by themselves.[125]

One letter from Rubinowicz is a good example of this. The body of the letter is typically scribal; the "p.s.," however, is written very sloppily. Also, many words are apparently spelled according to the pronunciation of the writer's dialect rather than in standard Polish

no. 71 where the rabbi discussed the proper spelling of "Zamość." It is obvious from the discussion that he had just recently learned this.

[123] BC 4818, 4825; see also BC 4820, pp. 33–34.

[124] EW 127 "Kwity (receipts) 1695–1703;" BC 3499 pp. 364–68; EW 133, documents kept by Chaim the *pisarz*. The Polish *arenda* contracts, usually signed in Hebrew, may have been translated into Hebrew for the benefit of the arrendator (e.g., BC 3503, pp. 191–92, contract for Sieniawa *arenda*, 1728, written in Hebrew) or the arrendators may have been able to read the original Polish but signed in Hebrew. Probably both methods existed. Note M. Czaplic's remark to ES (?) BC 5782 1.5892 1/30/1715 that he did not write everything he wanted to because he was afraid that the Jews carrying the message would read it.

[125] See EW 255, undated appeal of Izak Jakubowicz to ES from the customs prison at Fordon, BC 5756 Lewek Abuszewicz to Karreta 1.11 10/18/1719; EW 176, *Suplika* of Szewel Faktor to AAC. It should be remembered, too, that the utilization of professional scribes does not necessarily imply illiteracy on the part of the correspondent. ES was literate, yet most of her correspondence was professionally written.

spelling.[126] This suggests that after having had his scribe write the letter Rubinowicz reread it and decided to add the postscript without bothering to dictate.

Judging from his letters, Mojżesz Fortis was perfectly fluent and literate in Polish. The texts and signature of his letters are all written in a neat but nonscribal script, which is uniform in all the extant letters, no matter whether they were written in Jarosław, Wrocław, Rzeszów, or Amsterdam.[127] This certainly indicates that Fortis wrote his Polish letters himself. He must have received a good Polish education, for his grammar, usage, and spelling are on a par with the scribes who wrote Elżbieta Sieniawska's correspondence.[128]

Of course, language acculturation is not only a matter of literacy. There should be a familiarity with the conventions of language as well. That Rubinowicz and Fortis had mastered these is apparent in a letter dated August 3, 1721, which Fortis sent to Rubinowicz from Wrocław.[129] The letter covers three topics:

- it suggests that Rubinowicz try to reinterest Sieniawska in buying some property she had already decided not to purchase;
- it alludes to medicine Rubinowicz had requested and Fortis had sent;
- it apologizes for not sending Rubinowicz a particular horse.

The interesting thing about this letter between the two Jews is that it was written in Polish. Fortis even addressed Rubinowicz in typically Polish fashion as "My Beloved Noble Sir and Brother," and signed himself, "The Fortunate Brother and Servant of the Great

---

[126] BC 5935 R to AAC 1.34927 2/4/1736. Some of the spelling variants not found in the body of the letter: "*dobrodzy*" for "*dobrodzieja*," "*dalieko*" for "*daleko*," "*iezeły*" for "*ieżeli*," "*Warsawy*" for "*Warszawy*." It is hardly possible that a second, inferior scribe is involved. It would not make sense for R to employ an incompetent scribe to finish a letter begun by a competent one. The more reasonable alternative, in my opinion, is that the postscript must have been written by R himself; cf. BC 5882 Łukszyński to ES 1.23632 8/6/1719, where the Polish administrator apparently did the same thing.

[127] BC 5809 F to ES 1.10736–54 1714–26.

[128] Compare BC 5943–46.

[129] BC 5809 F to R 1.10754 8/3/1721. The address on the envelope is in both Polish and Hebrew; see n. 113.

Sir. . . ." A letter with such salutations could easily be mistaken as a letter between two Polish noblemen. Were it not for the Hebrew address on the back, and the names, it would be impossible to tell that the correspondents were Jewish.

Such a high level of language acculturation might imply a concomitant lessening of commitment to Jewish tradition or, at least, to the outward signs of Jewish identity. The Jewish moralists of the era often lambasted the "intimates of the regime," who imitated the ways of their masters and slacked in their adherence to Jewish social and religious mores. This is how R. Shmuel Kaidanover described such people:[130]

> The second reason why our fathers were redeemed from Egypt is that they did not change their names. But now in this generation I have seen those of the people who throw off the traces, dressing in the style of the nations and, even worse, shaving their beards. . . . Thus sometimes a Jew cannot be recognized as such and when he is asked his name he calls himself by one of the names of the gentiles; and sometimes when he is going with noblemen on a road where no one knows him he sins by eating non-kosher food and drinking unfit wine. . . .

Perhaps Rubinowicz and Fortis were attracted to the noble lifestyle. There are no clear signs. There are, however, strong indications that their commitment to Judaism and Jewish mores was unshaken. Statements like "I am a Jew, but honorable," or "Because I am a Jew there will be more than one unkind charge"[131] show that, however

---

[130] Kaidanover, pt. 2, ch. 72, pp. 47a–47c; cf. Dinur, pp. 121–25; Hundert, "Security and Dependence," pp. 225–29; see also Gelber, "Letoldot Harofim Hayehudim Bepolin," p. 351, on how Jewish doctors—like Fortis—were the vanguard of the early *Haskala* in Poland.

[131] BC 5809 F to ES 1.10736 undated, BC 5934 R to ES 1.34588 12/19/1710. For similar expressions see: 1.34583 5/14/1710, 1.34633 4/16/1714, 1.34817 6/30/1724. R's intercessions on behalf of fellow Jews may also have been an expression of his Jewish identity; see 1.34562 undated, 1.34610 1/1/1713, 1.34615 4/11/1713, 1.34657 2/8/1715, 1.34661 7/6/1715, 1.34677 4/30/1717, 1.34686 7/30/1719, 1.34737 7/10/1722, 1.34749 9/9/1722, 1.34890 7/3/1726, 1.34903 11/13/1726. ES certainly suspected that this was the case, prompting R to insist that such petitions were based on the merits of the cases and not Jewish solidarity: ". . . God knows better that I am not writing this because it is on behalf of a Jew or because of a bribe." In fact R did intercede on behalf of non-Jews too (see n. 63), while non-Jewish administrators did

strong their associations with Polish society, Fortis and Rubinowicz were poignantly aware that their place was in the Jewish community, and that even if they forgot that fact, the Poles would remind them.

As far as commitment to traditional Jewish observance is concerned, one letter from Fortis to Elżbieta Sieniawska is apposite. The letter, written from Rzeszów on Friday, March 21, 1721, pointedly includes the time of day—3:00 p.m.—in the heading. Fortis wrote, "I am deeply sorry that I cannot do very much in fulfillment of My Lady's command today because I have only three hours until *Shabbos* [Sabbath]. . . .[132]

Fortis, so afraid of running afoul of Sieniawska's good graces in the diamond brooch episode, here offered no long explanation or apology. He obviously expected Sieniawska to understand and accept the religious constraints as a matter of course. Undoubtedly Sieniawska was familiar with the Sabbath as a basic Jewish institution, knew that Jews could not travel or do work after sunset on Friday, and made allowances accordingly.

Rubinowicz wrote no such clear-cut statement of his adherence to Jewish practice. Emden's praise of him as a "fearer of Heaven" and as regretting the loss of the opportunity to fulfill the *mitzva* of supporting a scholar in his home signifies Rubinowicz's commitment to Jewish tradition, however. It is, moreover, doubtful that a rabbi of the stature and integrity of the Hakham Zvi would have accepted Rubinowicz's hospitality had the latter's religious punctiliousness been wanting.[133]

The Perils of Prominence

Rubinowicz's and Fortis's attempts to balance a steadfast Jewishness with close ties to Polish society did entail risks. A letter Rubi-

---

so on behalf of Jews (e.g., BC 5897 Morzycki to ES 1.26450 11/16/1715).

[132] BC 5809 F to ES 10742, 3/21/1721. Cf. BC 5806 Fejga Arrendator to ES 1.10138 6/12/1722: "On Friday *Shabbos* came and I couldn't go to conclude the contract for My Lady."

[133] Emden, pp. 44–45. On the Hakham Zvi Ashkenazi see: *EJE*, vol. 3, pp. 733–35 and bibliography there.

nowicz wrote on July 7, 1736[134] to August Aleksander Czartoryski reads, "I write, not with ink but with bloody tears. I am sick and my weak condition approaches final ruination."

The cause of Rubinowicz's great indisposition was that during his recent absence, his daughter was taken by a local noblewoman with the aim of converting her to Christianity. The noblewoman claimed that she had acted because the girl had voluntarily promised several weeks earlier that she wanted to convert.[135] The only obstacle, presumably, was finding a time when Rubinowicz would be away so that he could not stop her. To this claim, Rubinowicz's wife had said, "She did not promise and will not promise, but were she to promise I would not keep her from fulfilling her word."[136]

This incident suggests that by maintaining close ties with Polish society Rubinowicz and his family were not only subject to the pressures of acculturation but those of full assimilation as well. Rubinowicz ran the risk that his child would be tempted or forced into apostasy by one of his Polish acquaintances.[137]

Fortis also learned that Jews who rose too high could be compromised and that in Polish eyes conversion was always superior to loyalty to Judaism. Fortis was *dzierżawca* of a tract in the Stara Krupica *starostwo*. He had leased the *dzierżawa* for several years. When the *starosta* died and his son succeeded him (around 1723), the latter tried to remove Fortis from the *dzierżawa* by force. When this failed he accused Fortis of trying to convince a man named Winier—a Jewish convert to Christianity—to renounce his new faith and return to the

---

[134] 1.34934 7/7/1736.

[135] N. Samter, *Judentaufen im Neunzehnten Jahrhundert* (Berlin, 1906), p. 34, mentioned a bull of Pope Benedict XVI, issued in 1747, which confirmed the right of children from the age of seven to convert voluntarily without parental permission. On kidnapping Jewish children for the purpose of conversion, see N. M. Gelber, "Die Taufbewegung unter den Polnischen Juden im XVIII Jahrhundert," *Monatschrift für Geschichte und Wissenschaft des Judentums* 68 (1924), p. 239. See also *PML*, no. 365 p. 74, which authorized funds to prevent such kidnapping. On the fate of Jewish converts to Christianity in Polish society, see J. Goldberg, "Die getauften Juden in Polen-Litauen im XVI–XVIII Jahrhundert," *Jahrbücher für Geschichte Osteuropas* 30 (1982), pp. 54–99.

[136] BC 5935 R to AAC 1.34934 7/7/1736. It is clear from 1.34934, 1.34936–37 that R's daughter was returned to her family shortly after her disappearance.

[137] Compare *SB*, pp. 163–64, 246.

fold. This was a grave charge, and Fortis was to be tried on it before the Supreme Tribunal in Piotrków. The protection he sought from Sieniawska and Józef Potocki was—initially at least—to no avail in getting the charge dropped. Fortis escaped to Amsterdam, hoping that his magnate protectors would vindicate his honor and that he would be able to return to Poland.[138]

These two cases show that no Jew, no matter how well connected, was completely secure. Their service to the magnates opened many opportunities to Rubinowicz and Fortis, but it also laid them open to malevolent designs. Intervention by their magnate protectors in their hour of need was never assured or guaranteed to succeed. While he enjoyed wealth, status, and influence due to the personal support of his magnate, a Jewish administrator had to remain alert to the danger generated by his good fortune.

Conclusion

Jews like Fortis and Rubinowicz who succeeded in attaining high places in the magnate administration are extreme and visible representatives of some common patterns of Jewish-magnate relations and Jewish life generally in Poland. Many Jews were commercially oriented. The magnates encouraged Jewish commerce as a means of increasing their own income and as a source of commercial service for the latifundium. Fortis and Rubinowicz had developed their commercial skills and contacts to such a degree that they were called upon to provide personal commercial services for the Sieniawskis, and each in his own way helped to increase income.

Jewish status entailed dependence on the lord. In the case of highly placed men like Fortis and Rubinowicz this dependence was acute. Their security in Polish society and their status in Jewish society were directly linked to the visible support of their lord. They had to strive continually to provide efficient service and remain in good graces. Such vulnerability must have added to their appeal as employees.

---

[138] See: Gierowski, "Wrocławskie interesy," p. 233; BC 5809 F to ES 1.10736, 1.10747–53 ca. 1724–26. Judging from Borgolt's reports on the use of Fortis's services in Jarosław in 1730–31 (see n. 26), Fortis was ultimately allowed to return to Poland and regain his honor.

Jews in Poland had to be politically aware and active. They were always on the lookout for threats to their existence or well-being and acquired a reputation as sharp lobbyists.[139] Fortis and Rubinowicz were assailed by rivals and had to be politically adroit in order to maintain their positions. In a way analogous to Jewish communities securing charters, Rubinowicz even persuaded Czartoryski to grant a privilege forbidding anyone to interfere with him or his family.[140]

One aspect of Jewish life in Poland was an ongoing tension between the demands of religion and economics.[141] Commerce and leasing entailed such halakhically questionable practices as dealing in gentile wine, charging interest, pig-breeding, and running a tavern or customs house on the Sabbath. Rubinowicz and Fortis were faced with conflicts of this nature. The sources do not reveal how they resolved them. Perhaps Fortis was able to observe strictly the rabbinic strictures against Jews and gentiles eating even kosher food together. It may be that Rubinowicz suffered qualms about supervising the building of Sieniawska's chapel and altar in Lubnice. We can only speculate.

Another general pattern of Polish Jewry exemplified by Fortis and Rubinowicz is the tendency not to specialize occupationally. Like many other Jews, they took advantage of available opportunities and combined collateral pursuits. Their training and magnate contacts joined to enable each of them to engage in a whole range of enterprises, assuring them secure and substantial incomes.

Men in positions like Rubinowicz's and Fortis's were not, however, only exemplary cases of the conventional pattern of Polish Jewry. They also, by virtue of their high position, exercised an important influence over the Jewish community. Their connection with the magnate entitled them to special leadership positions in their communities. Rubinowicz may have served as a magnet for the development of a whole Jewish community as a result of the economic opportunities he controlled and the *protekcja* he could muster. The magnate connection also opened up a conduit through which the magnate could work his will on the *kehalim*.

---

[139] I. Lewin, *Z historii i tradycji: szkice z dziejów kultury żydowskiej* (Warsaw, 1983), pp. 35–63; Ber of Bolechow, p. 143.

[140] 1.34934 7/7/1736.

[141] Katz, pp. 64–75; Ben-Sasson, "Takanot," *Zion* 21 (1956), pp. 183, 194.

The poise with which Rubinowicz and Fortis functioned in the non-Jewish world was of more subtle significance. Their ease was facilitated by acquaintance with non-Jews and non-Jewish culture. These magnate men learned languages, acquired non-Jewish learning, and observed non-Jewish life close up. In doing so, they crossed the frontier between Jewish and non-Jewish culture, clearing a path for others.[142] As enlightenment set in, this path began to be traveled more and more heavily.

The characteristics of the Jews who reached high status in the latifundium administration appear to group them with the famous court Jews of Central Europe.[143] As commercial agents, administrators, and confidants, they were engaged in many of the same activities as the *Hofjude* attached to the German states. As founders and key members of Jewish communities, patrons of Jewish learning, and spokesmen for Jewish interests, the two types fulfilled similar roles within the Jewish communities in which they lived. Similar to court Jews, men like Rubinowicz and Fortis had wealth, felt comfortable with non-Jewish culture, and were on cordial terms with high-ranking and powerful gentiles. Yet in both regions men like these were beholden to the favor of their masters and perched precariously in their positions. They were subject to intrigue and precipitous falls from grace.

Despite all of these similarities, however, the Polish Jew who managed a part of a latifundium differed in fundamental ways from the German court Jew. In the first place, the scale of his activities was not comparable to that of at least the more famous court Jews, men like Samuel Oppenheimer, Samson Wertheimer, Behrend Lehmann, Leffman Behrens, and Jud Suess. The Polish Jew handled a budget in the tens of thousands annually; his German counterpart managed millions.

More important, the German Jew served a state or principality—a political entity. The Polish Jew worked on an estate—basically an economic institution and, despite the pretensions of the owners, only a constituent part of a larger political unit. Consequently, while the German court Jew had a role to play in politics, diplomacy, and war, the Polish magnate's Jew was in essence a household employee. His

---

[142] Gelber, "Letoldot Harofim Hayehudim Bepolin," p. 157; Stern, Preface, especially, pp. xvi – xv.
[143] Stern.

mandate was to run an efficient and profitable household, not to counsel a state's ruler.

The essential feature of the German court Jew was his ability as a financier. His job was to supply funds or arrange loans needed to finance wars and projects. He somehow had to find the resources to underwrite the discrepancy between the prince's ambition and his material capabilities. Very few Polish Jews could muster large sums of money.[144] The magnates depended upon their close Jewish associates as managers, comptrollers, and marketers, but not, typically, as financiers. Rubinowicz was juggling the Sieniawskis's resources, not arranging large-scale loans or pumping money of his own into the latifundium.

As feudal Poland differed from the absolutist German states, so the role of the Jews closest to the elite of each region differed. Absolutism required Jews who, beyond exploiting resources, could supply money which the traditional groups (peasants, guilds, nobility, church) would not or could not provide to the central government. Their most important task was to make the prince or king financially independent of his constituency and thus able to control it better politically.

Although the Polish lord was interested in consolidating his rule over his latifundium by curbing the influence of rival elements such as the Polish central government, the church, the town councils, and the Jewish *kehalim*, he was still committed to the feudal system. He was operating an estate designed to enrich himself. He wanted to rule his estate absolutely, but he had neither the desire, nor the need, nor the means to make it into an absolutist state. The Polish lord needed the Jew to maximize the profit potential of his domain. Through trade and administration, the Jew's task was to ensure levels of income that would strengthen the magnate *vis-à-vis* his rivals and permit him his high standard of living.

The Jews in the magnate's administration as controllers and distributors of resources, or even as managers and factors, were fulfilling a subordinate role within Polish feudalism. Unlike their German cousins, they were not helping to catalyze a new economic and political system.

---

[144] G. D. Hundert, "Jews, Money and Society in the Seventeenth Century Polish Commonwealth: the Case of Kraków," *Jewish Social Studies* 43 (1981), p. 269.

CHAPTER SEVEN

The Magnates and the Jewish Community

Roles filled by individuals—town resident, merchant, arrendator, administrator—served as one framework for magnate-Jewish interaction. There was another context, however, in which the relationship developed. This was the realm of interplay between the magnate and the collective representative institutions of the Jewish community.

As a medieval-style corporation, the official Jewish community, the *kehilla,* and its governing council, the *kahal,* played a key role in regulating relations between the Jewish community collectively and its individual members on the one hand, and the surrounding Polish society on the other. This was a traditional role, which can be traced to talmudic times, that prevailed wherever the Jews lived in Europe. In principle, the *kehilla* was responsible for the actions of its members. In order to ensure that no member acted against the interests of the community, the *kehilla* forbade individual members to enter into relations, particularly of an economic nature, with non-Jews without communal approval. Only a person licensed by the *kahal* could bid on an *arenda.* No loan could be taken from a non-Jew without prior approval. Non-Jews could not be told Jewish trade secrets. *Kehilla* members were prohibited from turning to non-Jewish courts. The *kehalim* also instituted sumptuary laws designed to prevent conspicuous consumption, which could incite non-Jewish jealousies.[1]

---

[1] Buber, pp. 82, 83, 86–87, 106–15; *PHo* nos. 82–84, 111, 112, 226, 228; *PML* nos. 60–61, p. 12, 70–87 pp. 13–17, 104–106 pp. 24–25, 148 p. 36, 163–65 p. 38, 249 p. 51, 404 p. 83, 541 p. 128, 545 p. 129, 637 pp. 155–56, 670–73 p. 160, 690 p. 167, 724 p. 177, 746 p. 186, 929 p. 245; *PVAA* nos. 1 p. 1, 297 pp. 124–25, 352 pp. 148–50; *TSCHPJ* Poznań nos. 77–79, 106–108, 120, 171–78.

The Polish *kehilla* system derived much of its strength from the overt support it enjoyed on the part of the Polish central government. In the late sixteenth century, the Polish kings decided to entrust the collection of Jewish taxes to the Jewish community. The *Sejm* set a sum which the Jews as a whole were to pay into the royal treasury. This was known as the Jewish head tax (*pogłówne żydowskie*). It was left to the Jewish central and regional councils to apportion this lump sum among individual communities. The king endorsed the tax apportionment decisions of the Jewish authorities, and this royal support was assimilated into other areas as well. Thus *kahal* authority in Poland rested on both Jewish tradition and Polish sponsorship.[2]

The significance of the *kehalim* was not, however, construed identically by the Jews and the Polish authorities. The Jews looked upon the *kehilla* system as a whole as "a bit of Redemption and a modicum of honor."[3] In other words, the *kehalim* from the local *kahal* on up to the Council of Four Lands were an expression of Jewish unity and autonomy and provided the basis for maintaining Jewish life and values intact. The local *kahal* was, for the Jews, the local embodiment of traditionally sanctioned Jewish authority.

For the Polish authorities, the *kahal* was an extension of their administration. It was a convenient means of collecting taxes, preserving order, and exercising authority over part of the population. As such it was the functional equivalent of the Christian municipal councils. To the Poles, the status of the local *kahal* in Jewish history was moot. What concerned them was that the local *kahal* embody *their* authority among the Jews. When the Poles were finally convinced that the Council of Four Lands was much better at fulfilling its own financial needs than it was at gathering revenue for the Polish treasury, they dissolved it.

For magnates, the question of subordination of the *kahal* to their objectives was even more important than it was for the king. In order

---

[2] Baron, *History,* vol. 16, pp. 156–57; S. A. Cygielman, "Iskei Hakhirot shel Yehudei Polin Ukesharam Lehithavut 'Vaad Arba Aratzot'," *Zion* 47 (1982), pp. 129–37; Schorr, *Organizacja Żydów,* p. 73.

[3] Ber of Bolechow; the Hebrew edition, p. 88; reads: Vehayah zot livnei yisrael geulah ketanah umeat kavod.

Note that my translation here differs from that of Wischnitzer in the English edition, p. 145.

to exploit his estate or royal leasehold to the fullest, a magnate desired to consolidate his rule over it. He wanted maximum freedom to manipulate all variables, including urban ones. Among the forces that could interfere with the magnate's ambitions was the Jewish communal organization. Because of the comprehensiveness of its activities and the natural and legal ties of the Jews to it, the *kahal* was the magnate's most formidable rival for control over his Jewish subjects. Consequently, although the magnates might have appreciated the *kahal*'s tax-collecting and administrative capabilities, they regarded other *kehilla* activities and prerogatives as an annoyance at best and a threat at worst. To the extent that regulations of the central councils or the local *kahal* prevented individual communities or individual Jews from devoting all of their energies towards benefiting the lord, there was a serious clash of interests between the lord and the community. The most common instance of this is the issue of *arenda* licenses.[4] Another example is taxation. The more tax money that a community paid toward the general Jewish head tax, the less it would have left to pay in taxes or other forms to its lord. Likewise, an individual's ability to put his financial resources at his lord's disposal was harmed by a high individual tax burden. Hence every magnate had an interest in reducing the *kahal*-imposed tax burden on his Jewish subjects.[5]

The magnate-*kahal* opposition of interests extended into the judicial field as well. While, in general, the magnate might welcome relief from the onus of judging cases between Jews, in cases affecting an individual's economic productivity he wanted his interests to be taken into account and might take steps to guarantee a favorable outcome.[6]

---

[4] See Chapter 5.

[5] BC 5943 ES to AMS 1.37174 8/29/1707; *ABK* nos. 192, 195; *PML* pp. xix – xx, no. 908 pp. 240 – 41; *PVAA* nos. 438 p. 208, 698 pp. 379 – 80, 825 pp. 440 – 41; *AGZ*, vol. 22 nos. 21.15, 31.53, 212.33, 261.20, 280; vol. 23 no. 25.1; M. Schorr, *Żydzi w Przemyślu do końca XVIII wieku* (Lviv, 1903), nos. 101, 124, 139; cf. Baron, *History*, vol. 16, p. 157; Mahler, *Toldot*, pp. 388 – 93; Szmeruk, pp. 182 – 84.

[6] For an expression by Poles of how important rabbinic courts were to the proper functioning of Polish commerce see: A. Freimann, ed., *Sefer Teka Shofar* (Frankfurt am Main, 1909), pp. 23 – 25. For examples of magnate interference in rabbinic courts see: BC 2702 3/17/1730, 6/6/1730. Note also the inclusion of several Hebrew court decisions in the magnate's archive; e.g., BC 3823 no. 52; BC 3826 no. 45.

Magnates ventured to prevent or control *kahal* involvement in matters of consequence to them in several ways. They injected themselves as much as possible into *kahal* internal affairs, lent their authority to the *kahal* only in instances where the *kahal* was serving them, and tended to bypass the *kahal,* relating directly to individual Jews.

Magnate involvement and interference in *kahal* affairs took different forms. One indirect way in which they weakened and co-opted *kahal* authority was by creating a group of rich arrendators and administrators who were more dependent on the magnate than on their *kahal.* While the primary motivation for the development of this group was economic, the political ramifications were significant. According to seventeenth- and eighteenth-century rabbinic literature, Jews who were "intimates of the authorities" often disregarded the demands of communal welfare and discipline in favor of their own narrow interests.

The *protekcja* offered by noblemen to their favorites enabled the latter to ignore community edicts and laws. In seventeenth-century Poznań, for example, the well-connected toll farmers blithely ignored communal resolutions ordering them to pay a special levy and to discharge an unscrupulous employee.[7] Both the Lithuanian and Polish councils railed against Jews who "saved themselves" from paying taxes and fulfilling other obligations by gaining the permission and protection of their nobility patrons.[8] The problem was sufficiently widespread that it came to the attention of the Polish authorities, who repeatedly stressed the illegality of Jews using their nobility affiliations to evade taxes or to obtain exemptions from trade restrictions.[9]

---

[7] *TSCHPJ,* Poznań nos. 75–76, 209–11.

[8] *PML* nos. 215 p. 44, 690 p. 167, 518 p. 122; 908 p. 240; *PVAA* nos. 231 pp. 89–90, 297 pp. 124–25; note 5 above. Cf. Goldberg, "Poles and Jews," p. 261.

[9] *AGZ,* vol. 22, nos. 2.19, 21.75, 42.74, 261.20, 280; vol. 23 nos. 25.1, 60.9, 162.10, 203.7–8; *ABK* no. 148; *PVAA* includes several proclamations by Polish authorities against "private" Jews who did not bear their share of the general Jewish tax burden; nos. 231 pp. 89–90, 253 p. 102, 438 p. 208. Such proclamations were probably issued in response to pressure by the Jewish communal authorities. Another way in which the communal establishment sought to fight these flouters was to try to restrict *a priori* their contact with potential magnate protectors. There were decrees requiring authorization by the communal leaders before any such direct contact could occur; e.g., *PML* nos. 163–65 p. 38, *PVAA* nos. 1 p. 1, 352 pp. 148–50; *PHo* nos. 83,

Jews with magnate ties could achieve a measure of independence from their community; they could even turn against it. In 1700, for example, a certain Jewish community (probably Poznań) tried to dismiss its *shtadlan,* Barukh Halevi. In retaliation he "informed and delated to a well-known lord, causing Jewish money to wind up in alien hands ... and he wrote despicable things to the lord here."[10] Thus the possibility existed that a powerful Jew would use his influence with non-Jews to harm the Jewish community.

In the Sieniawski-Czartoryski sources there is an extreme example of defiance of *kahal* authority by an arrendator. Around 1720, Jakub, arrendator of Oleszyce, was accused as follows: "Jakub, subject and citizen of Oleszyce, due to a claim he had against the late Zelman [of Jarosław] ... wrongly assailed, plundered and harassed the Jarosław Jews, causing them significant losses and damages. Moreover, he forced them into his custody as debt security. ... "[11]

The ability of magnate-backed individuals to defy *kahal* authority demonstrated the weakness of this authority, causing the *kahal* to lose its prestige and its capacity to control the behavior of its members. Concomitantly, the image of the Polish lord as the true repository of power and authority was reinforced.

The Magnates did not benefit solely from their Jewish clients' defiance of the *kehalim,* however. Much more common, and more advantageous to the magnates, were situations where magnate-sponsored Jews attained a controlling position in the economic and political life of the community.[12] If the amount and tone of Jewish criticism of this phenomenon are any indication, this was one of the great issues of eighteenth-century Jewish life in Poland. For instance, *Hasdei Avot,* a popular commentary on *Pirkei-Avot,* pilloried the type of leader who said, "Even though I have no pedigree and I do not act for the sake of Heaven, I will nonetheless succeed in my actions by

---

111, 112, 228. While such edicts are often ascribed to a desire to keep individuals out of risky financial ventures for which the community would ultimately be held accountable, I think that the desire to control potential rebels was at least as strong a motivation; cf. Dubnov, *History,* vol. 1, pp. 188–89.

[10] *PVAA* no. 530 pp. 254–55.

[11] EW 133 Uniwersał ES. See also: BC 5881 Łukszyński to ES 1.23429, undated.

[12] H. Alexandrov, "Derzhavtses un Kohol," *Tsaytshrift* 4 (1930), p. 121; M. Bałaban, *Stan kahału krakowskiego na przełomie XVII i XVIII w.* (Warsaw, 1931), pp. 1–8; P. S. Marek, "Istoricheskie soobshchenia," *Voshod* (May, 1903), pp. 74–76.

the power of the ruler and the owner of the town.''[13] Another important eighteenth-century book, *Darkhei Noam,* complained about those who "lavish huge sums on the lord in order to achieve greatness.''[14] The aims of such a leader are "firstly, to lord it over the community, that everyone should be subject to him; and secondly, to deny justice and to wrong a man in his cause, to favor his friends and relatives and to take revenge on his enemies.''[15]

So pervasive are critiques of this nature that the historian B. Z. Dinur was moved to remark, "I think that on the basis of all these we can establish that the locus of the general plight of the age was in the rule of the despotic—men of the nobles' courts and intimates of the authorities—over the communities, in the worsening of social cleavage, and in the moral decay of the community.''[16]

Other sources confirm the opinion that "intimates of the authorities" were often despotic. The community of Poznań was continually fighting the imposition of excess tolls by the toll farmers, in addition to combating their attempts to monopolize merchandise entering the town—a move that would guarantee them control of commerce.[17] Monopolization of opportunity by powerful arrendators was also a problem in the late seventeenth century in the community of Horki where the *Yehidim* (people without contracts from the Polish lord) were engaged in a constant struggle to carve out a sector of the economy where they could earn their livelihood. The final result was an arrangement whereby the arrendators were guaranteed a high degree of political power in exchange for relinquishing some of their economic predominance.[18]

Even where arrendators and administrators did not monopolize economic opportunities, they often controlled a large portion of them. Their ability to make appointments or to grant leases to subarrendators assured them a solid base of dependent clients.

---

[13] Aharon b. Yehuda, *Hasdei Avot,* (Nesterov [Zhovkva], 1771), p. 8b.

[14] Shmuel b. Eliezer of Kalaveria, *Darkhei Noam* (Koenigsberg, 1764), pp. 100a–101b. See also: Peretz b. Moshe, pp. 52d–53a.

[15] Shmuel b. Eliezer, pp. 100a–101b; cf. Mahler, *Toldot,* p. 69; *SB,* p. 217; Rapoport, no. 18.

[16] Dinur, p. 100.

[17] *TSCHPJ* Poznań, pp. 59–61, nos. 75–76, 209–19.

[18] *PHo,* nos. 83, 84, 108, 111, 112, 227, 228, 230; Alexandrov, pp. 121–24; Trunk, "Vaad Medinas Rusya," pp. 73–75.

It is evident from the Sieniawski-Czartoryski archival material that Jews with close ties to the owners enjoyed a dominant position in the Jewish community. As Maria Zofia Czartoryska reminded the rabbi of Sataniv in 1730: "You should remember, sir, that according to ancient custom the arrendators have an important place among the elders of the *kahal*."[19] Two of the Sieniawski-Czartoryski Jews introduced in earlier chapters exemplify this statement. Lejba Anklewicz Sukiennik enjoyed close connections with Elżbieta Sieniawska, being both a supplier of cloth to her staff and the general arrendator of Sieniawa. He also played a leading role in the operation of the Jewish community of the town.[20] The *ekonom,* Yisrael Rubinowicz, though his formal position in his community, if any, is unknown, was obviously a power to be reckoned with. According to Emden in *Megilat Sefer,* Rubinowicz was "an important notable, one of the distinguished men of the land of Poland."[21] The sources confirm his influence by preserving the record of his machinations ensuring rabbinic posts for his son-in-law and grandson.[22]

The ramifications of this phenomenon are far-reaching. The magnate could be certain that those dependent on him, who occupied positions of economic and political power in the Jewish community, would be on call to defend his interests. If it appeared that the *kahal* was stepping out of bounds, it was easy enough for the magnate to apply pressure to those whose livelihood he directly controlled. Magnates were not, however, hesitant to interfere themselves when they deemed it necessary.

It was traditional in Poland for the non-Jewish authority to confirm *kahal* election results and to supervise Jewish communal officials.[23] Magnates exploited this privilege both as a method of extorting money from the successful candidates[24] and as a means of exercising

[19] BC 2702 6/6/1730.

[20] BC 3826 nos. 59, 66, 69 – 72; see also Chapter 3.

[21] Emden, p. 44.

[22] See Chapter 6.

[23] M. Bałaban, "Die Krakauer Judengemeinde-Ordnung von 1595 und ihre Nachträge," *JJLG* (1912), p. 315; Pazdro, nos. 22, 63, 64. For examples of actual magnate certification of *kahal* elections, see: Pinkas Zabłudowa, nos. 283, 367; Pinkas Boćki, pp. 25 – 26, 30, 34 – 36, 55, 61 – 64; PHo no. 140.

[24] Shmuel b. Eliezer, pp. 100b – 101a: "And they lavish much money on the nobleman in order to achieve greatness."

control over the communities. Jan Potocki, owner of the town of Boćki, wrote in the Jewish communal record book there that he was confirming the election of the officials listed "for one year, reserving the right to change any or all of them if they prove to be incompetent in the exercise of their offices or if they commit any transgressions against me."[25]

Magnates also kept control by reserving the rights to approve the communal budget and to inspect the communal record books. The duties of the Medzhybizh Jews listed in the 1730 inventory specify that "accounts of all income and expenditures must be made yearly before the *zamek* official."[26]

In the eighteenth century magnates went beyond the exercise of traditional supervisory prerogatives and involved themselves in matters that lay at the heart of Jewish autonomy. The *raison d'etre* of the Council of Four Lands and its subdivisions was to arrange equitable, orderly distribution of the Jewish tax burden. In the early eighteenth century, however, in the Lviv region there was a continuing struggle for authority between the *kahal* of the city of Lviv and the *kehalim* of the surrounding towns. In an earlier period one would have expected the problem to be arbitrated by one of the central councils. Instead, in 1713, Adam Mikołaj Sieniawski ordered the representatives of the Jews of the Red Russian region to gather in his town, Burshtyn, to settle the matter.[27]

Similarly, as the dispute between Lviv and its hinterland festered, and attempts by the Council of Four Lands to mediate failed, a *modus vivendi* was arranged only in 1740 at a meeting of the communities in question at Berezhany under the patronage of August Aleksander Czartoryski in his capacity as the governor of Ruś.[28]

The magnates not only took a hand in mediating disputes between Jewish communities, they also helped their own communities and

[25] Pinkas Boćki, p. 43; cf. AAC's direct intervention in the Medzhybizh *kahal* elections, BC 4078 Międzybóż 1740 pt. 9; Pazdro, no. 11, pt. 2.

[26] BC 4047, p. 23, pt. 9.

[27] Trunk, "Vaad Medinas Rusya," pp. 75–79; Bałaban, "Z zagadnień," pp. 46–47, 62 (n. 21).

[28] Bałaban, "Z zagadnień," pp. 48–50; see also: I. Trunk, "An Umbekanter Dokument Vegn dem Kamf in di Kehilos fun Lemberger Sevivo, 1735–1758," *YB* 40 (1956), pp. 221–24; idem, "Ketovot Beivrit-Yiddish al Mismakhim Polaniim Mehameah ha-17–18," *N. M. Gelber Jubilee Volume* (Tel Aviv, 1963), pp. 83–88.

favorite individuals flout the authority of the established Jewish institutions. In 1727 the Jewish Council of the Red Russian district demanded 1,950 *zł.* as the tax assessment of the Jews of Stryi, Sieniawska's *starostwo.* The Stryi *kahal* paid only 1,200 and the intervention of Sieniawska prevented the Council from obtaining any more.[29] When the Jews of Jarosław fell into arrears in their tax obligations to the Council of Four Lands, Sieniawska's administrator, Łukszyński, advised her to write a threatening letter to the head of the regional Jewish council to forestall an *egzekucja.*[30] In 1707 Sieniawska herself wrote to her husband urging him to intervene with the Lublin *kahal* on behalf of the Jews in their town of Kozienice.[31]

The lords' interference in Jewish affairs also extended to local disputes. When Ajzyk Jachimowicz sued Lejba Sukiennik and the rest of the *kahal* of Sieniawa for monopolizing power and misusing funds, Sieniawski saw it as his obligation to have his court investigate the matter thoroughly.[32] In 1725, Elżbieta Sieniawska wrote to Zabagłowicz, administrator of Tenczyn:[33]

> The Jewish court does not deign to render justice or make restitution to the Tenczyn arrendator who has a just claim against the bankrupt Cracow Jew holding his merchandise. When the relatives of the bankrupt one return from Wrocław through Tenczyn, arrest and hold them until they fully compensate the arrendator.

In 1719 when the arrendators of Żuków and Bilov disagreed with their *kahal* on what percentage of the *arenda* income should be earmarked for the *kahal,* it was Czartoryski's father, Kazimierz, and not a Jewish court, who adjudicated the matter.[34] In February 1732, August Aleksander Czartoryski forced the Sieniawa *kahal* to pay a debt they owed to Jakub Cieplicki, Jewish supervisor of the Sieniawa stackyard.[35] The apportionment of occupational monopolies was traditionally a prerogative of the *kahal.* Yet, in an undated petition, the Jewish

---

[29] Prochaska, *Historja,* p. 119.

[30] BC 5881 Łukszyński to ES 1.23529 8/5/1715.

[31] BC 5943 ES to AMS 1.37174 8/29/1707; cf. Shmuel b. Elkanah, no. 101.

[32] BC 3826 nos. 59, 66, 69–72.

[33] BC 5946 ES to Zabagłowicz 1.37987 11/28/1725.

[34] EW 185 3/10/1719.

[35] EW 189 *Supl.* Jakub Cieplicki 1732.

physician, Rubin Molszowicz, complained to Sieniawski that another Jew had begun practicing medicine in Shkłoŭ and was stealing his livelihood.[36]

Each of these cases, and many similar ones,[37] related to an area where, traditionally, *kehilla* authorities were empowered to keep their own house in order. Despite this, time and again these authorities were defied or circumvented in favor of the authority of the Polish lord.

In general in this period, Polish authorities, and the magnate latifundium owners in particular, tried to preempt the prerogatives of the *kehalim* in matters both large and small. Whether it was imposing taxes on members, granting settlement rights, regulating economic competition, granting publishing or *arenda* licenses, regulating weights and measures, contracting debts, settling disputes, or even punishing religious transgressions and organizing synagogue life, the tendency in the eighteenth century was for the non-Jewish authorities to intrude more and more.[38]

A classic expression of this trend toward usurping *kahal* autonomous functions is contained in a memorandum sent by Sieniawski to the administrator of Shkłoŭ in 1725. One of the pillars of *kehilla* organization and authority was its court system. *Kehilla* courts were authorized to act as the court of the first instance in all noncriminal matters between Jewish litigants.[39] Sieniawski, however, was apparently dissatisfied with the traditional competence of the *kehilla*

---

[36] EW 525 *Supl.* Rubin Molszewicz.

[37] EW *Supl.* Irsz Pinkasów vs. Satanów *Kahal,* 1741, Response of Satanów *Kahal* to accusation by Melech, 1737; EW 196 *Regestr papierów grodzkich różnych:* Protest of Jura of Lubaczów, 1721; BC 3499 p. 429; BC 2702 p. 565; BC 3822 nos. 59, 60; BC 3756 M. Abramowicz to MZSC 1.9 3/24/1731(?); BC 5829 Hayzyk wnuk Chaimow to ES 1.14238–40 undated. Pazdro, pp. 29–31, observed that as the eighteenth century progressed the number of cases between Jews brought directly to the *podwojewoda* "Jews' court," came to outnumber those brought on appeal after having been heard in the rabbinic courts.

[38] EW 189 *Supl.* Gotel zięć Berko Fajbowicz of Sieniawa; BC 3503 pp. 89, 354; BC 5972 Chaim Tywlowicz to ES 1.45321 1/3/1719; *ABK* no. 219; *AGZ,* vol. 22, no. 212.33; Pazdro, pp. 72–73, 139–47, nos. 23, 52, 57, 69, 83, 84, 102; Brekhia Berekh b. Getzel, *Zera Berekh Hashlishi* (Halle, 1714), p. 37d; Peretz b. Moshe, p. 5a; Baron, *History,* vol. 16, p. 377, n. 54; Bergerówna, pp. 304–305, 318; Goldberg, "Bein Hofesh Lenetinut," pp. 110–12.

[39] See Chapter 3.

courts. In a bid to limit their authority he issued the following order on July 18, 1725:[40]

> For a long time due to our ignorance, the Jews have adjudicated matters involving Jews among themselves; and, moreover, without recourse to appeals to my *zamek* court. Therefore I am issuing an order that Jews dare not adjudicate any matters except for religious questions pertaining to their faith as well as cases involving marriage, divorce, baptism [*sic*] and the like. In such cases they are free to appeal to the elders of the ecclesiastical authorities of the region. When, however, a Jew and a Jew, or a Jew and a Catholic or a Catholic and a Jew are involved in a case concerning debt, commerce, assault, or when it pertains to my revenues or related matters, then my court is to judge and not the Jews . . . subject to a fine of 100 t.b.

This directive represents a radical departure from the traditional Polish policy of allowing, even encouraging, internal Jewish autonomy. It can be understood, however, as a logical move in the ongoing process of magnate interference in *kahal* affairs. Limiting Jewish judicial competence was not too large a step from mediating the apportionment of the Jewish tax burden.

Another way in which the authority of the local *kahal* with regard to its members was weakened in favor of the authority of the lord was the manner in which the lord entered into direct relationships with individual Jews without benefit of *kahal* intermediation. The most obvious instance of this was all the direct dealings owners had with Jewish arrendators, factors, and administrators. Even if all *kahal* restrictions on *entering* into relationships with non-Jews had been observed (they were not), once these relationships were formed, the *kahal* had almost no role to play. It is hard to serve two masters, and these individuals knew that their economic interests lay with absolute loyalty to the lord. In fact, in the case of these magnate-connected

---

[40] EW 525 Szkłów 1725 *Informacje*. Whether this was enforced cannot be determined. If it was, it probably did not apply beyond Shkłoŭ. Note that AAC, albeit in his capacity as governor (*wojewoda*), confirmed the traditional competence of the Jewish courts in his area in 1732, Pazdro, p. 45. But there were limits on the power of Jewish courts. For instance, EW 179 *Supl.* Herszko to AAC observes that rabbinic courts could not attach real estate in payment of debts without the express confirmation of the lord.

Jews the traditional relationship was reversed. Rather than these individuals being dependent on the community organization to tend to affairs with respect to the non-Jewish authorities, it was often the *kahal* that depended upon these individuals to gain the favor of the magnate owner.[41]

But it was not only chosen individuals who enjoyed a direct relationship with the owner, without involvement of the *kahal*. Two of the principal functions of the *kehilla* were tax apportionment and aid in time of disaster. In the Sieniawski-Czartoryski sources, however, there are numerous examples where these duties were filled by the Polish lord and not the *kehilla*. Given the sorry financial state of the *kehillot* in the eighteenth century, it is perhaps not surprising to find Jewish subjects turning to the owner's treasury for loans and grants to rebuild their homes after fires or destruction caused by invading armies. The fact that the lord and not the *kehilla* was the natural source of aid in time of disaster, and that such aid was secured by individual petition without the need of *kahal* intercession could not but take a toll on the standing of the *kehalim* in the eyes of their members. A community that could not help its members in their personal misfortune could not demand their absolute loyalty when communal interests were at stake.[42]

Also potentially detrimental to communal authority and discipline was the trend, apparent in the Sieniawski-Czartoryski holdings, for town real estate taxes (*czynsz*) to be assesssed and collected from each individual property owner rather than as a lump sum from the *kahal*.

---

[41] Buber, p. 84; Goldberg, *Privileges,* pp. 10–11; BC 5972 Chaim Tywlowicz to ES 1.45318, undated, 1.45327 12/12/1714 on behalf of the Stryi community.

[42] On the indebtedness of the Jewish communities in this period see J. Morgensztern, "Zadłużenie gmin żydowskich w ordynacji Zamojskiej w. II połowie XVII w.," *BŻIH* 73 (1970), pp. 47–65; I. Schiper, "Finanzialer Hurban fun der Tsentraler un Provintsialer Oytonomia fun Yidn in Altn Poiln," *Yivo Ekonomishe Shriftn,* vol. 2, Y. Leshtchinsky, ed. (Vilnius, 1932), pp. 1–19; I. Galant, "Zadlozhennost' evreiskikh obshchin v XVII vek," *EvS* 6 (1913), pp. 129–32. For examples of petitions addressed to the lords see: EW 189 *Supliki* of the following Sieniawa Jews ca. 1730–36; Berko Fajbowicz, Lemuś Jakubowicz, Irsz Dawidowicz, Majer Jakubowicz, Szmul Abramowicz, Lejbuś syn Moszko Krakowski, Leja Krakowska, Widow of Berko Gorlicki. See also BC 5757 Aron Szmuklerz to ES 1.265 9/13/1719; cf. Szmeruk, p. 192. *Kehalim* did petition the lord with regard to problems involving the whole community; e.g., EW 189 *Supl.* of Sieniawa Jewish community to ES and Szumanczowski, re: debts and inability to pay the rabbi's salary.

While in some locales the lump sum method persisted, in places like Shkłoŭ, Tarnoruds'ka, Sieniawa-Oleszyce, and Medzhybizh, after 1730, the *kahal* was excluded from fulfilling its traditional role.[43] Removing the *kahal* from the tax collection process removed one of the Polish lord's basic incentives to support the authority of the *kahal,* one of the foundations on which that authority rested.

While in this period the magnates tended to by-pass and usurp the autonomous functions of the *kahal,* they continued to make use of it to serve their own administrative and financial ends. Basing themselves on the medieval notion that the corporation was responsible for all of its members,[44] the lords were able to hold the *kahal* responsible for the enforcement of edicts on all Jews. Whenever an owner was faced with lawbreaking on the part of individual Jews, he might impose punishment on the *kahal.* If, for example, Jews were avoiding paying taxes, or illegally employing Christian servants, or leaving the latifundium in large numbers, the most common remedy was to force the *kahal* elders, by threat of fine or imprisonment, to stop *kehilla* members from engaging in their objectionable practices.[45]

In the sphere of finance, too, the doctrine of collective responsibility dictated that the *kehilla* assume responsibility for the financial obligations of its members. If an individual owed a debt to an outsider, the *kahal* was expected to collect the money or sell off the debtor's assets.[46] When, around 1730, the arrendator of Sieniawa went bankrupt, the *kahal* was expected to make good on his debts.[47] If no

---

[43] See tax lists: BC 4047, 4052, 4053, 4101, 4474, 4477, 4482, 4486; GOSP 345, 991, 1008.

[44] This notion is clearly expressed in the *arenda* contracts betwen Kazimierz Czartoryski and the *Kahal* of Klewań, EW 185.

[45] *AGZ*, vol. 22 nos. 21.75, 195.10, 269.2; vol. 25 nos. 107.2 – 107.11, 107.12, 119.10, 121.6, 132.11. AGAD AR cc/1 Ustawy Appendix pt. 1. This use of the communal organization and its officials was not limited to the *kahal.* The peasant *gromada* in the village was similarly utilized; see Burszta, *Wieś,* pp. 72 – 79; Szkurłatowski, pp. 187 – 90.

[46] BC 2702 p. 601.

[47] EW 189 *Supl.* Sieniawa community to Szumanczowski; see similarly BC 2702 7/30/1730.

one could be found to lease an *arenda,* it was frequently the *kahal* that was forced to find a candidate.[48]

The *kahal* could also be an important revenue-gathering arm. Besides receiving a share of certain *kahal* revenues, when it suited him the owner continued to utilize the *kahal* to collect taxes. In addition, the lord received gifts, bribes, and loan repayments from the *kahal.*[49]

The tendency of the magnates to try gradually to deprive Jewish communal institutions of autonomous functions and real power, while reinforcing their functioning as agents of the owner's interests, is most apparent in the magnate relations with the rabbinate. Normally, every main *kehilla* engaged a rabbi who was one of the employees of the *kahal,* serving at its pleasure. He filled several roles. First, he was the decisor in questions of Jewish law. If a housewife wanted to know if a chicken with a broken bone was indeed kosher; if an arrendator sought a way to keep his tavern functioning on Saturdays without violating Sabbath laws; if a woman whose husband was missing wanted permission to remarry—all of these would consult the community rabbi.

Second, the rabbi usually served as the chairman of the *kehilla* court. This court judged mostly questions of civil law, although it could also impose punishments for religious transgressions and breaches of communal discipline.

Third, the rabbi was the facilitator of many social acts having a religious-legal-ceremonial character. He officiated at weddings, divorces, contract signings, oath takings, testimony depositions, and elections.

Finally, the rabbi was expected to serve as the chief educator and moral guide of his community. He taught classes and delivered occasional sermons.[50]

The rabbi's pay for serving in these capacities typically consisted of

[48] See Chapter 5.

[49] GOSP 1566 1732, pp. 33–44; AKP K.01 Rachunki Starszemi Synagogi Międzyrzecki pp. 229–31, 1604–1704.

[50] S. Assaf, "Lekorot Harabanut Beashkenaz, Polin Velita," *Reshumot* 2 (1927), pp. 282–86. Since the basic source of a rabbi's authority was his expertise in Jewish law, and not his appointment, there were often times when a rabbi could find himself at odds with the communal elders; Assaf, pp. 288–89; PHo no. 297, *PML* no. 364, p. 74; R. Yoel Sirkes, *(New) Responsa,* (Korzec, 1795), no. 43.

a regular salary, "commissions" paid by those who directly benefited from his services (litigants in a lawsuit or parents of a bridegroom for example), and gifts given to him by many families of the community in honor of Jewish holidays. Some rabbis augmented their income by writing books or itinerant preaching. In addition, many rabbis had time to deal in ancillary occupations such as real estate investment, commerce, and petty moneylending.[51]

The right to appoint their own rabbis was one of the oldest and most fundamental rights of Polish-Lithuanian Jewry. The rabbinate and the rabbinic-led courts were among the most tangible aspects of Jewish autonomy.[52] In light of this, it is natural to find that the magnates' approach to the rabbinate mirrored their approach to Jewish autonomy in general.

Traditionally, the Polish authority, whether royal or private, had the right to approve a community's choice for rabbi. This right was exercised by means of the Polish authority granting a license (*konsens*) to the rabbi in question authorizing him to judge "in accord with ancient rabbinic practice" and exhorting the Jews not to turn to anyone else.[53]

This granting of a license by the magnate to the rabbi was but a formal expression of a reality clearly illustrated in the Sieniawski-Czartoryski territories in the eighteenth century. That is, the rabbi, though supposedly an employee of the *kahal,* was, in the last analysis, an appointee of the magnate. Like any other magnate official, he could wield authority with or without the *kahal*'s consent. When the magnate saw fit he could completely discount the considerations of the *kahal* when appointing the rabbi.

Thus in 1744 Hersz Lejbowicz, the incumbent rabbi of Medzhybizh, pleaded before Czartoryski's commissioner, Walicki, that he

---

[51] Assaf, pp. 277–81, 288–89. In Sieniawa in 1726 the rabbi was paid a minimum of 200 *zł*. In 1731 the rabbinic license there cost over 300 *zł*. per year. Cf. *TSCHPJ* Poznań nos. 138, 139; Trunk, "Vaad Medinas Rusya," p. 71. On rabbinic sidelines, see: BC 5870 Rabbi Hersz Lejbowicz to A. Walicki 1.21169 12/21/1744; Assaf, pp. 388–89; Bałaban, "Z zagadnień," p. 57; Dinur, p. 104; D. Wachstein, "Sridim Mipinkaso shel Rabbi Yaacov Yoshua Baal 'Penei Yehoshua'," *Studies in Jewish Bibliography in Honor of A. S. Freidus* (New York, 1929), Hebrew section, pp. 15–31.

[52] Assaf, pp. 267–69; cf. Goldberg, *Privileges,* pp. 22–23.

[53] BC 5281/2 no. 72 Jarosław 10/7/1723; Archiwum PAN Cracow 3795 (HM 6739) 6/3/1751.

ignore the petition the *kahal* had registered expressing dissatisfaction with Hersz's service and proposing a new candidate. Hersz insisted that the new man bribed the community and begged "that I might be held in My Lord's favor and maintain the license granted by the Prince [Czartoryski]."[54]

The magnate, not the *kahal,* was the ultimate power behind the rabbi. Therefore, in discouraging young men from entering the professional rabbinate, the author of *Hasdei Avot* wrote:[55]

For if you want to enter the rabbinate and make a living from it you will be forced to obtain the sanction of the [non-Jewish] authorities. . . . It would be better for you to earn your living from the work of your hands rather than trust in princes who only bring a person close to them when it is to their advantage, but do not support a person when he is in trouble.

Magnate control of rabbinic appointments was also the apparent motivation behind the Lithuanian Council's edict in 1720 that if a town owner deposed a rabbi from his position, no new rabbi was permitted to replace him until the contract of the deposed man expired.[56] This edict, the case of Hersz, and the comment in *Hasdei Avot* reflect the fact that magnate involvement with rabbinic appointments was not merely a means to derive financial advantage by placing an excise tax on the process by which *kehalim* hired rabbis. The significance of magnate interference was much more fundamental. In effect the magnates converted the rabbinate from an institution controlled by Jewish authoritative bodies to one controlled by themselves.[57]

Rabbinic posts were transformed into a type of *arenda.* The rabbi purchased from the owner a "lease" on the right to collect the rabbinic salary, commissions, and gifts from the community. Like an arrendator, his calculation was that these revenues would cover the price of the rent—in this case the license fee—and provide an income besides. Rabbinic posts were like *arendy* in another way too; they

[54] BC 5870 Hersz Lejbowicz to A. Walicki 1.21168 4/2/1744.

[55] Aharon b. Yehuda, p. 6a; cf. Peretz b. Moshe, p. 37d; D. Hakaro, *Ohel Rahel* (Shkłoǔ, 1790), pp. 15b–d; Schorr, *Organizacja Zydow*, pp. 42–43; Dinur, pp. 106–107.

[56] *PML* no. 915, pp. 243–44.

[57] Compare Katz, p. 228.

went to the highest bidder. When Rubinowicz sought to secure the Sieniawa rabbinate for his son-in-law, Judka, he had to promise payment of 30 *cz. zł.*[58] When the Jews of Yarychiv decided that they wanted the son of their former rabbi appointed to the post they were told that they would have to outbid the rival candidate by submitting a higher "honorarium" to Elżbieta Sieniawska.[59]

The rabbi also resembled an arrendator to the extent that he depended on the lord's authority to protect his rights to the revenues coming to him. In 1726, the *kahal* of Sieniawa felt that they could not afford to pay the rabbi his normal salary. They did not turn to any Jewish council or court to intercede on their behalf with the rabbi. Rather, they petitioned Sieniawska to release them from this obligation. Since she granted the rabbi the right to the income, only she could decide if he was to be forced to forego it.[60] In 1731, the rabbi of Sieniawa died after serving only a few months of a three-year license. His widow demanded from Czartoryski that no new rabbi be hired until the community reimburse her for the cost of the license, which her husband's untimely death had left to be recouped.[61] Thus, by the eighteenth century, as can be seen in the Sieniawski-Czartoryski territories, the rabbi was not a salaried employee of the *kehilla*, who owed them his livelihood and hence his loyalty. He was a lessee whose lease was the magnate's to give and to enforce. In this light the many complaints in the homiletical literature against rabbis who bought their positions from the Polish authorities should be viewed not so much as an indication of moral failing on the part of rabbis, but as a reflection of the loss of this central institution from the control of the Jewish authorities into the hands of the magnates.[62]

---

[58] BC 5935 R to Królikiewicz (secretary to ES) 1.34908 2/23/1727; see Chapter 6.

[59] BC 5899 S. Nahaczowski to ES 1.26904 11/26/1726.

[60] EW 189 *Supl. Kahal* Sieniawa to ES 1726; cf. *SB* p. 202.

[61] BC 2904 no. 119; cf. BC 5886 Chaim Tywlowicz et al. to ES 1.24374 7/11(?)/1717.

[62] Dinur, pp. 106–109; Katz, p. 228; M. Piekarz, *Bimei Tzmihat Hahasidut* (Jerusalem, 1978), pp. 178–83 quotes several complaints against magnate control of the rabbinate as well as some berating purchase of the rabbinic positions from the *kahal*. This type of purchase was a step prior to magnate control. Once the *hazaka* system broke down, as was true of other types of *arenda*, the rabbinate passed from the hands of the *kahal* to those of the magnate. Magnate control did not necessarily render the *kahal* helpless in dealing with its rabbi. Sometimes *kehalim* used the

Magnate control of the rabbinate did not stop with appointments. Magnates were very concerned with rabbinic activity because rabbis served an important function on the latifundium. Just as the owners expected arrendators to generate revenue and serve as banks, so they expected their rabbis to help guarantee the orderly functioning of society and the smooth flow of commerce. For example, the file of Maria Zofia Czartoryska's papers relating to Sataniv for 1730 shows that usually when the *kahal* was directed to enforce an edict or collect a debt the order was addressed to the rabbi and the *kahal*.[63] The rabbi bore responsibility in addition to the *kahal*.

The rabbi's judicial function was considered to be of paramount importance. Sieniawski's 1725 directive notwithstanding, the Polish authorities remained in need of rabbinic courts. Commerce in a town could be severely impaired if the local rabbinic court ceased to operate.[64] Czartoryski and other magnates and governors set down detailed guidelines as to how they expected rabbis in their territories to act. The main demand from the rabbi was "that justice in the ecclesiastical courts not be absent, and that order be preserved in the best way possible according to ancient Jewish laws and customs."[65]

Ordinarily the magnates upheld the authority of the rabbinic courts,[66] but the magnates were not subtle about their interest in certain cases. As Czartoryska observed to the rabbi of Sataniv in a brief she sent on behalf of her arrendator, "You should remember, sir, that the case is liable to come up before my court."[67]

The guidelines that the magnates set down for rabbis were designed to promote rabbinic honesty and reduce friction between the rabbi and

---

magnate's authority over the rabbi to combat rabbinic excesses. Thus, for example, in Lviv, in 1726 and 1752, the Polish governors issued rabbinic guidelines apparently in response to community complaints against the rabbis, see Pazdro nos. 13, 14; cf. Yaakov Yosef of Polnoe, *Zofnat Paneah* (Koretz, 1782), p. 93d.

[63] BC 2702; cf. *AGZ*, vol. 25, nos. 121.6, 132.11.

[64] Freimann, *Sefer Teka Shofar*, pp. 23–25; *PVAA* nos. 565–78 pp. 273ff.; *AGZ*, vol. 22, no. 261.21. In some localities the reputation of Jewish courts was such that even non-Jews agreed to utilize them, see Aryeh Leib b. Yosef Hakohen, *Avnei Miluim*, Responsa, pt. 3 (Tel Aviv, 1957), no. 23, p. 112.

[65] Pazdro, no. 66, pt. 2, 1760; BC 2581/2 no. 72 1723.

[66] For example, *Supl.* Irsz Pinkasów Satanów 1741

[67] BC 2702 6/6/1730; sometimes rabbinic court decisions were translated and filed with the magnate's chancellery, see n. 6.

the *kahal* elders. Rabbis were exhorted to judge honestly; their relatives were banned from positions in the *kehilla*; and their remuneration was carefully specified. They were also instructed to respect the prerogatives of the *kahal*: not to break *kahal* ordinances limiting the number of marriages, not to boycott *kahal* meetings, and not to issue bans unilaterally.[68]

Such regulations are an indicator of the potential for conflict between rabbi and *kahal*. In these conflicts the power of the magnate over both the *kahal* and the rabbinate often played a significant role. August Aleksander Czartoryski and his predecessor as governor of Rus', Jabłonowski, were integrally involved in the most famous *kahal*-rabbi dispute of the period.

The rabbinate in the eighteenth century was one of the loci of the struggle between the older established *kehillot* and their younger satellite communities. Throughout the first half of the century the hinterland of the city of Lviv sought not only recognition as a separate taxation authority, but the right to hire its own rabbi as well.[69] So in 1721 or 1724[70] when R. Moshe Haim Lazarus purchased the right to the rabbinate of Lviv and its region from Jabłonowski, the towns of Zhovkva, Brody, and Ternopil', among others, insisted that the previous incumbent, Yaacov Yoshua Falk was still *their* rabbi. The Council of Four Lands concurred, decreeing that R. Falk was still rabbi of the region at least and should be compensated for losing the city of Lviv itself. Of course the Council could not impose its decision on Jabłonowski, and R. Falk was forced to flee for his life to the town of Buchach, owned by Jabłonowski's rival, Kinowski. R. Falk eventually went to Berlin. Jabłonowski's candidate, R. Lazarus, served in Lviv until 1728, when he fled to Bessarabia as a result of a charge that he tried to reconvert an apostate.

---

[68] Pazdro, nos. 13, 14, 15, 35, 59, 91. Despite such measures conflicts between rabbis and their communities persisted; e.g., BC 5860 A. Kowalski to MZSC 1.19709, 1.19711 7/23, 8/7/1730.

[69] For documentation and analysis of this dispute see: M. Bałaban, "Z zagadnień," pp. 52–60; J. H. Simchovitz, "Zur Biographie R. Jacob Josua's des Verfassers des Sefer Penai Yehoshua," *Monatsschrift für Geschichte und Wissenschaft des Judentums* 54 (1910), pp. 608–21; D. Zunz, *Sefer Ateret Yehoshua*, (Bilgoray, 1935); Z. H. Horwitz, *Kitvei Hageonim* (Piotrków, 1928), pp. 27–32; *PVAA*, no. 594, pp. 296–98.

[70] Bałaban and Simchowitz gave the earlier date; Zunz preferred the later one, see Zunz, pp. 90–92.

Even with the two rabbinic rivals gone, however, the double rabbinate persisted until 1752, when the vacancy of the hinterland rabbinate gave the rabbi of the city, Haim Rapoport, the opportunity to unite the territory once again. Not for long, though, for in 1755 the Lviv hinterland, led by the head of the regional council, Berko Rabinowicz, once again nominated its own rabbi, Meir b. Zvi Hersh Margulies. By this time, the governor for the Lviv region (Rus') was Czartoryski. As with the taxation issue in 1740 he took an active role in resolving the dispute over the rabbinate. He believed that the territory should remain united and supported R. Rapoport as rabbi of the *whole* territory, in 1763 and 1769.[71]

It should be noted, however, that while Czartoryski clearly attempted to exercise authority over *kahal* and rabbinate, in this instance he was not completely successful. There is no evidence that R. Margulies was ever forced out of his position.[72] This points up the reality that despite the fact that the magnate exercised a large measure of control over the rabbinate and the *kahal* in this period, there were limits to his ability to impose his will. A cohesive, determined *kahal* could still challenge the magnate's power. Even as late as 1765, Czartoryski decried the fact that *kehalim* defied his authority. He complained that sometimes when a Jew defaulted on a loan and the local administrator tried to sell the Jew's house to raise the necessary cash, the Jew left town and the *kahal* prevented other Jews from bidding on the house.[73]

Conclusion

Practically every survey of the history of Polish Jewry in this period has described the crisis of the Jewish community and its autonomous institutions. This crisis is generally perceived as resulting from a combination of internal Jewish problems—oligarchic rule, bad leadership, social gap, spiritual aridity, multiplicity of interests—and objec-

---

[71] Bałaban, "Z zagadnień," pp. 57–58 (nn. 70, 73, 74); Pazdro, nos. 35, 66.

[72] Bałaban, "Z zagadnień," p. 59. Note that R. Rapoport's confirmation had to be repeated.

[73] BC 4495 Szkłów 1765 *Instrukcja* Appendix pt. 5. As to the frequency of this ploy, he said that the number of such cases was "considerable" (*niemało*).

tive external conditions—lack of law and order, the general financial crisis in Poland.[74]

The material marshaled here demonstrates that in addition to the centrifugal forces enumerated in the preceding paragraph, the Jewish communal structures were beset by the magnates' concerted efforts to weaken them. The magnates, in their drive to consolidate their rule over their latifundia, had an interest in dislodging the *kahal* from its medieval position as intermediary between the Jews and the surrounding society. They therefore exacerbated the existing internal tensions within Jewish society and tried to circumscribe *kahal* powers, usurp *kahal* prerogatives, and gain more direct control over the individual community members. While not completely successful, their endeavors made a significant contribution to the decline of the institutions that embodied Jewish communal autonomy in Poland. They may also have indirectly encouraged the development of Hasidism, which was based on a charismatic leadership operating independently of the autonomy structures.

---

[74] Dinur, pp. 84–86, 92–139; Dubnov, *Toldot Hahasidut*, pp. 20–21; P. S. Marek, "Krizis evreiskogo samoupravleniia i Hasidizm," *EvS* 12 (1928), pp. 45–101; S. Ettinger, "The Hasidic Movement—Reality and Ideals," in H. H. Ben-Sasson and S. Ettinger, eds., *Jewish Society Through the Ages* (London, 1971), p. 251; S. Ginzburg in *Istoriia evreiskogo naroda*, vol. 11, A. I. Braudo, ed. (Moscow, 1914), pp. 487–90; Katz, pp. 227–29; Mahler, *Toldot*, pp. 357–415; Szmeruk, p. 192.

Conclusion

Polish proverbs, anti-Jewish tracts, and speeches and legislation in the *Sejm* all reveal a basically negative stereotype of the Jews. The Jews' economic success was resented, their commercial practices suspect, their religion mocked, and their difference feared.[1] Under certain circumstances this theoretical hostility could be kindled into actual persecution, as attested by the events accompanying the 1648 Cossack-Peasant Uprising and the precipitous rise in the number of blood libels during the first half of the eighteenth century.[2]

The most active antagonists of the Jews were members of the clergy, townsmen, and petty nobility; but magnates shared the negative images about Jews that were part of Polish popular culture. Adam Mikołaj Sieniawski felt that the Jews had somehow tricked the Poles into allowing them a measure of judicial autonomy. August Aleksander Czartoryski believed that Jews slyly exploited the *protekcja*. Elżbieta Sieniawska employed anti-Jewish expressions in her correspondence. Yet, while their opinion about Jewish character may have been unfavorable, opinion was not characteristically the consideration that informed magnate policy toward the Jews.

A good example of this is the case of the Jewish convert to Christianity, Jan Serafinowicz. Serafinowicz, allegedly a rabbi, decided to undergo baptism in 1710. Although he was apparently an erratic personality, his baptism, like that of a later outlandish apostate, Jacob Frank, was made into a grand celebration. He was privileged to have as his godmother Elżbieta Sieniawska. In addition, at the behest of the

---

[1] Baranowski, *Życie,* p. 245; H. Hekker, "Iudofobia v Polshe XVIII veka," *EvS* 6 (1913); cf. R. Mahler, "Anti-Semitism in Poland," *Essays on Anti-Semitism,* K. Pinson, ed. (New York, 1942), pp. 111–26. Mahler pointed out that the Jews were not the only object of such a negative image.

[2] Dubnov, *History,* vol. 1, pp. 172–80. A. Bruckner, *Dzieje kultury polskiej,* vol. 3 (Warsaw, 1958), pp. 36–38.

anti-Jewish cleric Żuchowski, Serafinowicz testified at the 1710 Sandomierz blood libel trial that Jews were specifically commanded by the Talmud to use Christian blood. In response to this, officials of the Council of Four Lands wrote to Sieniawska asking her to arrange a disputation where they could refute the accusation. They probably believed that while Sieniawska had participated in the baptism out of a sense of religious obligation, her basic sympathies did not include a desire to persecute Jews and she would guarantee their rebuttal a fair hearing and wide publication. She did not disappoint them. Sieniawska arranged for the disputation to take place. On the appointed day, however, Serafinowicz did not appear. Sieniawska promptly issued an edict exonerating the Jews, specifically calling for a halt to the suffering caused to the Jews by Serafinowicz's accusations.[3] She was not interested in perpetuating the cloud of suspicion.

In light of the material analyzed in this study, Sieniawska's help to the Jews is not surprising. Whether it was providing *protekcja,* enforcing *arenda* monopolies, aiding Jewish commerce, dealing rationally with Jewish arrendators, granting financial relief to Jews in trouble, rescuing Rubinowicz's daughter or refusing to believe bad reports about Rubinowicz himself, the benevolent tendencies of the magnate lords toward their Jews are manifest. Moreover, the Jews fully expected such benevolence.

The reason for this is clear. The determining factor in magnates' relations with their Jews was not abstract principle or fundamental attitudes, but concrete economic interest. Jewish economic interests were often at odds with those of other groups in Poland, but they usually complemented the economic aims of the magnates, prompting them to support Jewish endeavors and protect Jewish existence. In the preceding chapters I have tried to demonstrate how this intertwining of interests actually operated.

We have seen that the Jews as a group were the economic mainspring of the magnate towns, that they played a central role in controlling the distribution of latifundium resources, and that they were the magnates' most reliable source of cash. As important as the Jews' contribution of revenue and service was, however, this was surpassed by the benefit derived by the magnates as a by-product of Jewish

---

[3] Bałaban, *Letoldot Hatenuah Hafrankit,* pp. 56–59; Dubnov, *History,* vol. 1, p. 173; *PVAA* no. 549, p. 265.

economic activity in which they were not directly involved.

The Sieniawski-Czartoryski material, in addition to illustrating the interests that motivated magnates to treat their Jews favorably, also affords a glimpse of the limits on the effectiveness of shared economic interests in serving as such a motivation. The first of these limitations is contained in the maxim that the motivation to be gracious cannot be stronger than the economic incentive on which it is based. Hence, magnates were willing to accommodate the requirements and even the demands of Jewish individuals and communities as long as they believed that such accommodation would result in financial gains in the long run. If, however, they became convinced that lowering *arenda* prices or providing financial relief was not an investment in future revenues, they lost patience. Arrendators were sometimes imprisoned or beaten, and requests for aid could be refused. Jews, it will be recalled, cited their commercial utility when petitioning for favors.

Economic interests were varied and could conflict with each other. Sometimes the economic interests represented by other latifundium constituencies—peasants, townsmen, administrators—were perceived as overriding those advanced by the Jews.

It is also true that, while intertwined, Jewish and magnate interests were not identical. The *kahal* had an important economic stake in the *hazaka* licensing system. For the magnate this institution was a barrier to maximum profit.

Another limiting influence is the fact that sometimes there were noneconomic considerations that took precedence. The magnates brooked no competition in ruling their latifundia. This led them to look askance at Jewish political institutions that embodied Jewish autonomy.

The limits on magnate benevolence notwithstanding, Jews took full advantage of the magnates' favorable inclinations toward them. The magnate latifundium offered the most congenial environment in Poland for the conduct of Jewish business and religion and was a place where Jews could live with a large measure of confidence and security.

The influence of the magnate connection on Jewish life was not merely passive, providing a fertile substratum on which Jewish society could grow. Magnate policies and behavior had a profound effect on the dynamics of Jewish life. Individuals with direct links to the magnates enjoyed wealth and power. They occupied an important niche in the economic, political, and social elite of the Jewish, and sometimes the non-Jewish, communities. Like Yisrael Rubinowicz, they could fulfill a pivotal dual cultural role, serving as maecenas of Jewish learning and culture and paving the way for meaningful cultural contact with the non-Jewish world.

In the sphere of economics and commerce, the opportunities and facilities magnates made available were a major factor in determining the contours of Jewish economic activity and the Jewish occupational structure, as well as the material success or failure of individual Jews. The magnates' governing style contributed to the weakening of Jewish communal authority and the decline of Jewish autonomous structures and institutions, like the rabbinate.

The impact of the magnates on Jewish life was reciprocated by the prominent functions filled by the Jews on the latifundium. The Jews contributed the strength of their numbers and their economic activity to the magnates' towns. They guaranteed the viability of central economic institutions, like the *spław* and *arenda,* and provided the latifundium population with important commercial services. Jewish arrendators circulated cash and served banking functions. Jewish merchants marketed and procured goods for the entire population and offered the magnates marketing flexibility. Jewish administrators helped to control and distribute latifundium resources. Most of all, Jews showed their value to the magnates as generators of profit and wealth.

The Jews did not vegetate on the margins of the latifundium economy. Neither did aristocratic magnates like the Sieniawskis and Czartoryskis blindly commit their economic fate to the hands of the Jewish entrepreneurs. In reality, Jews and magnates developed complementary economies. As a result, the latifundium was better able to realize its full profit potential while the Jews could achieve a degree of productivity and prosperity.

Beyond economics, the Sieniawski-Czartoryski example implies that Jews could not help but be drawn into the main arena of society. Jews were not involved in the marketplace only. They had an interest in and an influence on what transpired in the *Sejm*, the town and village councils, the church institutions, and the magnate palaces. Jews not only did business with Poles, they lived with them; social, cultural, and political associations were unavoidable. Poles and Jews related to each other in numerous contexts: in the marketplace, in the tavern, at the mill, in the courts, in the latifundium administration, as neighbors, as fellow town residents, as doctor and patient, on *spław* expeditions, in times of physical danger, as religious opponents, and as political allies or antagonists.

With such a variety of settings, Polish-Jewish interaction cannot be conveniently schematized or glibly characterized as utilitarian. Marriages of convenience are still marriages. They generate a dynamic and entail responsibilities that go beyond the original utilitarian motivations. The Jewish-magnate nexus once formed—for whatever reasons—took on a life of its own and was a potent factor in society; just how potent is apparent if we consider the magnate-Jewish connection in relation to the events and trends of Polish-Jewish history in the seventeenth and eighteenth centuries.

As devastating as the depradations of the 1648 Uprising and subsequent Muscovite-Swedish Invasion were, the evidence of the Sieniawski-Czartoryski latifundium, parts of which were located in areas hit directly by these events, indicates that the economic and demographic effects were temporary. By the turn of the eighteenth century the Jews had reestablished flourishing communities with strong economic infrastructures and growing populations. The data with regard to taxes, *arendy,* and commerce, presented here, imply that even during the Northern War period the people managed to keep their lives on an even keel. None of this would have been possible without the support of the magnates. Jews could return to the communities that were the sites of the persecutions because they were assured of the physical protection, economic support, and political advocacy of the magnates.

While the eighteenth century may have brought increased anti-Jewish religious and legal manifestations, the Jews continued to flock to magnate-owned territories because these still offered the best promise of physical security, benign legal status, and prosperity. Communal debts mounted, but the example of the freighters and the powerful arrendators demonstrates that these financially strapped communities were not bereft of prosperous members.

The oft-cited eighteenth-century crisis of Jewish religious and lay leadership and the decay of the organs of Jewish autonomy cannot be explained simply as the result of the deleterious effects of 1648–60 or the financial crisis of the early eighteenth century. It is clear that the magnates had a stake in weakening the Jewish community and in exercising control over institutions like the rabbinate and *kahal*. The abolition of the Council of Four Lands in 1764 can be understood as the culmination of a process of displacing the official Jewish community from its medieval role as intermediary between the Jews and the surrounding society. As we have seen, this process was fostered on the magnate latifundia.

With regard to the rise of Hasidism, the picture of Jewish life on the eighteenth-century magnate latifundia presented here cannot support the idea that Hasidism was a response of downtrodden people seeking a mystical release from the desperation of everyday life[4] or of disillusioned messianists needing an outlet to diffuse their frustrated beliefs.[5] Hasidism did not begin in the wake of 1648, nor in response to the abolition of the Council of Four Lands, nor in the aftermath of Frankism. Hasidism began in the 1740s in a town on the Sieniawski-Czartoryski latifundium where the Jews were flourishing. Medzhybizh, the headquarters of Israel Baal Shem Tov, Hasidism's founder, was not a small secluded village populated by mystics and saintly hermits. It was an important regional center with a Jewish population of over two thousand (large by eighteenth-century standards) where, already by 1730, Jews owned 45 out of 75 stores and 110 out of 124 wooden or stone houses. It was dominated by hard-headed merchants and arrendators.

That it was in such a place that Hasidism got its start suggests that the movement was neither born in poverty nor was it as inimical to the Jewish establishment as has often been supposed.[6] The new forms of leadership and communal organization that it established may have been welcomed by the official Jewish community. Perhaps the traditional leadership found ways to employ the charisma-based power of the Hasidic *rebbe* as reinforcement for its own weakening coercive authority, anchored as it was to waning magnate support. The new forms may also have been to the liking of the magnates, who may have felt less threatened by a religious leadership which focused on the soul, yet could serve as an address for dealing with the Jews. Such leaders were preferable to a political leadership with all the trappings

---

[4] Dubnov, *Toldot Hahasidut*, p. 36.

[5] G. Scholem, *Major Trends in Jewish Mysticism* (New York, 1961), pp. 325–30.

[6] Dinur, pp. 131–47.

of a rival government that was not always effective in marshaling its minions when the magnate desired.

In terms of Polish history the Jews' role on the latifundia proved to be one of the most durable features of the Polish-Lithuanian Commonwealth. The magnate connection had placed the Jews in a key economic function as the main link between the agricultural and commercial sectors; in a central political position as allies in the struggle against royal absolutism; and in an important social capacity as the predominant urban element in the Polish countryside.

The Jewish role became part and parcel of Polish society and persisted throughout the eighteenth century and beyond. Anyone who sought to rule or transform Poland was forced to deal with the Jewish phenomenon. The shrunken Polish state, attempting between 1772 and 1793 to change its fundamental economic, political, and social constellations, considered several proposals intended to alter the traditional Jewish role. For absolutist Prussia, Russia, and Austria, which, beginning in 1772, partitioned Poland and found themselves with hundreds of thousands of new Jews, the magnate-generated Jewish role was an anomaly. These governments went to considerable trouble to try to reduce the number of Jews and to change their economic, political, and social status. They made concerted efforts to break the links connecting the Jews, peasantry, and nobility, and to remove the Jews from the small urban communities in the countryside. Despite their determination, however, up until World War I, and in some regions until World War II, many East European Jews continued in much the same role their great-great-great-grandfathers had filled under the magnates. They were still leasing estates, forests, and taverns; still marketing nobility and peasant produce in the towns; and still selling finished goods in the countryside. The magnate-Jewish connection, crystallized in the sixteenth century, continued to resonate in the twentieth.

Through the centuries the magnate-Jewish relationship had been one of the most significant factors in the social, economic, and political dynamics of Poland and one of the main determinants of the overall condition of the Jews in Poland. As Poland was in many ways the land of the aristocratic magnates, Poland's Jews were in many respects the lords' Jews.

Appendix 1

The Jewish Population in the Czartoryski Territories ca. 1766

In 1764, so as to set the number of Jews liable for head tax, the Polish *Sejm* ordered a census of Jews above the age of one year in the Commonwealth. While the results of this census cannot be accepted uncritically, it is generally recognized as the starting point for calculating the Jewish population in Poland-Lithuania at the time. (See R. Mahler, *Yidn in Amolikn Poiln in Likht fun Tsifirn* / The Jews in Old Poland in the light of numbers/, 2 vols. [Warsaw, 1958].) The list of Jewish Head Tax in the Territories of August Aleksander Czartoryski for 1766 (AGAD Arch. Potockich z Łancuta 168) is based on this census and includes its results for twenty of the *Kehillot* located on the Czartoryski latifundium. They are:

Kehilla	*Number of Jews Older Than One Year*
Baranów	513
Berezhany (Brzeżany)	1270
Granów	1024
Jarosław	1884
Kalush (Kałusz) (*Starostwo*)	1662
Klevan' (Klewań)	973
Końskowoła	789
Liatychiv (Latyczów) (*Starostwo*)	652
Medzhybizh (Międzybóż)	2039

Międzyrzec Podlaski	1075
Mykolaiv	1142
(Mikołajów)	
Naraiv	286
(Narajów)	
Peremyshliany	789
(Przemyślany)	
Sataniv	1625
(Satanów)	
Sieniawa	1115
Skole	1063
Stara Syniava	851
(Stara Sieniawa)	
Staszów	776
Tarnoruda	771
Zin'kiv	522
(Zińków)	
TOTAL	20,812

Since this figure omits babies younger than a year, Mahler suggested adding approximately 6 percent to compensate. Moreover, it is generally acknowledged that the census data, supplied primarily by Jews, understated the true number of Jews. Therefore, following Mahler again, it is necessary to add a minimum of 20 percent to the official total. Hence the number of Jews in these twenty communities was probably close to 25,000 (or an average of 1250 per community). This list excludes another approximately five communities of Jews in Czartoryski's holdings in Lithuania and Belorussia. Only one of those communities, Shkłoŭ, was large and so the average concentration of Jews in this region was probably somewhat lower than it was in the communities listed above. The Czartoryski holdings around Warsaw and Gdańsk were in areas of minimal Jewish settlement. Therefore I estimate the total Jewish population of these additional holdings at 5,000–7,000. Thus the total number of Jews in the Czartoryski territories was somewhat more than 30,000.

Appendix 2

Currency in Poland in the Early Eighteenth Century

The currency situation in Poland in the late seventeenth and early eighteenth centuries was unstable and confusing. (See J. Rutkowski, *Historia gospodarcza Polski/Economic history of Poland* [Warsaw, 1953], pp. 153–57, 193–95, 263–74; B. D. Weinryb, *The Jews of Poland* [Philadelphia, 1973], pp. 304–305.) The basic Polish monetary unit was the silver *złoty* containing, in 1650, 8.15 grams of silver and equaling 30 *groszy*, 90 *szelągów*, or 5 *szóstaków*. In 1663, a new, mostly copper *złoty* was circulated. This was popularly called *tymf* or *tynf* after the treasury official who introduced it. By the early eighteenth century the *tynf* was denominated as 36–38 *groszy* or 6 *szóstaków* and was equal in value to 18 silver *groszy*. Thus a two-tiered currency system developed: *bona moneta* signifying the old silver *złoty* and *currentis moneta* signifying the newer, debased coins. In addition there were in circulation Prussian silver thalers (*talar bity*) worth 6–8 *złoty*, as well as golden ducats (*czerwony złoty*) worth up to 18 *złoty*. The situation was further occluded by the widespread practices of coin-clipping and counterfeiting. All of this vastly complicates the task of a scholar seeking to compare and interpret monetary data.

Glossary

akta grodzkie	official documents issued by or filed with the magnate's court in a particular town
arenda	a lease of monopoly rights
arendarz	arrendator
ashir*	a wealthy person
asygnacja	a payment order
aukcja	a price or rent increment
balchazaka*	holder of a *hazaka*
bona moneta	money with a high silver content
chałupa	shack
currentis moneta	money with a high copper content introduced after 1663
czerwony złoty	golden ducat, worth up to 18 *złoty*
czopowy	excise tax on liquor
czynsz	real estate tax
dobra	a large section of a latifundium comprising several *klucze*
dom	house
dozorca	supervisor
dwór	court-residence
dwornik	assistant to *podstarosta*
dzierżawa	a leasehold, usually of real estate
dzierżawca	lessee of a *dzierżawa*
ekonom	general manager of a unit of a latifundium
faktor	factor
folga	a discount granted to a person owing some financial obligation
folwark	a feudal manor

frokt	freight
froktarz	freighter, i.e., a person who shipped *frokt* by riverboat
gospodyni	woman in charge of dairy and poultry production on a manor
gromada	village council
grosz	1/30 *złoty*
grzywna	48 *groszy*, by the eighteenth century a currency of account only, usually used to express the amounts of monetary fines
gummienny	stackyard supervisor
Hasid*	member of a religious movement, begun by Israel Baal Shem Tov, which emphasized piety and joyous communion with God
Haskalah*	Jewish enlightenment movement
hazaka*	license granted by a *kahal* entitling a person to hold the monopoly on some economic enterprise
hevra*	a mutual benefit society made up of people in the same occupation or who were devoted to performing some social or religious task (charity, burial, early morning prayer, etc.)
heter iska*	a legal circumvention of the biblical prohibition of loaning on interest
hetman	a marshal of the Polish-Lithuania army
hrabstwo	a very large hereditary estate
ImP	(*Jego Mości Pan*) Polish honorific meaning: "His Powerfulness, Sir . . ."
informacja	an information bulletin circulated among latifundium administrators
instancja	a brief submitted on behalf of an accused person or a victim of some calamity
instrukcja	instructions given to latifundium administrators

inwentarz	inventory of equipment, buildings, tax-payers, and income of a unit of a latifundium
kahal*	the governing council of a *kehilla*
karczma	tavern or inn
kasa centralna	master ledger, recording the finances of an entire latifundium
kasztelan	palatine of a given area, having no real administrative duties, but holding a seat in the upper house of the Sejm
katzin*	title applied to leading non-rabbinic figures in the Jewish community; translated as *notable*
kehilla*	an organized Jewish community
klucz	the basic unit of a latifundium consisting of town or towns, villages, and several manors
komisariat	an administrative district of a latifundium
komisarz	an official in charge of a *komisariat* or a commissioner charged with executing some specific task
konsens	a monopoly license granted by a town owner
królewszczyzna	a royal land grant given for life
łaszt	a large volume measure used for grain, of variable size depending on the grain, the region, and the period
leśnik	forest warden
Liberum Veto	a rule of procedure in the *Sejm*, whereby any single member could defeat a bill and cause the dissolution of the house by voicing his objection
mahazik*	a general arrendator
mamram*	letter of credit
marszałek	palace steward
mieszczanin	townsman
mihya*	means of livelihood
mishar*	commerce

mitzva*	a Jewish religious duty; more colloquially: a beneficent act
obywatel	citizen
ordynacja	a Polish estate that was not divided among heirs upon the death of the owner, but passed intact to one of them
Pan	"Sir," title usually applied to a Polish nobleman
pinkas*	communal minute book
pisarz, pisarz prowentowy	clerk, bookkeeper, comptroller
podskarbi	treasurer
podstarosta	an administrator of the agricultural production of a manor
podwojewoda	deputy provincial governor whose main function was to sponsor a "court of the Jews," which heard appeals from rabbinical courts and cases involving Jews and Christians
pogłówne żydowskie	Jewish head tax in Poland
pręt	a measure of area equaling 7 1/2 ells
protekcja	protection, patronage, use of influence on behalf of a client or dependent
rachunki	financial accounts
rata	an installment payment
rebbe*	a leader of a group of *Hasidim*, not necessarily a rabbi, whose authority was charismatic
Sejm	the Polish legislature, diet
sejmik	regional legislative assembly, dietine
shtadlan*	a Jewish lobbyist with the non-Jewish authorities
skarb	treasury
służba folwarczna	the corps of manorial service employees
sohair*	merchant
spław	river trade
sprawiedliwość	justice, equity
starosta	holder of a *starostwo*
starostwo	a royal land grant limited in time
suplika	a petition

szafarz	a steward
szeląg	1/3 *grosz*
szóstak	1/5 *złoty*, 1/6 *tynf*
szynk	a bar
szyper	skipper of a riverboat or flotilla of boats
taler bity (or: talar bity)	6–8 *złoty*
tanti	possessing much cash
targownik	market-tax lessee
tynf	18 silver *groszy* or 36–38 copper ones
uniwersał	an edict
vaad*	council
Vaad Arba Aratzot*	The Council of Four Lands
Vaad Medinat Lita*	The Council of Lithuania
vaad galil*	a regional council
włość	a large section of a latifundium including several *klucze*
wojewoda	governor of a province, also holding a seat in the Polish senate
yehidim*	individuals who did not have contracts with Polish noblemen, i.e., nonarrendators
zamek	castle, *klucz* administrative headquarters
złoty	basic Polish monetary unit

Note: Words are defined according to their context in this study. Words marked by an asterisk (*) are Hebrew or Yiddish. All other words are Polish or of Latin origin (bona moneta, currentis moneta, liberum veto, tanti).

Abbreviations

AAC	August Aleksander Czartoryski
ABK	*Akty Vilenskoi Komissii*, vol. 29
AGAD	Archiwum Główne Akt Dawnych
AGZ	*Akta Grodzkie i Ziemskie*
AKP	Archiwum Krzeszowickie Potockich
AMS	Adam Mikołaj Sieniawski
APH	*Acta Poloniae Historica*
AR	Archiwum Radziwiłłów
Arch.	Archiwum (archive)
BC	Biblioteka Czartoryskich
b.	ben (= son of)
b.m.	*bona moneta*
BZIH	*Biuletyn Żydowskiego Instytutu Historycznego*
c.m.	*currentis moneta*
cz. zł.	*czerwony złoty*
EJE	*Encyclopedia Judaica*, Jerusalem 1972
EJG	*Encyclopedia Judaica*, Berlin 1928 – 1932
ES	Elżbieta Sieniawska
EvS	*Evreiskaya Starina*
EW	Ewidencje (section of Czartoryski Archive)
F	Fortis
G	Gdańsk
GOSP	Gospodarcze (section of Czartoryski Archive)
gr.	*grosz*
HM	Prefix of call number of microfilm in the Central Archive for the History of the Jewish People, Jerusalem
Inwent.	Inwentarz
JJLG	*Jahrbuch der Jüdisch-Literarischen Gesellschaft*
KH	*Kwartalnik Historyczny*
l.	letter

MZSC	Maria Zofia z Sieniawskich Czartoryska
OSS	Ossolineum
PAN	Polska Akademia Nauk
PH	*Przegląd Historyczny*
PHo	Pinkas Horki
PML	*Pinkas Hamedina* (= *Pinkas Medinat Lita*)
PSB	*Polski Słownik Biograficzny*
pt.	Part (of a book)
pt.	point (in a document)
PVAA	*Pinkas Va'ad Arba Aratzot*
R	Rubinowicz
R.	Rabbi
RDSG	*Roczniki Dziejów Społecznych i Gospodarczych*
SB	*Shivhei HaBesht* (*In Praise of the Baal Shem Tov*)
S-C	Sieniawski-Czartoryski
Sien.	Sieniawa
Supl.	*Suplika*
t.b.	*taler bity*
TSCHPJ	*Texts and Studies in the Communal History of Polish Jewry*
WAP	Wojewódzkie Archiwum Państwowe
WKL	Grand Duchy of Lithuania
YB	*Yivo Bleter*
YBLBI	*Year Book of the Leo Baeck Institute*
zł.	*złoty*

Archival Sources

File Numbers

Archiwum Główne Akt Dawnych (AGAD), Warsaw.

Arch. Potockich z Łańcuta 168 (HM 366)
Arch. Radziwiłłów (AR) Dział V 14275
Arch. Roskie provisional number 321 (Pinkas Boćki)

Archiwum Polskiej Akademii Nauk (PAN), Cracow.

3795 (HM 6739)

Biblioteka Czartoryskich (BC) Cracow.

220, 221, 2514, 2525, 2527, 2529, 2581/1 – 2, 2599, 2628, 2647, 2677, 2693/1 – 2, 2702, 2898, 2899, 2900, 2901, 2903 – 2905, 3499, 3500, 3502, 3503, 3507, 3813 – 26, 4035 – 39, 4041, 4042, 4044 – 48, 4061, 4074, 4117, 4474 – 78, 4481 – 83, 4489 – 91, 4495, 4818 – 35.

Ewidencje (EW):

11, 86, 127, 128, 133 – 35, 144, 152, 171, 172, 176, 179, 185, 188, 189, 196, 255, 282, 297/2 – 3, 341, 394, 402, 449c, 506, 525, 1509.

Gospodarcze (GOSP)

50, 51, 232, 328, 340, 344, 348, 407, 428, 441, 478, 537, 574, 597, 602, 770, 773, 777, 784, 853, 991, 993, 1008, 1014, 1015, 1084, 1104, 1472, 1505, 1566.

Korespondencja (BC):

5756, 5757, 5767, 5782, 5806, 5809, 5829, 5840, 5844, 5860, 5870, 5881, 5882, 5884, 5886, 5897, 5899, 5934, 5935, 5943 – 46, 5963, 5972, 5997.

Jewish National and University Library, Jerusalem.

Heb. 4^0	920	Pinkas Horki (PHo)
Heb. 4^0	103	Pinkas Zabłudowa

Ossolineum, (OSS) Wrocław.

2122/II	(HM 6653)
5167 – 68/II	(HM 6678 – 79)

Wojewódzkie Archiwum Państwowe (WAP), Cracow.

Arch. Krzeszowickie Potockich (AKP)
D.S.: 2, 6, 79, 80, 84.
Krzesz.: 6, 137, 141.

Note: Files followed by an HM number were examined on microfilm at the Central Archives for the History of the Jewish People, Jerusalem.

Bibliography*

Aharon ben Yehuda. *Hasdei Avot*. Nesterov (Zhovkva), 1771.

Akty Vilenskoi Kommissii dlia razbora drevnikh aktov. Documents of the Vilna Commission for the analysis of old documents. Vol. 29. Vilna, 1902.

Alexandrov, Hillel. "Derzhavtses un Kohol." Large lessees and the Jewish community. *Tsaytshrift* 4 (1930), 121–24.

Altbauer, Moshe. *Achievements and Tasks in the Field of Jewish-Slavic Language Contact Studies*. Los Angeles, 1972.

Aryeh Leib ben Yosef Hakohen. *Avnei Miluim*. Tel Aviv, 1957.

Assaf, Simha. "Lekorot Harabanut Beashkenaz, Polin Velita." On the history of the rabbinate in Germany, Poland and Lithuania. *Reshumot* 2 (1927), 259–300.

Bałaban, Meir. *Beit Yisrael Bepolin*. Vol. 1. I. Halpern, ed. Jerusalem, 1948.

_____ *Historja Żydów w Krakowie i na Kazimierzu*. History of the Jews in Cracow and Kazimierz. 2 vols. Cracow, 1931–36.

_____ *Die Judenstadt von Lublin*. Berlin, 1919.

_____ "Die Krakauer Judengemeinde-Ordnung von 1595 und ihre nachträge." *JJLG* 10 (1912), 296–360; 11 (1913), 88–113.

_____ *Letoldot Hatenuah Hafrankit*. On the history of the Frankist movement. Tel Aviv, 1934.

_____ "Stan kahału krakowskiego na przełomie XVII i XVIII w." The state of the Cracow Jewish community at the turn of the eighteenth century. Warsaw, 1931.

*The titles of Hebrew primary sources are not translated.

———— "Z zagadnień ustrojowych żydostwa polskiego." On the structural problems of Polish Jewry. *Studja Lwowskie*. Lviv, 1932.

———— *Żydzi lwowscy na przełomie XVI i XVII w.* Lviv Jewry at the turn of the seventeenth century. Lviv, 1906.

Baranovich, A. I. *Magnatskoie khoziaistvo na iuge Volyni v XVIII v.* Magnate economy in southern Volyn in the eighteenth century. Moscow, 1955.

Baranowski, Bohdan. *Instrukcje gospodarcze dla dóbr magnackich i szlacheckich z XVII–XIX wieku.* Economic instructions for magnate and nobility holdings, seventeenth–nineteenth centuries. 2 vols. Wrocław, 1961–63.

———— et al., eds. *Historia Polski 1648–1764.* History of Poland 1648–1764. Warsaw, 1956.

———— *Polska karczma-restauracja-kawiarnia.* The Polish tavern-restaurant-cafe. Wrocław, 1979.

———— *Życie codzienne małego miasteczka w XVII i XVIII w.* Small town daily life in the seventeenth and eighteenth centuries. Warsaw, 1975.

Baron, S. W. "Ghetto and Emancipation." *The Menorah Treasury.* L. W. Schwarz, ed. Philadelphia, 1973.

———— *The Jewish Community.* 3 vols. Philadelphia, 1942 [Westport, Conn., 1972].

———— "The Jewish Factor in Medieval Civilization." *Proceedings of the American Academy for Jewish Research* 12 (1942), 1–48.

———— *A Social and Religious History of the Jews.* 2d ed. 18 vols. New York–Philadelphia, 1937–83.

Bartoszewicz, Kazimierz. *Antysemityzm w literaturze polskiej XV–XVII w.* Anti-Semitism in Polish literature, fifteenth–seventeenth centuries. Warsaw, 1914.

Ben Amos, Dan and Mintz, Jerome, eds. and trans. *In Praise of the Baal Shem Tov [Shivhei Habesht].* Bloomington, 1971.

Ben-Sasson, H. H. *Hagut Vehanhagah.* Theory and practice. Jerusalem, 1959.

———— "Poland." *EJE*, vol. 13.

———— "Takanot Issurei Shabbat Shel Polin Umashmautan Hahevratit Vehakalkalit." Statutes for the enforcement of the observance of the Sabbath in Poland. *Zion* 21 (1956), 183–206.

Ber, of Bolechow. *Memoirs*. M. Wischnitzer, ed. and trans. Berlin, 1922 [New York, 1973].

Bergerówna, Janina. *Księżna pani na Kocku i Siemiatyczach*. The Princess, lady of Kock and Siemiatycze. Lviv, 1936.

Berliner, Abraham. "Aus den Memoiren eines Römischen Ghetto-Jünglings." *Jahrbuch für Jüdische Geschichte und Literatur* 7 (1904), 110–32.

Bershadskii, S. A. *Russko-Evreiskii arkhiv*. 3 vols. St. Petersburg, 1882–1903.

Bersohn, Mateusz. *Dyplomataryusz dotyczący Żydów w dawnej Polsce*. Official documents concerning the Jews in Old Poland. Warsaw, 1911.

Biernat, Czesław. *Statystyka obrotu towarowego Gdańska w latach 1651–1815*. Statistics of the mercantile trade in Gdańsk, 1651–1815. Warsaw, 1962.

Bobińska, Celina, ed. *Studia z dziejów wsi małopolskiej w drugiej połowie XVIII w*. Studies in the history of the villages of Little Poland in the second half of the eighteenth century. Warsaw, 1957.

Bobrzyński, Michał. "Prawo propinacji w dawnej Polsce." The right of propination in Old Poland. *Szkice i studja historyczne*. Vol. 2. Cracow, 1922.

Bogucka, Maria, and Samsonowicz, Henryk. *Dzieje miast i mieszczaństwa w Polsce przedrozbiorowej*. History of towns and townspeople in pre-partition Poland. Wrocław, 1986.

Bohdziewicz, Piotr, ed. *Korespondencja artystyczna Elżbiety Sieniawskiej z lat 1700–1729*. The artistic correspondence of Elżbieta Sieniawska, 1700–1729. Lublin, 1964.

Brablec, Wanda. "Elżbieta z Lubomirskich Sieniawska." Doctoral dissertation, Jagiellonian University. Cracow, 1949.

Braudo, A. I. et al. *Istoriia evreiskogo naroda*. History of the Jewish People. Vol. 11. Moscow, 1914.

Brawer, A. Y. *Galicia Veyehudeha*. Studies in Galician Jewry. Jerusalem, 1965.

———— "Makor Ivri Hadash Letoldot Frank Vesiyato." A new source for the history of the Frankists. *Hashiloah* 38 (1917), 16–31, 231–38, 349–54, 446–57.

Brekhia Berekh ben Getzel. *Zera Berekh Hashlishi*. Halle, 1714.

Bruckner, Alexander. *Dzieje kultury polskiej*. History of Polish culture. Vol. 3. Warsaw, 1958.

Buber, Shlomo, ed. *Kirya Nisgava*. The Jewish Community of Nesterov (Zhovkva). Cracow, 1903.

Buczek, Karol. "Z dziejów polskiej archiwistyki prywatnej." On the history of Polish private archive organization. *Studia historyczne ku czci Stanisława Kutrzeby*. Vol. 2. Cracow, 1938.

Burszta, Józef. "Handel magnacki i kupiecki między Sieniawą nad Sanem a Gdańskiem od końca XVII do połowy XVIII wieku." Magnate and merchant commerce between Sieniawa-on-the-San and Gdańsk from the end of the seventeenth to the mid-eighteenth centuries. *RDSG* 16 (1954), 174–223.

———— "Materiały do techniki spławu rzecznego na Sanie i średniej Wiśle z XVII i XVIII w." Material on the technical aspects of the San and Vistula river trade in the seventeenth and eighteenth centuries. *Kwartalnik Historii Kultury Materialnej* 3 (1955), 752–82.

———— Wieś i karczma. Village and tavern. Warsaw, 1950.

———— "Zbiegostwo chłopów znad Sanu w I ćwierci XVIII wieku." Desertion of peasants from the San region in the first quarter of the eighteenth century. *RDSG* 17 (1955), 55–84.

Burzyński, Andrzej. "Struktura dochodów wielkiej własności ziemskiej XVI–XVIII w." The income structure of the large estates in the sixteenth–eighteenth centuries. *RDSG* 34 (1973), 31–66.

Cieślak, Edmund. "Z dziejów żeglugi i handlu gdańskiego w połowie XVIII wieku." An outline of the history of the navigation and sea trade of Gdańsk in the mid-eighteenth century. *Rocznik Gdański* 24 (1965), 61–89.

———— and Czesław, Biernat. *Dzieje Gdańska*. History of Gdańsk. Gdańsk, 1975.

Cohen, Benjamin. "Hareshut Havoyevodit Vehakehilla Hayehudit Bameiot Ha-16–18." The wojewoda authority and the Jewish community in the sixteenth–eighteenth centuries. *Gal-Ed* 3 (1976), 9–32.

Cohen, Tuvia. *Maaseh Tuvia*. Venice, 1707.

Cygielman, S. A. "Iskei Hakhirot shel Yehudei Polin Ukesharam Lehithavut 'Vaad Arba Aratzot'." Leasing and contracting interests [public incomes] of Polish Jewry and the founding of 'Va'ad Arba Aratzot'. *Zion* 47 (1982), 112–44.

Cynarski, Stanisław. "The Shape of Sarmatian Ideology in Poland.' *APH* 19 (1968), 5–17.

Czapliński, Władysław. "Rządy oligarchii w Polsce nowożytnej." Oligarchic rule in Poland. *PH* 52 (1961), 445–65.

———— *Dwa Sejmy w roku 1652: Studium z dziejów rozkładu Rzeczypospolitej Szlacheckiej*. Two Diets in 1652: A study in the history of the disintegration of the Noblemen's Commonwealth. Wrocław, 1955.

———— and Długosz, Józef. *Życie codzienne magnaterii polskiej w XVII wieku*. Daily life of the Polish magnates in the seventeenth century. Warsaw, 1976.

Czartoryski, A. J. *Memoirs*. Adam Gielgud, ed. and trans. 2 vols. London, 1888.

Czwojdrak, Tadeusz and Żak, Zenon. "Przemysł propinacyjny i karczmarstwo w dobrach biskupa poznańskiego w XVII i XVIII wieku." The liquor and tavern industry in the territories of the Poznań bishopric in the seventeenth and eighteenth centuries. *Studia i materiały do dziejów Wielkopolski i Pomorza* 2 (1956), 79–197.

Dąbkowski, Przemysław. *Prawo prywatne polskie*. Polish private law. 2 vols. Lviv, 1910–11.

Davies, Norman. *God's Playground: A History of Poland*. Vol. 1. New York, 1982.

Dębicki, Ludwik. *Puławy*. 4 vols. Lviv, 1887–88.

Dernalewicz, Maria. *Portret familii*. Warsaw, 1974.

Dinur, B. Z. *Bemifne Hadorot*. Historical writings. Vol. 1. Jerusalem, 1955.

Dubnov, S. M. "Arendy kontrakty v Litve XVII–XVIII v." Arenda contracts in Lithuania, seventeenth–eighteenth centuries. *EvS* 2 (1909), 105–11.

—— *History of the Jews in Russia and Poland.* 3 vols. Philadelphia, 1916–18.

—— "Sotsialnaia i dukhovnaia zhizn' evreiev v Polshe v pervoi polovin XVIII veka." Social and religious life of the Jews in Poland in the first half of the eighteenth century. *Voshod.* Jan.–Feb., 1899, 1–18, 49–62.

—— *Toldot Hahasidut.* History of Hasidism. Tel Aviv, 1931 [1975].

—— *Weltgeschichte des Jüdischen Volkes.* Vols. 6–7. Berlin, 1927–28.

—— ed. *Pinkas Hamedina.* Minute book of the Lithuanian Council. Berlin, 1925.

Dworzaczek, Włodzimierz. *Genealogia.* Warsaw, 1958.

—— "La mobilité sociale de la noblesse Polonaise aux XVI et XVII siècles." *APH* 36 (1977), 147–61.

Echt, Samuel. *Geschichte der Juden in Danzig.* History of the Jews in Gdańsk. Leer, Ostfriesland, 1972.

Eliyahu ben Yehezkeil of Bilgoray. *Har Hakarmel.* Frankfurt/Oder, 1782 [Jerusalem, 1973].

Emden, Y. Y. *Megilat Sefer.* New York, 1956.

Ettinger, Shmuel. "The Hasidic Movement—Reality and Ideals." *Jewish Society Through the Ages.* H. H. Ben-Sasson and S. Ettinger, eds. London, 1971.

—— "Hayishuv Hayehudi Beukraina min Haihud Halublini ad Legezeirot Takh." The Jewish colonization of the Ukraine from the Union of Lublin until 1648." Doctoral dissertation, Hebrew University. Jerusalem, 1957.

—— "Helkam Shel Hayehudim Bekolonizatzia shel Ukraina." Jewish participation in the colonization of the Ukraine. *Zion* 21 (1956), 107–42.

—— "Maamadam Hamishpati Vehahevrati shel Yehudei Ukraina Bameiot Ha-15–17." The legal and social status of Jews in the Ukraine from the fifteenth to the seventeenth centuries. *Zion* 20 (1955), 128–52.

Eybeshutz, Y. *Luhot Eidut.* Altona, 1755.

Falk, Yaacov Yoshua. *Penei Yehoshua*. Amsterdam, 1739.

Feldman, Eliyahu. "Heikhan Ubishvil Mi Nitkanu Hatakanot Leissur Hamelakha Beshabbat Shel R. Meshullam Faibish." Where and for whom were composed the regulations forbidding work on the Sabbath of R. Meshullam Faibish of Cracow. *Zion* 34 (1969), 90-97.

Freimann, Aaron. "Briefwechsel eines Studenten der Medizin in Frankfurt a.d. Oder mit dem in Halle Medizin studierenden Isak Wallach im Jahre 1702." *Zeitschrift für Hebräische Bibliographie* 14 (1910), 117-23.

———— ed. *Sefer Teka Shofar*. Frankfurt am Main, 1909.

Friedenwald, Harry. *The Jews and Medicine*. 2 vols. Baltimore, 1944.

Friedman, N. Z. *Otzar Harabanim*. Treasury of Rabbis. Bnei Brak (n.d.).

Gajewski, Jacek. "Elżbieta Sieniawska i jej artyści. Z zagadnień organizacji pracy artystycznej i odbioru w XVIII w. w Polsce." Elżbieta Sieniawska and her artists. A chapter from the organization of artistic life and art reception in eighteenth-century Poland. *Mecenas, Kolekcjoner, Odbiorca*. Warsaw, 1984.

Galant, Ilya. "Zadolzhennost' evreiskikh obshchin v XVII vek." The indebtedness of the Jewish communities in the seventeenth century. *EvS* 6 (1913), 129-32.

Gelber, N. M. *Brzeżany Memorial Book*. M. Katz, ed. Haifa, 1978.

———— "Letoldot Harofim Hayehudim Bepolin Bameah Ha-18." On the history of Jewish doctors in Poland in the eighteenth century. *Shai Leyeshayahu*. Tel Aviv, 1957.

———— "Letoldot Hayehudim Bestaszów." On the history of the Jews in Staszów. *Sefer Staszów*. E. Ehrlich, ed. Tel Aviv, 1962.

———— "Oyslandishe Reisende Vegen Poilishe Yidn inem 18ten Yarhundert." Foreign travelers on Polish Jews in the eighteenth century. *YIVO Historishe Shriften*. Vol. 1. Warsaw, 1929.

———— "Die Taufbewegung unter den Polnischen Juden im XVIII Jahrhundert." *Monatschrift für Geschichte und Wissenschaft des Judentums* 68 (1924), 225-41.

———— *Toldot Yehudei Brody.* History of the Jews of Brody. Jerusalem, 1956.

Gierowski, J. A. *Historia Śląska.* History of Silesia. Vol. 1, pt. 3. K. Maleczyński, ed. Wrocław, 1963.

———— *Między saskim absolutyzmem a złotą wolnością.* Between Saxon absolutism and the golden freedom. Wrocław, 1953.

———— "Personal oder Realunion." *Um die Polnische Krone: Sachsen und Polen während des Nordischen Krieges 1700–1721.* J. Kalisch and J. A. Gierowski, eds. Berlin, 1962.

———— *W cieniu Ligi Pólnocnej.* In the shadow of the Northern league. Wrocław, 1971.

———— "Wrocławskie interesy hetmanowej Elżbiety Sieniawskiej." The Wrocław interests of Elżbieta Sieniawska. *Studia z dziejów kultury i ideologii.* Wrocław, 1968.

———— ed. *Rzeczpospolita w dobie upadku 1700–1740.* The Polish Commonwealth in the period of decline. Wrocław, 1955.

———— and Kamiński, Andrzej. "The Eclipse of Poland." *The New Cambridge Modern History.* Vol. 6. J. S. Bromley, ed. Cambridge, 1970.

Gieysztor, Aleksander et al. *A History of Poland.* Warsaw, 1979.

Goldberg, Jacob. "Bein Hofesh Lenetinut—Sugei Hatlut Hafeiudalit shel Hayehudim Bepolin." Between freedom and bondage: forms of feudal dependency of the Jews in Poland in the sixteenth–eighteenth centuries. *Proceedings of the Fifth World Congress of Jewish Studies.* Vol. 2. Jerusalem, 1972.

———— "De Non Tolerandis Iudaeis." *Studies in Jewish History Presented to Professor Raphael Mahler.* S. Yeivin, ed. Merhavia, 1974.

———— "Die getauften Juden in Polen-Litauen im XVI–XVIII Jahrhundert." *Jahrbücher für Geschichte Osteuropas* 30 (1982), 54–99.

———— *Jewish Privileges in the Polish Commonwealth.* Jerusalem, 1985.

———— "Poles and Jews in the Seventeenth and Eighteenth Centuries: Rejection or Acceptance." *Jahrbücher für Geschichte Osteuropas* 22 (1974), 248–82.

———— "Społeczność żydowska w szlacheckim miasteczku." A Jewish community in a town owned by a nobleman. *BZIH* 59 (1966), 13–28.

———— *Stosunki agrarne w miastach ziemi wieluńskiej w drugiej połowie XVII i w XVIII wieku.* Agrarian conditions in the towns of the Wieluń region in the late seventeenth and eighteenth centuries. Łódz, 1960.

Gostomski, A. *Gospodarstwo.* Economy. S. Inglot, ed. Wrocław, 1951.

Grabski, A. F. et al. *Zarys wojskowości polskiej do roku 1864.* Outline of Polish military history to 1864. Vol. 2. Warsaw, 1966.

Grodecki, Roman. "Konfederacje w Polsce XV w." Confederations in fifteenth century Poland. *Sprawozdania PAN* 52 (1951), 880–85.

Grodziski, Stanisław. "Les devoirs et les droits politiques de la noblesse polonaise." *APH* 36 (1977), 163–76.

Guldon, Zenon. *Związki handlowe dóbr magnackich na prawobrzeżnej Ukrainie z Gdańskiem w XVIII w.* Commercial ties between magnate territories in the western Ukraine and Gdańsk in the eighteenth century. Toruń, 1966.

Hakaro, David. *Ohel Rahel.* Shkłoŭ, 1790.

Halecki, Oscar. *A History of Poland.* Rev. ed. London, 1978.

Halpern, Israel. "Gezeirot Voshchilo." The Woszczyło Uprising. *Zion* 22 (1958), 56–67.

———— "Hevrot Baalei Melakha Yehudim Bepolin Velita." Jewish artisans' guilds in Poland and Lithuania. *Zion* 2 (1937), 70–89.

———— "The Jews in Eastern Europe." *The Jews.* Vol. 1. L. Finkelstein, ed. New York, 1960.

———— ed. *Beit Yisrael Bepolin.* The Jews in Poland. 2 vols. Jerusalem, 1948–53.

———— ed. *Pinkas Vaad Arba Aratzot.* Proceedings of the Council of Four Lands. Jerusalem, 1948.

Hannover, N. N. *Yeven Metzulah.* Tel Aviv, 1966.

Haugen, Einar. *Bilingualism in the Americas.* Alabama, 1956.

Hekker, Helena. "Evrei v polskikh gorodakh vo vtoroi polovin XVIII veka." The Jews in Polish cities during the second half of the eighteenth century. *EvS* 6 (1913), 184–200, 325–32.

——— "Iudofobia v Polshe XVIII veka." Judeo-phobia in Poland in the eighteenth century. *EvS* 6 (1913), 439–541.

Historia Polski. History of Poland. Vols. 1 and 2. Tadeusz Manteuffel, ed. Warsaw, 1957–1960.

Homecki, Adam. *Produkcja i handel zbożowy w latyfundium Lubomirskich w drugiej połowie XVII i pierwszej XVIII wieku.* Grain production and commerce in the Lubomirski latifundium in the late seventeenth and early eighteenth centuries. Wrocław, 1970.

Horn, Maurycy. "Żydzi województwa bełskiego w pierwszej połowie XVII w." Jews in the voivodeship of Bełzec in the first half of the seventeenth century (a statistical assessment). *BZIH* 27 (1958), 22–61.

Horwitz, Z. H. *Kitvei Hageonim.* Writings of the Sages. Piotrków, 1928.

——— *Letoldot Hakehillot Bepolin.* On the history of the communities in Poland. Jerusalem, 1978.

Hoszowski, Stanisław. "Handel Gdańska w okresie XV–XVIII wieku." Gdańsk commerce in the fifteenth–eighteenth centuries. *Prace z Zakresu Historii Gospodarczej* 11 (1960), 3–71.

Hrushevs'kyi, Mikhailo. *Istoriia Ukrainy-Rusy.* History of Ukraine-Rus'. Vol. 9. New York, 1957.

Hundert, G. D. "Jewish Urban Residence in the Polish Commonwealth in the Early Modern Period." *Jewish Journal of Sociology* 26 (1984), 25–34.

——— "Jews, Money and Society in the Seventeenth-Century Polish Commonwealth: The Case of Kraków." *Jewish Social Studies* 43 (1981), 261–74.

——— "Security and Dependence: Perspectives on Seventeenth Century Polish-Jewish Society Gained Through a Study of Jewish Merchants in Little

Poland." Doctoral dissertation, Columbia University. New York, 1978.

Iaroshevych, A. I. "Kapitalistychna orenda na Ukraini za polskoi doby." Capitalist arenda in the Ukraine during the Polish period. *Zapysky sotsialno-ekonomichnoho viddilu Ukrainska Akademiia Nauk* 5–6 (1927), 116–259.

Kaczmarczyk, Zdzisław. "Oligarchia magnacka w Polsce jako forma państwa." Magnate Oligarchy in Poland as a form of government. *Pamiętnik VIII powszechnego zjazdu historyków polskich w Krakowie.* Warsaw, 1958.

———— and Leśnodorski, Bogusław. *Historia państwa i prawa Polski.* History of Polish government and law. Vol. 2. J. Bardach, ed. Warsaw, 1966.

Kaidanover, R. Shmuel. *Kav Hayashar.* Frankfurt/Main, 1706.

Kamiński, Andrzej. *Konfederacja Sandomierska wobec Rosji w okresie poaltranstadzkim, 1706–1709.* The Sandomierz Confederation and Russia in the post-Altranstadt period, 1706–1709. Wrocław, 1969.

———— "Neo-Serfdom in Poland-Lithuania." *Slavic Review* 34 (1975), 253–68.

———— "Piotr I a wojsko koronne w przededniu szwedzkiego uderzenia na Rosję w 1707." Peter I and the Polish army on the eve of the Swedish attack on Russia in 1707. *Studia i materiały do historii wojskowości.* Warsaw, 1969.

———— "The Szlachta of the Polish-Lithuania Commonwealth and their Government." *The Nobility in Russia and Eastern Europe.* I. Banac and P. Bushkovitch, eds. New Haven, 1983.

Karo, Joseph. *Shulkhan Arukh.* New York, 1967.

Katz, Jacob. *Tradition and Crisis.* New York, 1971.

Kersten, Adam. "Les Magnats—élite de la société nobiliaire." *APH* 36 (1977).

———— "Problem władzy w Rzeczypospolitej czasu Wazów." The problem of authority in the Polish Commonwealth under the Wazas. *O naprawę Rzeczypospolitej.* J. A. Gierowski, ed. Warsaw, 1965.

Kluk, K. *O rolnictwie, zbożach, łąkach, chmielnikach, winnicach i roślinach gospodarskich.* On agriculture, grain crops, meadows, hop fields, vineyards, and farm vegetables. S. Inglot, ed. Wrocław, 1954.

Konopczyński, Władysław. *Liberum Veto: Studyum porównawczo-historyczne.* Liberum Veto: a comparative historical study. Cracow, 1918.

Kossower, Mordekhai. "Der Inlendisher Handel fun Poilishe Yidn in 16ten un 17ten Yarhundert." Internal trade of Polish Jews in the sixteenth and seventeenth centuries. *Yivo Bleter* 12 (1939), 533–45.

Kot, Stanisław. "Polska rajem dla Żydów, piekłem dla chłopów, niebem dla szlachty." Poland: paradise for Jews, hell for peasants, heaven for noblemen. *Kultura i nauka—praca zbiorowa.* Warsaw, 1937.

Krantz, Yaakov. *Kol Yaakov.* Lviv, 1804.

Kremer, Moshe. "Leheker Hamelakha Vehevrot Baalei Hamelakha Etzel Yehudei Polin." Jewish artisans in Poland in the sixteenth–eighteenth centuries. *Zion* 2 (1937), 294–25.

Kuchowicz, Zbigniew. "Społeczne konsekwencje postępującej degeneracji możnowładztwa polskiego w XVII–XVIII w." The social consequences of the progressive degeneration of the Polish magnates in the seventeenth–eighteenth centuries. *KH* 76 (1969), 21–43.

——— *Warunki zdrowotne wsi i miasteczek województw łęczyckiego i sieradzkiego w XVIII w.* Hygienic conditions in the villages and townlets of the Łęczycz and Sieradz regions in the eighteenth century. Łódz, 1961.

Kula, Witold. *An Economic Theory of the Feudal System.* L. Garner, trans. Bristol, England, 1976.

——— "L'histoire économique de la Pologne du XVIII siècle." *APH* 4 (1961), 133–46.

——— *Problemy i metody historii gospodarczej.* Problems and methods in economic history. Warsaw, 1963.

Kutrzeba, Stanisław. *Historya ustroju Polski.* History of the Polish system. Lviv, 1920.

Kuznets, Simon. "Economic Structure and the Life of the Jews." *The Jews.* Vol. 2. L. Finkelstein, ed. New York, 1960.

Lech, Marian. "Powstanie chłopów białoruskich w starostwie krzyczewskim (1740 r.)." The uprising of White Russian peasants in the Krzyczewski region in 1740. *PH* 51 (1960), 314–30.

Lehmann, Emil. *Der Polnische Resident Behrend Lehmann.* Dresden, 1885.

Leskiewiczowa, Janina. *Próba analizy gospodarki dóbr magnackich w Polsce.* An attempt at analysis of the economy of magnate territories in Poland. Warsaw, 1964.

———— and Michalski, Jerzy, eds. *Supliki chłopskie XVIII wieku.* Peasant petitions of the eighteenth century. Warsaw, 1954.

Leszczyński, Anatol. "Karczmarze i szynkarze żydowscy ziemi bielskiej od drugiej połowy XVII w. do 1795 r." Jewish tavernkeepers and bartenders in the Bielsko region from the mid-seventeenth century until 1795. *BZIH* 102 (1977), 77–85.

———— "Żydzi ziemi bielskiej od połowy XVII wieku do 1795 r.," The Jews of the Bielsko region from the mid-seventeenth century until 1795. Doctoral dissertation, Wyższa Szkoła Pedagogiczna im. Powstańców Śląskich w Opolu. Opole, 1977.

———— *Żydzi ziemi bielskiej od polowy XVII wieku do 1795 r.* Wrocław, 1980.

Levi, Isaia. "Famiglie Distinte e Benemerite della com. Isr. di Mantova." *Il Vessilo Israelitico* 54 (1906), 18–19, 75–77, 163–64.

Levine, Hillel. "Gentry, Jews, and Serfs: The Rise of Polish Vodka," *Review* 4 (1980), 223–50.

Lewin, Izaak. *Z historii i tradycji: szkice z dziejów kultury żydowskiej.* Out of history and tradition: sketches from Jewish cultural history. Warsaw, 1983.

Lewin, Louis. *Geschichte der Juden in Lissa.* Pinna, 1904.

———— "Jüdische Aerzte in Gross-Polen." *JJLG* 9 (1911), 367–420.

———— "Die Jüdischen Studenten an der Universität Frankfurt a.d. Oder." *JJLG* 14 (1921), 216–38, 15 (1923), 59–96, 16 (1924), 43–86.

Łukasik, Ryszard. *Rachunkowość rolna w dawnej Polsce.* Agricultural accounting in Old Poland. Warsaw, 1963.

Luria, R. Shlomo. *Responsa.* Jerusalem, 1969.

Maciszewski, Maurycy. *Brzeżany.* Brody, 1910.

Madurowicz-Urbańska, Helena. *Gospodarstwo folwarczne w dobrach biskupstwa krakowskiego na pograniczu polsko-śląskim w XVII–XVIII w.* The manor economy in the territories of the Cracow bishopric in the Polish-Silesian border area in the seventeenth–eighteenth centuries. Cracow, 1962.

Mahler, Raphael. "Anti-Semitism in Poland." *Essays on Anti-Semitism.* K. Pinson, ed. New York, 1942.

———— *A History of Modern Jewry.* London, 1971.

———— *Toldot Hayehudim Bepolin.* History of the Jews in Poland. Merhavia, 1946.

———— *Yidn in Amolikn Poiln in Likht fun Tsifirn.* The Jews in Old Poland in the light of numbers. 2 vols. Warsaw, 1958.

Maimon, Solomon. *Autobiography.* J. Clark Murray, ed. and trans. London, 1954.

Majewski, Jan. *Gospodarstwo folwarczne we wsiach miasta Poznania w latach 1582–1644.* The manor economy in the villages belonging to the city of Poznań, 1582–1644. Poznań, 1957.

Makkai, Laszlo. "Neo-Serfdom: Its Origin and Nature in East Central Europe." *Slavic Review* 34 (1975), 225–38.

Makowska, Alicja. "Pracownicy najemni wielkiej własności na przykładzie dóbr sandomierskich Czartoryskich w XVIII wieku." Hired labor in the large latifundia as seen in the Czartoryski Sandomierz territories in the eighteenth century. *Społeczeństwo Staropolskie.* Vol. 2. A. Wyczański, ed. Warsaw, 1979.

Marek, P. S. "Istoricheskie soobshcheniia." Historical notes. *Voshod* (May, 1903), 74–91.

———— "Krizis evreiskogo samoupravleniia i Hasidizm." The crisis of Jewish autonomy and Hasidism. *EvS* 12 (1928), 45–101.

Margoliot, Meir b. Zvi Hersh. *Meir Netivim*. Polonne, 1791–92 [Brooklyn, 1960].

Markina, W. A. *Magnatskoe pomeste pravoberezhnoi Ukrainy vtoroi poloviny XVIII veka*. Magnate estates in the western Ukraine in the second half of the eighteenth century. Kiev, 1961.

Meir b. Eliakim Getz. *Even Hashoham Umeirat Einaim*. Dyhernfürth, 1733.

Meisl, Josef. "Behrend Lehmann und der Sächsische Hof." *JJLG* 16 (1924), 227–52.

Modena, Abdelkader and Morpugo, Edgardo. *Medici e Chirughi Ebrei Dottorati Licenziati nell' Universita di Padova dal 1617 al 1816*. Bologna, 1967.

Mordekhai b. Naftali Hertz. *Pithei Yah*. Lviv, 1799.

Morgensztern, Janina. "O działalności gospodarczej Żydów w Zamościu w XVI i XVII w." On the economic activities of the Jews in Zamość in the sixteenth and seventeenth centuries. *BZIH* 53 (1965), 3–32, 56 (1965), 3–28.

———— "Operacje kredytowe Żydów w Zamościu w XVII w." Credit operations of the Jews of Zamość in the seventeenth century. *BZIH* 64 (1967), 3–32.

———— "Zadłużenie gmin żydowskich w ordynacji zamojskiej w II połowie XVII w." Indebtedness of the Jewish communities in Zamość in the second half of the seventeenth century. *BZIH* 73 (1970), 47–65.

Nadav, Mordekhai. *Pinsk*. Tel Aviv, 1973.

Namaczyńska, Stanisław. *Kronika klęsk elementarnych w Polsce i w krajach sąsiednich w latach 1648–1696*. A chronicle of natural catastrophes in Poland and neighboring countries, 1648–1696. Lviv, 1937.

Nisenboim, S. B. *Lekorot Hayehudim Belublin*. On the history of the Jews in Lublin. Lublin, 1899.

Nycz, Michał. *Geneza reform skarbowych Sejmu Niemego*. The genesis of the Silent Sejm treasury reform. Poznań, 1938.

Obuchowska-Pysiowa, Honorata. *Handel wiślany w pierwszej połowie XVII w.* The Vistula trade in the first half of the seventeenth century. Wrocław, 1964.

Olszewski, Henryk. *Doktryny prawno-ustrojowe czasów saskich.* Legal-structural doctrines of the Saxon period. Warsaw, 1961.

――――― *Sejm Rzeczpospolitej epoki oligarchii.* The Diet in the period of oligarchy. Poznań, 1966.

Opas, Tomasz. "Miasta prywatne a Rzeczpospolita." Private towns and the Commonwealth. *KH* 78 (1971), 28–48.

――――― "Powinności na rzecz dziedziców w miastach szlacheckich województwa lubelskiego w drugiej połowie XVII i w XVIII wieku." Obligations to the owners in the nobility towns of the Lublin region. *Rocznik Lubelski* 14 (1971), 121–44.

Pazdro, Zbigniew. *Organizacya i praktyka żydowskich sądów podwojewodzińskich w okresie 1740–1772.* The organization and conduct of the Jewish podwojewoda courts, 1740–1772. Lviv, 1903.

Peretz b. Moshe. *Beit Peretz.* Nesterov (Zhovkva), 1759.

Piekarz, Mendl. *Bimei Tzmihat Hahasidut.* The beginnings of Hasidism. Jerusalem, 1978.

Pikulski, Gauden. *Złość żydowska.* Jewish malice. Lviv, 1758.

Pinhas Eliyahu b. Meir. *Sefer Habrit.* Brünn, 1797.

Pinkas Hakehillot. Encyclopedia of Jewish communities. *Poland,* Vol. 2. Jerusalem, 1980.

Podraza, A. *Jakub Kazimierz Haur, pisarz rolniczy XVII wieku.* Jakub Kazimierz Haur, agricultural bookkeeper of the XVII century. Wrocław, 1961.

Polski słownik biograficzny. Vols. 1+. Dictionary of Polish biography. Cracow, 1935+.

Pośpiech, Andrzej and Tygielski, Wojciech. "Społeczna rola dworu magnackiego XVII–XVIII wieku." The social role of the magnate court in the seventeenth–eighteenth centuries. *PH* 69 (1978), 215–37.

Powidaj, Ludwik. *Rytwiany i ich dziedzice.* Rytwiany and its owners. Cracow, 1880.

Prochaska, Antoni. *Historja miasta Stryja.* History of the town of Stryi. Lviv, 1926.

_____ and Hejnosz, Wojciech, eds. *Akta Grodzkie i Ziemskie*. Court and legislative documents. Vols. 22, 23, 25. Lviv, 1914–35.

Ptaśnik, Jan. *Miasto i mieszczaństwo w dawnej Polsce*. Town and townspeople in Old Poland. Warsaw, 1949.

Puczyński, Bohdan. "Ludność Brzeżan i okolicy w XVII i XVIII w." The population of Berezhany and vicinity in the seventeenth–eighteenth centuries. *Przeszłość demograficzna Polski* 4–5 (1971–72), 177–214, 15–64.

Rafacz, Józef. "Przymus propinacyjny w dobrach królewskich koronnych w epoce nowożytnej." The propination obligation in the royal territories of Crown Poland in the modern era. *Themis Polska* 8 (1933), 35–102.

_____ *Ustrój wsi samorządnej małopolskiej w XVIII wieku.* The structure of the self-governing village in Little Poland in the eighteenth century. Lublin, 1922.

Rapoport, Haim. *Responsa*. Lviv, 1861.

Rawita-Gawronski, Franciszek. *Żydzi w historji i literaturze ludowej na Rusi*. Jews in the history and folk literature of Rus'. Warsaw, 1923.

Reddaway, W. F. et al. *The Cambridge History of Poland*. 2 vols. Cambridge, 1941–50.

Richarz, Monika. *Der Eintritt der Juden in die Akademischen Berufe*. Tübingen, 1974.

Rieger, Paul. "Deutsche Juden als Heidelberger Studenten im 18. Jahrhundert." *M. Philippson Festschrift*. Leipzig, 1916.

Rosman, M. J. "Helkam shel Hayehudim Bemishar Hashayit Midrom Mizrah Polin Legdansk: 1695–1726." The Jewish role in the river trade between southeast Poland and Gdańsk: 1695–1726. *Gal-Ed* 7–8 (1985), 83–70.

Rostworowski, Emanuel. "Zdrowie i niezdrowie polskich magnatów XVI–XVIII wieku." Health and sickness of the Polish magnates in the sixteenth–eighteenth centuries. *KH* 76 (1969), 865–87.

Rusiński, Władysław. *Uwagi o rozwarstwieniu wsi w Polsce XVIII wieku*. Observations on the stratification of the village in Poland in the eighteenth century. Poznań, 1953.

Rutkowski, Jan. *Badania nad podziałem dochodów w Polsce w czasach nowożytnych.* A study of the division of income in Poland. Warsaw, 1938.

———— *Historia gospodarcza Polski.* Economic history of Poland. Warsaw, 1953.

———— *Przebudowa wsi w Polsce po wojnach z połowy XVII wieku.* Village reconstruction in Poland after the wars of the mid-seventeenth century. Cracow, 1916.

———— "Studya nad położeniem włościan w Polsce w XVIII wieku." Studies on the position of the villager in Poland in the eighteenth century. *Ekonomista* 14 (1914), no. 1: 87–131, no. 2:71–121, no. 3:129– 53.

Rybarski, Roman. *Skarb i pieniądz za Jana Kazimierza, Michała Korybuta i Jana III.* Treasury and currency under Jan Kazimierz, Michał Korybut and Jan III. Warsaw, 1939.

Rychlikowa, Irena. *Klucz wielkoporębski Wodzickich w drugiej połowie XVIII wieku.* The Wodzicki's Wielkoporębski complex in the second half of the eighteenth century. Wrocław, 1960.

———— *Produkcja zbożowa wielkiej własności w Małopolsce w latach 1764–1805.* Grain production on the large estates in Little Poland 1764–1805. Warsaw, 1967.

———— *Szkice o gospodarce panów na Łańcucie.* Sketches of the economy of the lords of Łańcut. Łańcut, 1971.

Samter, Nathan. *Judentaufen im Neunzehnten Jahrhundert.* Berlin, 1906.

Schiper, Ignacy. *Dzieje handlu żydowskiego na ziemiach polskich.* History of Jewish commerce in Polish lands. Warsaw, 1937.

———— "Finanzialer Hurban fun der Tsentraler un Provintsialer Oytonomia fun Yidn in Altn Polin." The financial ruin of the central and provincial autonomy of the Jews in Poland. *Yivo Ekonomishe Shriftn.* Vol. 2. Y. Leshtchinsky, ed. Vilna, 1932.

Scholem, Gershom. *Major Trends in Jewish Mysticism.* New York, 1961.

Schorr, Mojżesz. *Organizacja Żydów w Polsce.* Organization of the Jews in Poland. Lviv, 1899.

———— *Żydzi w Przemyślu do końca XVIII wieku.* The Jews in Przemyśl to the end of the eighteenth century. Lviv, 1903.

Serczyk, W. A. *Gospodarstwo magnackie w województwie podolskim w drugiej połowie XVIII wieku.* Magnate economy in Podillia in the second half of the eighteenth century. Wrocław, 1965.

Shlomo of Helma. *Mirkevet Mishna.* Jerusalem, 1975.

Shmuel b. Eliezer of Kalaveria. *Darkhei Noam.* Koenigsberg, 1764.

Shmuel b. Elkanah. *Mekom Shmuel.* Altona, 1738.

Simchovitz, J. H. "Zur Biographie R. Jacob Josua's, des Verfassers des Sefer Penai Yehoshua." *Monatschrift für Geschichte und Wissenschaft des Judentums* 54 (1910), 608–21.

Sirkes, Yoel. *(Old) Responsa.* Frankfurt/Main, 1697.

———— *(New) Responsa.* Korzec, 1795.

Słownik geograficzny królestwa polskiego. Polish geographical dictionary. 15 vols. Warsaw, 1880–1902.

Smoleński, Władysław. *Stan i sprawa Żydów polskich w XVIII wieku.* The condition and problems of the Polish Jews in the eighteenth century. Warsaw, 1876.

Sobczak, Tadeusz. "Zmiany w stanie posiadania dóbr ziemskich w województwie łęczyckim od XVI do XVIII wieku." Changes in the state of possession of lands in the Łęczyca region. *RDSG* 18 (1955), 163–93.

Solnik, Binyamin. *Masat Binyamin.* Cracow, 1633.

Sosis, Yisrael. "Tsu der Sotsialer Geshikhte fun Yidn in Vaysrusland." On the social history of the Jews in White Russia. *Tsaytshrift* 1 (1926), 1–24.

Śreniowski, Stanisław. "Oznaki regresu ekonomicznego w ustroju folwarczno-pańszczyźnianym w Polsce od schyłku XVI wieku." Signs of economic regression in the manorial structure of Poland from the end of the sixteenth century. *KH* 61 (1954), 165–96.

———— "Państwo polskie w połowie XVII w. Zagadnienia ekonomicznej i politycznej władzy oligarchiów." The Polish state in the mid-seventeenth century: The economic and political problems of oligarchic rule.

Polska w okresie drugiej wojny północnej. Vol. 1. Warsaw, 1957.

Steinberg, Mojżesz. *Żydzi w Jarosławiu.* The Jews in Jarosław. Jarosław, 1933.

Stern, Selma. *The Court Jew.* Philadelphia, 1950.

Szczepaniak, Marian. *Karczma, Wieś, Dwór.* Tavern, village, court. Warsaw, 1977.

Szczygielski, Wojciech. "Zmiany w stanie posiadania i w strukturze własnościowej szlachty powiatu wieluńskiego od połowy XVI do końca XVIII wieku." Changes in the state of possession and the structure of noble ownership in Wieluń county from the mid-sixteenth to the end of the eighteenth centuries. *Rocznik Łódzki* 1 (1958), 259–81.

Szkurłatowski, Zygmunt. "Organizacja, administracja i praca w dobrach wielkiej własności feudalnej w Polsce w XVII i XVIII wieku w świetle instruktarzy ekonomicznych." Organization, administration, and labor in the territories of the large feudal estates in Poland in the seventeenth and eighteenth centuries. *Zeszyty Naukowe Universytetu Wrocławskiego,* Ser. A, no. 7 (1957), 147–93.

Szmeruk, Chone. "Hahasidut Veiskei Hahakhirot." Hasidism and the 'arendars'. *Zion* 35 (1970), 182–92.

Tazbir, Janusz. "Les modèles personnels de la noblesse polonaise au XVII siècle." *APH* 36 (1977), 135–45.

———— *A State Without Stakes.* New York–Warsaw, 1973.

Topolska, M. B. *Dobra szkłowskie na Białorusi wschodniej w XVII i XVIII wieku.* The Shkłoů territory in eastern Belorussia in the seventeenth and eighteenth centuries. Warsaw, 1969.

Topolski, Jerzy. "La régression économique en Pologne du XVI au XVII siècle." *APH* 7 (1962), 28–49.

———— ed. *Dzieje Polski.* History of Poland. Warsaw, 1976.

Toury, Jacob. "Jewish Townships in the German-speaking Parts of the Austrian Empire—Before and After the Revolution of 1848/1849." *YBLBI* 26 (1981), 55–72.

———— "Types of Municipal Rights in German Townships—The Problem of Local Emancipation." *YBLBI* 22 (1977), 55–80.

Trunk, Isaiah. "Ketovot Beivrit-Yiddish al Mismakhim Polaniim Mehameah ha-17–18." Hebrew-Yiddish inscriptions on Polish documents from the seventeenth–eighteenth centuries. *N. M. Gelber Jubilee Volume*. Tel Aviv, 1963.

———— "An Umbekanter Dokument Vegn dem kamf in di Kehilos fun Lemberger Sevivo, 1735–1758." An unknown document concerning the struggle among the communities of the Lviv region. *YB* 40 (1956), 221–24.

———— "Der Vaad Medinas Rusya." The council of White Russia. *YB* 40 (1956), 63–82.

Trzebiński, Wojciech. "Działalność urbanistyczna magnatów i szlachty w Polsce XVIII wieku." Urban activity of the magnates and nobility in Poland in the eighteenth century. Warsaw, 1962.

Trzyna, Edward. *Położenie ludności wiejskiej w królewszczyznach województwa krakowskiego w XVII wieku*. The position of the village population in the royal holdings of the Cracow region. Wrocław, 1963.

Urban, Wacław. "Umiejętność pisania w Małopolsce." Writing ability in Little Poland in the second half of the sixteenth century. *PH* 68 (1977), 231–57.

Volumina Legum. 10 Vols. St. Petersburg, Cracow, Poznań, 1859–1952.

Wachowiak, Bogdan. "Ze studiów nad spławem na Wiśle w XVI–XVIII w." From studies on Vistula commerce in the sixteenth–eighteenth centuries. *Przegląd Zachodni* 7 (1951), 122–36.

Wachstein, Duber. "Sridim Mipinkaso shel Rabbi Yaacov Yoshua Baal 'Penei Yehoshua'." Fragments from the account book of Rabbi Yaakov Yoshua, author of *Penei Yehoshua*. *Studies in Jewish Bibliography in Honor of A. S. Freidus*. New York, 1929.

Waligórska, Krystyna. "Konstrukcja statków pływających po Sanie i Wiśle w XVIII w." San and Vistula riverboat construction in the eighteenth century. *Kwartalnik Historii Kultury Materialnej* 8 (1960), 229–41.

Warchał, Jan. "Żydzi polscy na Uniwersytecie Padewskim." Polish Jews at the University of Padua. *Kwartalnik poświęcony badaniu przeszłości Żydów w Polsce* 1 (1912), 37–72.

Wąsowicz, Michał and Siegel, Stanisław. *Kontrakty Lwowskie, 1678–1724.* Lviv contracts, 1678–1724. Lviv, 1935.

Weinryb, B. D. *The Jews of Poland.* Philadelphia, 1973.

――――― *Mehkarim Betoldot Hakalkala Vehahevra shel Yehudei Polin.* Studies in the economical and social history of the Jews in Poland. Jerusalem, 1939.

――――― *Neueste Wirtschaftsgeschichte der Juden in Russland und Polen.* Hildesheim–New York, 1972.

――――― *Texts and Studies in the Communal History of Polish Jewry.* New York, 1951 (= *Proceedings of the American Academy for Jewish Research* 19 [1951]).

Wetstein, F. H. *Letoldot Yisrael Vehakhamav.* On the history of the Jews and their scholars. Vol. 2. Cracow, 1893.

Wexler, Paul. "The Reconstruction of Pre-Ashkenazic Jewish Settlements in the Slavic Lands in the Light of Linguistic Sources." *POLIN* 1 (1986), 3–18.

Wiatrowski, Leszek. "Z dziejów latyfundium klasztoru Klarysek z Starego Sącza." On the history of the Stary Sącz Clarist monastery's latifundium. *Zeszyty Naukowe Uniwersytetu Wrocławskiego,* Ser. A, no. 13 (1959), 93–177.

Wimmer, Jan. *Wojsko Rzeczpospolitej w dobie Wojny Północnej.* The Polish army during the Northern War Period. Warsaw, 1956.

Wirszyłło, K. S. "Stosunek duchowieństwa katolickiego na Wołyniu do Żydów w XVIII wieku." Relations between the Catholic clergy and the Jews in Volhynia in the eighteenth century. *Miesięcznik Diecezjalny Łucki* 9 (1934), 18–25.

Wolański, Marian. *Statystyka handlu Śląska z Rzeczpospolitą w XVII wieku.* Statistics of the commerce between Silesia and the Commonwealth in the seventeenth century. Wrocław, 1963.

——— *Związki handlowe Śląska z Rzeczpospolitą w XVII wieku.* Commercial ties between Silesia and the Commonwealth in the seventeenth century. Wrocław, 1961.

Wyczański, Andrzej. *Polska Rzeczpospolita szlachecka 1454–1764.* Poland: The Commonwealth of Nobles, 1454–1764. Warsaw, 1965.

——— "La structure de la noblesse polonaise aux XVI–XVIII siècles." *APH* 36 (1977), 109–17.

——— *Studia nad folwarkiem szlacheckim w Polsce w latach 1500–1580.* A study of the nobility manor in Poland, 1500–1580. Warsaw, 1966.

Wyrobisz, Andrzej. "Materiały do dziejów handlu w miasteczkach polskich na początku XVII wieku." Material on the history of small town Polish commerce at the beginning of the eighteenth century. *PH* 62 (1971), 703–16.

——— "Rola miast prywatnych w Polsce w XVI i XVII wieku." The role of private towns in Poland in the sixteenth and seventeenth centuries. *PH* 65 (1974), 19–46.

Yaakov Yisrael of Kremenets. *Shevet Miyisrael.* Nesterov (Zhovkva), 1772.

Yaakov Yosef of Polnoe. *Zofnat Paneah.* Koretz, 1782.

Yosef b. Yehuda Yidel. *Yesod Yosef.* Shkłoŭ, 1785.

Zielińska, Teresa. *Magnateria polska epoki saskiej.* The Polish magnates in the Saxon era. Wrocław, 1977.

Zinberg, Israel. *A History of Jewish Literature.* Vol. 6. B. Martin, trans. Cincinnati–New York, 1975.

Żuchowski, Stefan. *Proces kriminalny o niewinne dziecię Jana Krasnowskiego.* The criminal trial concerning the innocent child of Jan Krasnowski. [No place], 1713.

Zunz, David. *Sefer Ateret Yehoshua.* Bilgoray, 1936.

Zvi Hersh of Vilna. *Ateret Avi.* Yosenitz, 1722.

Żytkowicz, Leonid. "Okres gospodarki folwarczno-pańszczyźnianej XVI–XVIII w." The period of the manorial-courvée economy, sixteenth – eighteenth century. *Historia chłopów polskich.* S. Inglot, ed. Częstochowa, 1970.

————— "Struktura dochodu pańskiego w końcu XVIII wieku w dobrach Janów biskupstwa łuckiego." The structure of the owners' income at the end of the eighteenth century in the Janów territory of the Luts'k bishopric. *Studia historii w 35 – lecie pracy naukowej Henryka Łowmiańskiego.* Warsaw, 1958.

Index

Harvard Judaic Texts and Studies

Harvard Judaic Monographs

Any of the above volumes can be ordered by contacting the Harvard University Center for Jewish Studies, 6 Divinity Avenue, Cambridge, MA, 02138

Income from the Lecture and Publication Funds established at the Center for Jewish Studies by our many thoughtful friends and patrons, helps in the publication of important studies, revised doctoral dissertations, and conference proceedings.

Harvard Series in Ukrainian Studies

A complete catalogue including the Harvard Library of Early Ukrainian Literature and Renovatio is available upon request from the Harvard Series in Ukrainian Studies, 1583 Massachusetts Avenue, Cambridge, MA, 02138.

The publication series of the Harvard Ukrainian Research Institute are made possible in large part by donations to the Ukrainian Studies Fund.